THE CRUISING GUIDE
to the
VIRGIN ISLANDS

14th Edition

2009-2011

THE CRUISING GUIDE
to the
VIRGIN
ISLANDS

14th Edition

2009-2011

by Nancy and Simon Scott

A Complete Guide
for Yachtsmen, Divers and
Watersports Enthusiasts

Cruising Guide Publications, Inc.

is a special interest publisher of sailing guides to cruising in various areas around the world and other publications of nautical interest. CGP endeavors to provide comprehensive and invaluable materials to both inveterate sailors and less experienced seafarers seeking vital vacationing tips and navigational information relative to the journey to and the enjoyment of their destinations.

The Cruising Guide to the Virgin Islands is intended for use in conjunction with either U.S. National Ocean Survey charts, U.S. Hydrographic Office charts, Caribbean Yachting Charts, or British Admiralty charts. Every effort has been made to describe conditions accurately. However, the publisher makes no warranty, express or implied, for any errors or omissions in this publication. Skippers should use this guide only in conjunction with the above charts and/or other navigational aids and not place undue credence in the accuracy of this guide. The Cruising Guide to the Virgin Islands is not intended for use for navigational purposes.

Anchoring in coral is
STRICTLY PROHIBITED
in both the U.S. and B.V.I.

For regular V.I. information updates see our website: www.cruisingguides.com

Published by

Cruising Guide Publications, Inc.

P.O. Box 1017, Dunedin, FL 34697-1017
Telephone: (727) 733-5322
(800) 330-9542
Fax (727) 734-8179

Email: info@cruisingguides.com
www.cruisingguides.com

By Nancy & Simon Scott

Art Direction
Carol Dioca-Bevis

Advertising/Marketing Director
Maureen Larroux

Editor/Production Manager
Ashley Scott

Administration
Pat Kozemski

Illustrations
Roger Burnett
Roger Bansemer
Compass Rose courtesy of Phil Petot
Additional illustrations courtesy of
NOAA.gov

Photography
A.J. Blake
Dougal Thornton
Jim Scheiner
Julian Putley
Mauricio Handler
Simon Scott

Contributing writers
Claudia Colli
Julian Putley
Sue Wheatley
Emy Thomas

Contributing Photography Courtesy of:
Aragorn Studios
Andy Morrell – HIHO
Eric Norie – seahawkpaints.com
Virgin Islands National Park

Copyright © Maritime Ventures, Ltd.
2008
Fourteenth Edition
Printed in China

Front Cover Photography:
Mauricio Handler
Chris Doyle

ISBN 978-0-944428-86-3

TABLE OF CONTENTS

TABLE OF CONTENTS (con'

Jim Scheiner

:ARRIVE

YACHT HAVEN GRANDE
ST THOMAS, USVI

Yacht Haven Grande in spectacular Charlotte Amalie Harbor offers guests an unprecedented marina experience. The flagship property of IGY's incomparable collection, the marina destination features unparalleled amenities, world-class shopping, dining, recreation and much more.

- Extra-wide concrete docks with side-to berthing for yachts 450+'
- On-site customs & border protection office
- Up to 600 amps of 3 phase power
- In-slip fueling, oil removal, black water pump-out
- Hi-speed internet, WiFi, telephone and cable
- 24-hour video surveillance and on-site security
- World-class provisioning & NY Times fax daily
- Promenade with signature restaurants, bars, ice cream, music & more
- World-class designer and "local flavor" shopping
- Swimming, tennis, fitness club, access to golf

18°20'N / 64°50'W

T + 340-774-5030
F + 340-774-5035
9100 Port of Sale
St. Thomas, USVI 00802
marina@yachthavengrande.com
www.yachthavengrande.com

ISLAND GLOBAL YACHTING

AMERICAS | CARIBBEAN | EUROPE | MIDDLE EAST

an IGY destination

Jim Scheiner

INTRODUCTION

D o you need a mental health holiday? Put yourself on a sail or power boat in the Virgin Islands. The trade winds will help to whisk away those gnawing concerns and put them well in the back of your brain. The gentle rocking of the boat, the sails full as you head towards a new anchorage will make you forget you even have a job. If you have purchased this book then chances are that this dream will become a reality.

The Virgin Islands are perfect for cruisers. The anchorages are all within a couple of hours of each other. The trade winds are steady, the water is turquoise and clear and the sun is golden. You are always within sight of land, with panoramic views of the verdant mountains, swaying palm trees and white sand beaches. At night, at anchor, you may well hear the sounds of steel drum bands drifting in with the breeze calling you ashore to dance in the sand.

There is something for everyone here: sailing, snorkeling, kayaking, or sun bathing, shopping, reading a good book, gazing out to sea or star gazing from the bow of your boat at night. Your trip can be active and adventurous or as laid back and relaxed as you wish. Cruising Guide Publications has been safely guiding yachtsmen through the islands of the Caribbean for over 20 years. The guide is packed with information including sketch charts of the various anchorages, information on marinas, resorts, diving and snorkeling, customs and immigration procedures, beach bars, restaurants and just about anything else you will want to know. Even emergency procedures are listed for your peace of mind.

Leave your worries behind. Forget your watches and clocks –you're on island time here.

Welcome to the Virgin Islands!

Nancy Scott
Publisher

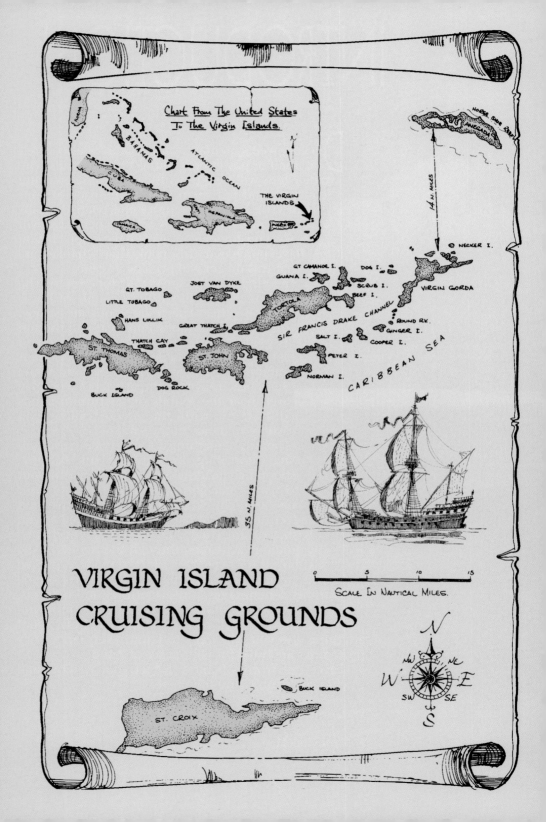

VIRGIN ISLAND
CRUISING GROUNDS

Sailing Ships   *Jim Scheiner*

The Virgin Islands

Nothing has influenced the history of the Virgin Islands more profoundly than their geography and physical makeup. Situated at the high point of the curving archipelago that swings from Trinidad to Florida, they survey strategically all of the Americas, and, with their steady trade winds and numerous sheltered harbors, it is not surprising that they rapidly became a center for sea routes to every point of the compass, providing a welcome pause in the lengthy trade lines between Europe and the riches of South and Central America. Having been described as "the place on the way to everywhere," they have long been desirable for both trading and military

advantage, from the days when Spaniards sailed through carrying Mexican and Peruvian bullion to Spain until this century when the United States paid $25 million to buy the U.S.V.I. from Denmark in order to forestall any unfriendly foreign power from parking on her doorstep.

Sailors and sailing have therefore been at the core of Virgin Islands history from the moment the first Amerindians brought their kanawa (canoes) from the South American mainland and populated the Antilles.

The various migrations that occurred into the Caribbean from South America over the last thousand years have been identified with various archaeological complexes such as the Ciboney, Arawak and Caribs. However, the relationship amongst these different archaeological traditions remains obscure, although the old story of fierce and cannibalistic Caribs eating their way across the islands at the expense of the peaceable Arawaks is now seen as rather more the lurid colonial fantasy than a credible anthropological reconstruction of the early Caribbean.

The Amerindians who settled throughout the Virgin Islands, cultivated the land, made attractive pottery and ornaments (which can still be found) and maintained a complex and intricately organized society. Indigenous people believed that spiritual power resided not just in human souls but also in trees, rocks and other natural phenomena. The form and character of such spirits could be revealed through carving of the wood and stone into idols called "zemis". The well known three-pointed stones recalled the volcanic terrain of the Caribbean and were believed to influence crops and weather. As a source of spiritual power the human body itself was also decorated and adorned with guanin (a gold/copper alloy), marked with paint and sometimes deformed to reflect aesthetic and spiritual meaning — as with head flattening or arm and leg binding (coiro).

When the first Europeans arrived, the wonder of the New World meant that many native words were adopted directly into European languages, as with canoe, tobacco, barbecue, potato, hurricane and, notoriously, cannibal.

The matter of cannibalism therefore deserves some explicit attention - not so much because of its importance in aboriginal Caribbean culture but also because of the obsessive fascination of outsiders with the topic. Although Spanish colonial policy cynically used the charge of cannibalism as a way of justifying the enslavement of Caribbean peoples, it is the Caribs (Kalinago) who were most closely associated with its practice. But this was partly because of their obdurate resistance to the Spanish. While the Amerindians of Hispaniola and Puerto Rico - with whom the Spanish initially allied - were certainly competitors and military enemies with the Caribs to the south - in fact the early documents make it quite clear the war-cannibalism was practiced as much by the supposedly "peaceful" Arawak as it may have been by the supposedly "fierce" Caribs.

Dougal Thorton

In fact the Caribs, as do some Arawaks or Taino, survive through to the present day and have recently revived some of their old canoe making crafts in order to re-unite Carib and other Amerindian communities scattered by the long colonial conquest in this region. The length of their jour-

neys used to be prodigious and they even had satellite "colonies" as far south as the mouth of the Amazon. Theirs is therefore a story of survival (as on Dominica, St. Vincent and in Belize) as well as resistance, which also made them a romantic category for European thinkers who, following Jean-Jacques Rousseau, even saw in their wildness a kind of noble savagery.

Columbus discovered the Virgin Islands in 1493 on his second voyage to the New World. He anchored off Salt River Bay in St. Croix for fresh water and then was driven by unfavorable winds to Virgin Gorda. Seeing the numerous islands, he named them "the Virgins" in honor of St. Ursula and the 11,000 virgins who, threatened by the marauding Huns in 4th-century Cologne, sacrificed their lives rather than submit to a fate worse than death. Virgin Gorda may have got its name (fat virgin) because Columbus, viewing it from seaward, thought that it resembled a reclining woman with a protruding belly.

The Spaniards, whose nation was one of the most powerful in Europe at this time, had laid claim to the West Indies as they had in their discovery of the Americas. They began to settle in various places throughout the islands to provide stop- over points for their ships carrying spoils from Central and South America to the mother country.

As Spanish settlement increased so did Carib resistance which only provoked Emperor Charles V to order that the Indians "should be treated as ene-

Simon Scott

Courtesy of seahawkpaints.com

This combination of privateering and piracy (the distinction between the two wearing very thin at times) was to continue for several hundred years. A vast array of colorful and bizarre characters paused in the Virgin Islands, among them the well-known pirate Henry Morgan and the legendary Sir John Hawkins, who visited the area four times. On his last voyage in 1595 Hawkins sailed with Sir Francis Drake to attack Puerto Rico, the two fleets apparently reconnoitering for a few days in the North Sound of Virgin Gorda to muster their men and prepare for battle.

It was a fateful trip for both of them: Hawkins sickened and died of the fever that was the scourge of the tropics; Drake, himself, after a failed assault on the heavy fortifications of San Juan, soon followed suit.

mies and given no quarter." Nevertheless, Carib military resistance to the Europeans lasted in one form or another until the start of the nineteenth century - and there was even a minor Carib War with the British in the 1930's, leading to the despatch (though thankfully not the use of) a gun ship to stand off the coast of Salybia on Dominica.

The Caribs also attacked shipping on occasion, especially as they called to "wood and water" on islands like St. Lucia, St. Kitts, Dominica or Martinique. In this way they mirrored the tactics of the first pirates of the Caribbean. Piracy arose in general because various European nations who were unable to challenge Spanish dominance in the region directly, gave these pirates unofficial backing, in the form of letters of marque, to follow private enterprise or to indulge in smuggling, piracy and the harassment of Spanish settlements. Even a famous personage like Sir Walter Raleigh was therefore known to the Spanish as "El Pirata Ingles".

As the power of Spain waned, other countries began to colonize the West Indies more seriously, although piracy continued for a while, the struggling settlers being happy to trade their agricultural produce and materials for a share of the Spanish gold. The Virgin Islands went through a lengthy period of "musical colonies" with the English, French, Dutch, Spanish and Danish moving from one island to another, shoving previous settlers on to the next, squabbling amongst themselves in Europe and, as a result, warring in the West Indies became so prevalent it was dubbed the "cockpit of conflict" for the Europeans.

Eventually, however, the bullion treasures from America dried up and a process of colonization for commercial profit emerged. The Danes formally took possession of St. Thomas and, later, St. John; the English ousted the Dutch and gained a firm foothold in Tortola and Virgin Gorda; and the French settled in St. Croix but later sold it to the Danish West India Company.

The Spaniards continued to raid

occasionally from their strongholds in Puerto Rico and Hispaniola through the late 1600s and piracy flared up intermittently in the early 1700s.

Considerable cleaning up and law enforcement took place as the casual farming that had begun, merely in order to colonize the islands and break the Spanish monopoly, gave way to serious plantations which, unsubsidized by stolen Spanish gold, needed to trade at a steady profit.

Following the example of the original Spanish settlers, early plantation owners brought slaves from Africa. When the introduction of sugar cane production in the 1640s required a large, cheap and stable labor force, the number of slaves began to increase. For some time the colonies thrived. Sugar and cotton were valuable commodities and the plantations diversified into the production of indigo, spices, rum, maize, pineapples, yams and coconuts. In 1717 the first census taken in Virgin Gorda showed a population of 625, about half of whom were black. By the mid-1700s this population had grown to nearly 2,000 and the proportion of slaves throughout the Virgin Islands had increased dramatically.

Life on the plantations was extremely hard for the slaves and, as their majority on the islands increased, so did the restrictions on them and the severity of the punishments meted out to them for the breaking of these. Conflict over the slave trade was increasing; it had been outlawed in England in 1772 and the impetus for its abolition was growing.

The obstacles to plantation life increased, several hurricanes and droughts ravaged the islands, and the American Revolution and Napoleonic wars created a revival of enemy raids, piracy and fighting within the islands. The slaves suffered as a result and, as news of abolition elsewhere began to filter through to the West Indies, they began to make use of their by now considerable majority to rebel.

The slave rebellions coincided, more or less, with the introduction of the sugar beet in Europe, which dealt a fatal blow to the once great "trade-triangle" based on West Indian cane. By the mid-1800s the slaves were free and the white population had deserted the colonies.

For almost 100 years the Virgin Islands dozed peacefully, the freed slaves living quietly off the land and sea, though with some difficulty in years of drought and famine. Government was minimal: In 1893, for example, there were only two white men in the B.V.I. — the Deputy Governor and the doctor.

The islands struggled on with tottering economies. Virgin Gorda was visited briefly by Cornish miners who reopened the old Spanish mine in search of copper. An earthquake leveled all the churches in Tortola and the H.M.S. Rhone was wrecked off Salt Island. As late as 1869 the steamship Telegrafo was detained in Tortola and charged with piracy. Labor riots and rebellions occasionally protested the hardships. The United States began to show an interest in buying the Danish islands, afraid that they would be sold to a hostile nation such as Germany.

The islands moved into the 20th century without much change. An agricultural station was established in Tortola in 1900 in hopes of boosting the faltering economy, various homestead projects were begun throughout the island with little effect and the parent governments of each colony were forced to accept financial responsibility for the islands, which were fast becoming a liability.

The first world was tightening the purse strings further, and by 1917 the Danes were happy to sell their Virgin Islands to the United States, which was eager to have a military outpost in the Caribbean.

St. Thomas had long been a useful coaling station and harbor for steamships and was well positioned to defend the approaches to the Panama Canal.

Over the first half of the 20th century there was gradual social reform and progress towards local government. This process began to speed up as the tourist trade, boosted by the increasing ease of casual travel, began to grow.

Finally the geography and physical advantages of the islands began once more to have a major influence on their fortunes. Situated conveniently close to the United States and blessed with a warm climate and a beautiful, unspoiled environment, the Virgin Islands rapidly became popular with tourists. This is an industry which needed only the natural resources of the islands to sustain their economies, and responsible tourism will also ensure that sustainability continues.

With the charter industry becoming the backbone of the islands, particularly in the B.V.I., sailors continue to make use of one of the finest sailing areas in the world. The quiet coves where Drake, Columbus and Blackbeard used to anchor are once more havens for fleets of sailing vessels and the modern adventurers who come to explore the Virgin Islands.

Thank you to Neil Whitehead, PhD for a history with less poetic license in the above article.

Simon Scott

Carnival in the Islands
"It's carnival time. Let the fun begin

Dougal Thorton

Carnival is a time of merrymaking. It involves indulging in food and drink, dancing with carefree abandon and parading in dazzling costume. The origin, as the name suggests, comes from the Latin and means 'caro' (meat) and 'vale' (farewell); in other words 'goodbye to meat'. It was the time of great feasting before the traditional Christian fasting of Lent. In the Virgin Islands the dates of the various festivals are not strictly adhered to but the fun is by no means diminished.

St. Thomas

The St. Thomas extravaganza, as with most Virgin Island carnivals, revolves around a central village. Here booths sell food and drinks; stalls offer games for prizes and there are fairground rides for children. In the middle of the circle of booths a stage lights up at night where shows and pageants are performed. One of the favorite shows is the calypso night when VI talent and other Caribbean songsters sing and perform renditions highlighting political scandals, male/female relations, crime and island satire.

J'ouvert, is the official beginning of the parade day, the highlight of carnival. At 4am revelers, often numbering in the thousands, begin a tramp through the streets of Charlotte Amalie to the accompaniment of mobile bands on the back of large flat-bed trucks. Most have been up all night and provocative dancing and wild cavorting are a hallmark of this event supposedly resembling the revelry that took place on the day of emancipation from slavery all those years ago.

The parade itself begins at the cemetery and winds its way through the streets of down town Charlotte Amalie culminating at the Lionel Roberts Stadium. Troupes can contain hundreds of revelers or a single participant representing a particular theme. Music fills the air from steel bands, reggae or calypso renditions performed live on slow moving flat-bed trailers. Performers in elaborately designed costumes sway to the music, wine and grind or cavort in rhythmic style as the parade moves slowly forward. Cleverly decorated floats designed to highlight local culture or a current event provide interest and excitement. The carnival queen sits atop a luxury vehicle, with attendant maids of honor, waving to

Jim Scheiner

the crowd. Mocko jumbies (costumed stilt walkers) weave their way alongside or through the troupes and floats displaying amazing acrobatic skill eliciting ooohs and aaahs from the awestruck crowd. Troupes and floats are judged along the route and at the stadium where a final exhibition is staged. Awards and prizes are the culmination to weeks of preparation and hard work.

A spectacular fireworks display by the harbour concludes the weeks of activities that make up the carnival extravaganza.

St. John

St. John's carnival takes place at the island's capital, tiny Cruz Bay. It follows the same format as the St Thomas event but its theme is more on the emancipation from slavery and independence from Denmark. Having said that the St John carnival is similar to all the others in that it's about fun.

The village and food fair is in the park at Cruz Bay and the parade is a much anticipated event. Ferries make almost non-stop trips to and from St Thomas on parade day and Cruz Bay is transformed from a quiet village atmosphere into a seething crowd of merrymakers. Like St. Thomas the event concludes with a fireworks display.

St. Croix

The two main towns in St. Croix, Frederiksted and the capital Christiansted, share the responsibility for carnival. Both provide venues for the various shows, contests and pageants that are the run-up to parade day. The carnival parade is an all day affair and as many as fifty masqueraders enter the competition

A day is devoted to horse racing

and another to water sports competitions and is highlighted here more than other carnival locations. St Croix's carnival coincides with Christmas celebrations and the climax of the parade takes place on Three King's Day in early January.

Tortola

Tortola in the BVI has renamed its carnival 'August Festival' since it no longer reflects the coming of Lent. Never-the-less it is the island's premier cultural event and attracts

Jim Scheiner

many visitors and participants from around the region. The festival village is erected close to the middle of Road Town and is 'party central'. There are booths selling food and drinks, a mini fairground with game stalls and rides for children, a haunted house and souvenir kiosks. The huge lighted stage is in the middle and provides the venue for bands, shows and pageants. Other events are held at the cultural center and the

Briercliffe Hall.

The pre-cursor to the parade of masqueraders is the 'rise and shine tramp' where participants tramp around the streets of Road Town to the accompaniment of a band on the back of a flatbed truck. Visitors can join in but often need a nap before the parade starts in the early afternoon

Imaginative floats and energetic troupes in masquerade wind their way along the waterfront to the rhythm of a steel band or reggae group. Trailers rock to the beat and hangers-on often throw sweets to the crowd. As the line of participants nears the judges stand the swaying, dancing and erotic wine and grinding reach fever pitch; entrants have their eyes on coveted prizes.

The spectacle finally over, weary participants head to the village for refreshments and spectators make their way home, satiated from an indulgence of food and drink, fun and games, and a show that will long be remembered.

Virgin Gorda

Virgin Gorda holds its own festival with a calypso monarch competition, a king and queen pageant, food fairs and bands. It all happens during the four days leading up to Easter with the parade on Easter Monday.

Schedule of Virgin Island Carnival Events. (Check for exact dates of shows and events just prior to previously published schedule)

St. Thomas Carnival:
The latter half of April

St. John:
4th July weekend

St. Croix:
Christmas to Three King's Day.

Tortola, BVI:
July 25 to August 10

Virgin Gorda:
Easter holidays

INTRODUCTION

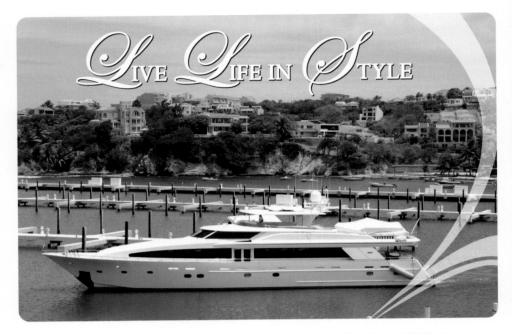

THE MOST COMPLETE MEGA-YACHT MARINA RESORT IN THE CARIBBEAN.

Designed as the ultimate berth for private yachts and mega-yachts, this new project features 162 slips, state of the art facilities for up to 200ft long vessels and world-class amenities within the most exclusive resort community in the Caribbean. Plus a 6 star Regent Hotel & Spa and Mandarin Oriental Hotel beginning construction in 2009.

With a unique hospitality focus, the staff provides concierge-style customer service to all yacht constituencies; sharing expertise and offering top notch services to captain, crew, guests and owners. Experience for yourself the best kept secret in Palmas del Mar; great big game marlin fishing just 2 miles to the south of Vieques.

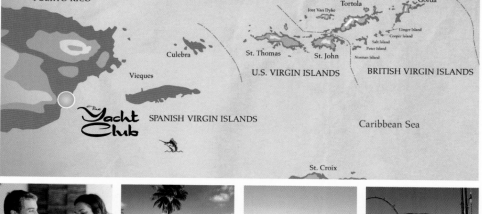

MARINA AMENITIES

- Yacht Club and Restaurant
- Tapas bar
- Infinity swimming pool
- Fuel dock
- In-dock fuel services
- Laundry services
- Wireless Internet
- Restrooms
- Showers
- Cable TV
- Ship Provisioning and Catering
- Ice

PALMAS DEL MAR AMENITIES

- Luxury Hotels
- Spa
- Fitness center
- Two 18-hole championship
  golf courses designed
  by Rees Jones and Gary Player
- Beach club with water features
- Largest tennis courts in the Caribbean
- World class equestrian facility
- Over 18 restaurants
- Casino

Visit us at the marina or contact us at:
787-379-7383 • 787-656-7300
www.palmasdelmaryachtclub.com
info@palmasdelmaryachtclub.com

The Yacht Club is professionally managed by
www.marinamanagement.com

Management Services, Inc.

Planning
The
Cruise

Soggy Dollar Bar   *Simon Scott*

Planning Your Cruise

Air Service

Traveling to and from the Virgins is very straightforward. Most of the larger bareboat companies have travel agents who work closely with them and are in touch with special air fares and hotel accommodations. San Juan, Puerto Rico is the main routing for passengers destined to the B.V.I., St. Thomas and St. Croix. There are numerous non-stop flights from major U.S. gateways with ample local connections. American Airlines is one of the main airlines that services the San Juan Airport. There are other airlines from the US, Europe, the UK and Canada, but with the changes taking place in the aviation industry due to fuel prices, it is best you check online or with your travel agent.

There are plenty of good hotels throughout the islands and it is advisable to plan a one night stay before checking in at the appropriate marina. This will enable you to "acclimatize" slowly, watching the sun set and sipping a rum punch

Tortola Looking West   *Dougal Thornton*

ISLAND AIR TRAVEL
AIRLINE ACCESS

The following airlines service the British Virgin Islands:

Air Sunshine
284-495-8900

American Eagle
284-495-2559

Cape Air
284-495-2100

Caribbean Star
284-494-2347

Caribbean Sun
284-494-2347

Caribbean Wings (charter)
284-495-6000

Flight Adventures Intl Ltd.
284-495-2311

Fly BVI (charter)
284-495-1747

Island Helicopters (charter)
284-499-2663

Island Birds
284-495-2002

LIAT
284-495-1187

The following airlines service the U.S. Virgin Islands:

Air Center Helicopters (charter)
340-775-7335

Air Sunshine
340-776-7900

American Airlines
800-474-4884

American Eagle
800-474-4884

Bohlke International Airways (charter)
340-778-9177

Cape Air
800-352-0714

Caribbean Sun
800-744-7827

Continental
800-231-0856

Delta Airlines
800-221-1212

LIAT
340-774-2313

Seaborne Aviation Inc.
340-773-6442

Spirit Airlines
800-772-7117

Sun Country
800-359-6786

US Airways
800-428-4322

United
800-864-8331

(Many of the airlines that fly in the British Virgin Islands also fly to the US Virgin Islands)
*See a complete listing of airline websites in the directory

while the frustrations of the day's travel diminish to insignificance.

The Virgins are an extremely popular tourist destination not only for sailors, but for all sorts of tourists and water sports enthusiasts; consequently, air travel and hotel accommodations should be reserved well in advance.

If you are planning to travel between the islands, there are numerous methods available to you.

Ferries

When traveling from one island to another, or between the British and U.S. Virgin Islands, ferries are a quick and convenient way to go when not using your yacht. The following schedules should be confirmed before making your plans, as schedules are subject to change. Most itineraries are scheduled at convenient times, and most ferries travel several times back and forth daily.

ISLAND FERRIES

Speedy's (284-495-5240):
*Underlined times are only effective Dec. 1st—Aug. 31st.

Virgin Gorda to Tortola
Monday-Sunday 8am
Monday-Saturday 8am, 10am,
11:30am, 12:30pm, 3:30pm
Mon, Tues, Thurs, Fri 5pm
Wednesday, Saturday 6pm, 10:30pm
Sundays & Holidays 8am, 1pm, 4:30pm

Tortola to Virgin Gorda
Monday-Sunday 9am
Monday-Saturday 9am, 10:30am,
12pm, 1:30pm, 4:30pm
Monday, Friday 6pm
Tuesday & Thursday 6:15pm
Wednesday, Saturday 6:45pm, 11pm
Sundays & Holidays 9am, 1:30pm, 5:15pm

St. Thomas to Virgin Gorda
Tuesday & Thursday 8:45am, 5pm
Saturday 4:30pm

Tortola to St. Thomas
Tuesday & Thursday 7:15am, 3:25pm
Saturday 9:15am

Virgin Gorda to St. Thomas
Tuesday & Thursday 6:30am, 2:45pm
Saturday 8:30am

Marina Cay Ferry (284-494-2174):

Marina Cay to Beef Island
9:15am, 10:15am, 11:15am, 12:15pm,
2:45pm, 3:45pm, 4:45pm, 5:45pm, 6:45pm

Beef Island to Marina Cay
9:30am, 10:30am, 11:30am, 12:30pm,
3pm, 4pm, 5pm, 6pm, 7pm

Inter-Island Boat Services (284-495-4166):

Cruz Bay, St. John to West End, Tortola
Monday-Thursday 8:30am,
11:30am, 3:30pm
Friday 8:30am, 11:30am, 3:30pm, 5pm
Saturday 8:30am, 11:30am, 3:30pm
Sunday 8:30am, 11:30am, 4:30pm

West End to Cruz Bay
Monday-Thursday 9:15am,
12:15pm, 4:15pm
Friday 9:15am, 12:15pm,
4:15pm, 5:30pm
Saturday 9:15am, 12:15pm, 4:15pm
Sunday 9:15am, 12:15pm, 5:15pm
every hour until 11pm

Smith's Ferry Services (284-495-4495):

West End, Tortola to Redhook, St. Thomas
Monday-Saturday 6:15/6:30am RT,
7:00am/7:30am, 10:00am/10:30am,
2:30pm/3pm
Saturday 6am (RT), 6:30am, 8:50am.
12:15pm, 3:45pm
Sunday 9:15am/9:30am,
12:15pm, 4:00pm

Red Hook, St. Thomas to Tortola
Monday-Saturday 8:25/55am,
12:15/45pm, 3:40pm, 4pm
Saturday 8am, 11:45am, 2:55pm,
5:30pm
Sunday 8am, 10:45am, 2:15pm,
5:15pm

Road Town to Virgin Gorda
Monday-Friday 7am, 8:50am,
12:30pm, 3:15 pm
Saturday 7am, 8:50am,
12:30pm, 4:15pm
Sunday 8:50am, 12:30pm, 4:15pm

Virgin Gorda to Road Town
Monday-Friday 7:50am, 10:15am,
2:15pm, 4pm
Saturday 7:00am, 8:50am,
12:30pm, 4:15pm
Sunday 8:50am, 12:30pm, 4:15pm

Native Son, Inc.(284-495-4617):

Tortola to Charlotte Amalie, St. Thomas
Monday-Friday 6:15/6:30am RT,
7:00am/7:30am WE,
10:00am/10:30am WE,
12:30pm WE, 2:30pm/3pm WE
Saturday 6:15/6:30am RT,
7:00am/7:30am WE, 8:45am RT,
10:00am/10:30am WE,
2:30pm/3pm WE, 5:45pm WE
Sunday 9:30am WE, 12:00pm WE,
3:50pm WE Daily to St. John
& Red Hook, St. Thomas 6am RT,
6:45am WE, 8:30am WE,
12:30pm WE, 4:00pm

Charlotte Amalie, St. Thomas to Tortola
Monday-Friday 8:25/55am, 1:30pm,
2:30pm, 4/4:30pm
Saturday 8:25/55am, 12:00pm,
1:30pm, 2:30pm, 4pm, 4:45pm
Sunday 8:00/8:30am, 10:45/11:15am,
1:45pm, 2:45pm, 4:00pm, 5:30pm
Daily from Red Hook to West End
7:45am, 11:15/11:45am, 3:15pm, 5pm

Nubian Princess(284-495-4999):

West End to St. John then St. Thomas
Monday, Thursday 6:30am, 8am,
11:30am, 3:30pm
Daily 8am, 11:30am, 3:30pm

Red Hook to St. John then West End
Monday, Thursday 7:30am, 10:45am,
2:30pm, 4:30pm Daily 10:45am,
2:30pm, 4:30pm

Road Town Fast Ferry (284-494-2323):

*Only direct ferry service to and from
Road Town and Charlotte Amalie
Road Town to St. Thomas
Monday-Saturday 7am, 10am, 2:30pm
Sunday 9am, 2:30pm

St. Thomas to Road Town
Monday-Saturday 8:40am,
12pm, 4:15pm
Sunday 12pm, 4pm

New Horizon Ferry Service (284-495-9278):

West End to Jost Van Dyke
Monday-Friday 8am, 10am, 1pm,
4pm, 6pm
Saturday, Sunday 9am, 10am, 1pm,
4pm, 6pm

Jost Van Dyke to West End
Monday-Friday 7am, 9:00am, 12pm,
2pm, 5:00pm
Saturday, Sunday 8:00am, 9:30am,
12pm, 2pm, 5pm

Peter Island Ferry (284-495-2000):

Road Town to Peter Island
Daily 5:30am, 7am, 8:30am, 10am,
12pm, 2pm, 3:30pm, 5:30pm, 6:30pm,
9:30pm, 10:30pm

Peter Island to Road Town
Daily 6:30am, 8am, 9am, 11:30am,
1:30pm, 2:30pm, 4:30pm, 6pm,
7:30pm, 10pm, 11:30pm

North Sound Express (284-495-2138, reservations required):

Beef Island to Virgin Gorda
Daily 8:15am, 11:15am, 1:45pm,
4:15pm, 6pm, 8pm

The Valley to Beef Island
Daily 8:30am, 11:30am, 4:30pm

Bitter End to Beef Island
Daily 6:45am, 9am, 12pm,
3:15pm, 5pm

Leverick Bay to Beef Island
(must call for LB pickup):
Daily 6:30am, 8:45am,
11:45am, 3pm, 4:45pm

Saba Rock Ferry (284-495-7711 or 495-9966 or VHF Channel 16)

A complimentary service for anyone wanting to travel to or from Saba Rock Resort to any dock within the North Sound. This includes Bitter End Yacht Club, Biras Creek Resort, Gun Creek, Leverick Bay, and Prickly Pear Island. The ferries operate on demand from 7:00 am until 11:00 pm. Just contact them by telephone or radio for pick up.

Check our website for links to ferries, airlines and other useful Virgin Islands websites.

Schedule subject to change without notice.

Packing for the Cruise

Almost without exception, most sailors coming to the Virgin Islands for a week's sailing bring far too much gear. Try not to carry hard suitcases as they do not stow easily on a boat. If possible, use duffel bags or sea bags that can be folded up when not in use.

If you are traveling from the northern climates during the winter months, try to shed your heavy overcoats and boots prior to boarding the airplane. You will only have to carry them around for the duration of your stay in the islands.

Lay out everything you intend to bring and ask yourself if you really need each item. During the days aboard the boat, you will need only bathing suits and perhaps a cover-up, shorts and a few casual shirts or blouses. If you intend to eat ashore at resorts like Caneel Bay, Little Dix and Peter Island Resort, include a jacket and tie for the men and a light cocktail dress for the ladies. Otherwise, in most island restaurants, casual slacks and shirts are acceptable.

You will need some reef shoes for wading in shallow water and T-shirts.

You may wish to include an inexpensive snorkel for each crew member… using a second hand snorkel can be like borrowing someone else's toothbrush.

The Baths   *Julian Putley*

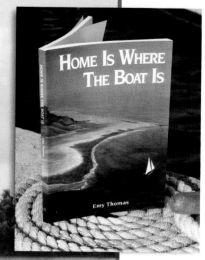
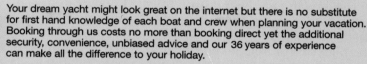
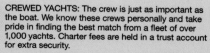

PLANNING THE CRUISE

Car Rental

Both the British and the U.S. Virgin Islands have developed adequate car rental agencies to cope with the needs of the growing tourist industry.

Prices are slightly higher than on the U.S. mainland, but considering the high cost of freight and the limited life expectancy that vehicles enjoy in the island environment, the differential is not excessive. Most of the major car rental companies have local branches throughout the Virgins and advance reservations can be made through your travel agent.

In addition, many locally owned and operated companies are also represented. If you are chartering during the peak months (December-April), try to reserve well in advance to avoid delays. In both the U.S. and British Virgins, remember to drive on the left.

Taxi Service

All points of debarkation are more than adequately serviced by taxis. The airports and ferry docks are often lined three deep, with the drivers pushing hard to capture their share of the market.

It is common in the islands to see open safari buses, which can carry up to 20 passengers in natural "air-conditioned" comfort. Taxi fares tend to be expensive throughout the islands and taxis are not metered! However, there are official taxi rates in both the British and U.S. Virgin Islands, and the prudent traveler should inquire of the rate beforehand so that there are no misunderstandings.

The major charter-boat companies will arrange transportation to pick you up upon arrival at the airport, but, such service should be arranged at the time of booking the charter.

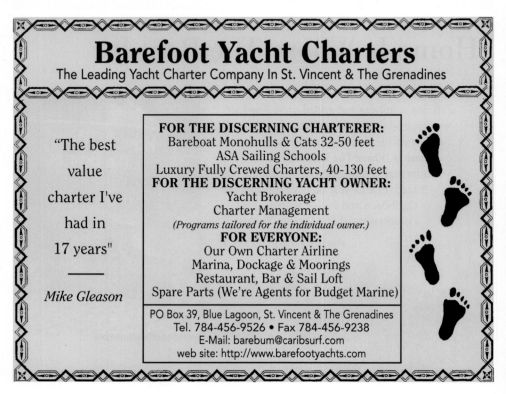

Currency

The U.S. dollar is the local currency in both the U.S. and British Virgin Islands. Since you will be spending a lot of time on small islands, it is a good

idea to keep traveller's checks in smaller denominations. Major credit cards are honored at most U.S.V.I. stores and hotels and the larger B.V.I. establishments, but do not expect to use them at small restaurants during your cruise. Personal checks are not accepted anywhere. There are a few ATM machines in more populated areas.

A SAMPLING OF TAXI FARES*

The fares listed below are "per person". Many fares will be "charter fares" and therefore should be lower. This is just to give you an idea of the maximum you should be expected to pay. Always inquire before accepting a taxi and if you have a question ask to see the government passenger fares regulations.

TORTOLA

From Beef Island Airport to:
East End, Long Look - $3.00
Maya Cove - $4.00
Wickhams Cay II (Moorings, Tortola Yacht Services), Road Town, $6.00
Nanny Cay - $8.00
West End, Long Bay, Cane Garden Bay - $12.00

From Road Town to:
Prospect Reef, Treasure Isle, Wickhams Cay II - $3.00
Baughers Bay - $4.00
Maya Cove, Brandywine, Skyworld, Nanny Cay - $5.00
Cane Garden Bay, West End, Beef Island Airport - $6.00

From West End Jetty To:
Frenchman's Cay - $3.00
Sugar Mill, Long Bay Hotel - $4.00
Cane Garden Bay, Nanny Cay - $5.00
Prospect Reef, Road Town,
Treasure Isle, Wickham's Cay II - $6.00
Beef Island - $12.00
Note: Tours of a maximum of 2 1/2 hours and 1-3 persons $50.00
Fixed Tours over 3 persons - $15.00 PP

ST. THOMAS

From downtown Charlotte Amalie to:
Airport Terminal - $6.00
Compass Point - $10.00
Crown Bay Dock - $4.00
Frenchman's Reef - $3.00
Frenchtown - $3.00
National Park Dock - $10.00
Red Hook - $10.00
St. Thomas Yacht Club - $13.00
Sapphire Resort - $12.00
Vessup Bay - $13.00

*Check our website for links to ferries, airlines and other useful Virgin Islands websites.

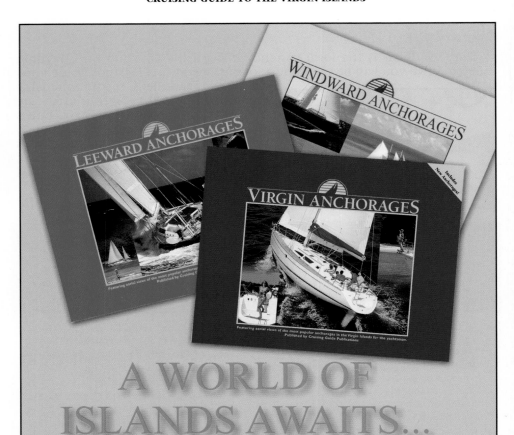

A WORLD OF ISLANDS AWAITS...

The Caribbean Islands are a magical world that awaits your exploration. Three books, *Virgin Anchorages, Windward Anchorages* and *Leeward Anchorages*, graphically, and through spectacular aerial photography, depict dozens of favorite anchorages in their respective areas.

Each anchorage is featured in a two-page full color spread. One page provides an aerial photograph of the anchorage. The adjoining page offers advice on approaching the anchorage with navigational instructions.

Virgin Anchorages can be used in conjunction with the *Cruising Guide to the Virgin Island*s. *Leeward Anchorages* is a companion to the *Cruising Guide to the Leeward Islands*. *Windward Anchorages* is a companion to the *Sailors Guide to the Windward Islands*. All should also be used with official navigational charts.

These guides are indispensable for the cruising yachtsman or charterer visiting these legendary Caribbean islands and they make a stunning memento for the coffee table.

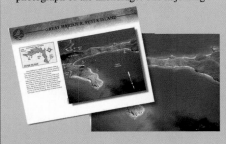

CRUISING GUIDE PUBLICATIONS

To Order:
Phone: (727) 733-5322 • (800) 330-9542
Fax: (727) 734-8179
www.cruisingguides.com

Virgin Anchorages $29.95
Leeward Anchorages $29.95
Windward Anchorages $29.95

Protection from the Sun

Although it may seem difficult to comprehend as you dig your car out of the snow to get to the airport, the tropical sun is hot, especially on pale bodies that have been kept undercover throughout a northern winter.

The constant trade breezes keep the temperature pretty much ideal, but be careful not to spend too long out in the sun, as the combined effect of overhead tropical sun and reflection from both sails and water can cause severe sunburns.

Most charter yachts are equipped with bimini tops; however, it is still a good idea to bring along a pair of lightweight or surgical pants and tops if you have access to them. These will enable you to cover up.

If you are fair, then perhaps you should think about a wide-brimmed hat.

Suntan lotions are available throughout the islands. Heed the warnings of dermatologists regarding excessive sun exposure and do not go out into the sun without using an appropriate sun block or coverup. Start with at least SPF-15. If you are careful, you will gradually develop a rich, golden tan without suffering a painful and potentially dangerous sunburn.

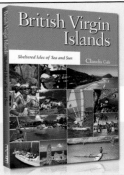

Smugglers Cove, Tortola

What Not to Bring

Apart from an abundance of clothing, there are a few items that don't make any sense to lug back and forth:

(A) Scuba gear — If you have your own regulator, face mask, etc., fine, but don't bring down weight belts and tanks. They are available for rent from many outlets and dive shops throughout the islands an will save you the hassle of lugging them around.

(B) Food items—Once again, unless you have special dietary needs, these items are readily available through out the islands and the marginal savings on some frozen steaks could be offset if the box thaws or goes astray.

(C) Surfboards and windsurfers — These items represent a problem for the major airlines and a nightmare for the smaller commuter airlines. They are available for rent and anyone interested should make prior arrangements with the appropriate charter company or agent.

Remember that you will probably purchase a few items while in the islands and some allowance should be made for such purchases when packing.

The ideal amount of luggage to bring on a sailing holiday should fit in a duffel bag underneath your airline seat. This will save your worrying about checking bags and waiting with baited breath to see if they show up on the other end.

Bringing Firearms into the Virgins

Some cruisers feel more secure with guns aboard for protection. If you are bringing firearms on your vessel into the U.S. Virgin Islands, the firearms must be licensed. When clearing customs all firearms and ammunition must be declared to Customs. Before arriving in the U.S. Virgin Islands call customs first to ensure the regulations have not changed.

Firearms in the British Virgin Islands are restricted and must be declared to Customs when you enter the British Virgin Islands. Customs will confiscate the firearms, leave them at Police Headquarters giving the owner a receipt. When leaving the B.V.I. the guns may be claimed from Police Headquarters with the receipt. Please check with B.V.I. Customs before arriving with guns in the event that regulations have changed.

Safety in the Virgin Islands

The Virgin Islands, both U.S. and BVI, are for the most part very safe. However, as with any other destination in the world, there is always a chance of having something of value targeted by a thief. If you take precautions in advance, then you can enjoy your holiday with less worry. If you are chartering a bareboat, direct any specific questions to your charter company.

The following are some suggestions to help keep your possessions safe from petty crime:

Valuables-- Expensive jewelry can be left at home. It is too easy to lose rings, earrings etc. when swimming, beaching and sailing. The islands are very informal for the most part, beach bars are casual and it's unlikely you would want to wear anything fancy. If you can't leave it behind, insure it.

Passports – You can keep your passport with you or put it in a very safe place when leaving the vessel. We suggest using waterproof pouches that can be worn around the neck, under a shirt, that will fit a passport, some cash and credit cards. Leave your passport number with someone at home so that if you do lose it, it will be easier for immigration to help you.

Cash – Of course you'll need some cash, but there are more and more ATM's located throughout the islands. Credit cards can be replaced if lost or stolen. Just make sure you have left your credit card number with someone at home and bring the telephone number listed on the card to call and report a lost or stolen card. Travelers Checks are always a good idea.

Cameras – About all you can do when leaving your camera behind on board is to lock your boat and put

PLANNING THE CRUISE

the camera out of sight.

Leaving your vessel – most boats can be locked at the companionway hatch after dogging the portholes.

Dinghies- most charter boats are equipped with metal cables and locks. When going ashore, lock your dinghy to the dock to avoid having it "borrowed". Also, at night or when leaving the dinghy with the boat make sure you lock it to the boat. Vessels with dinghy davits should raise the dinghy out of the water at night or when leaving the dinghy and the boat.

Nights aboard -- When sleeping at night, many people leave the hatches

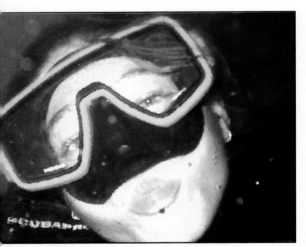

open to enjoy sleeping with the trade winds lulling them to sleep. If you prefer, lock the companionway, close the large hatches and leave the portholes open to capture the breeze.

For your personal safety, the usual rules apply. Don't go anywhere where you feel uncomfortable, especially alone. Use caution as you would anywhere else. After several rounds of rum punch anyone can become more vulnerable to crime, and it is not safe to be operating motor vessels after having a few too many.

The Virgin Islanders are very warm, friendly and helpful. The environment is mostly benign. As you would anywhere in the world, take a few simple precautions, relax, and enjoy your stay.

Seasickness

One of the downsides of a sailing holiday can be, of course, seasickness. This is one of the few times you can feel so badly that you are afraid that you won't die! Although the Virgin Islands have relatively little wave action there are those who just look at a boat and turn green. It can happen at the most unpredictable times, and seasickness is always every bit as embarrassing as it is miserable for the victim.

Over the years we have seen and heard all kinds of remedies, and have tried most of them. Here is a list of products to help you prepare for your trip and act like an old salt:

1. One favorite is Sea Bands. These elastic wrist bands have a small, plastic button that when placed in the right acupressure point on the inside of your wrist, help to relieve symptoms. The bands come with easy instructions. They have no side effects, and are comfortable to wear. You may purchase them at drug stores. There are also other similar brands available. We have tried these numerous times with people who suffer from motion sickness at the slightest movement and have found them very successful.

2. An old, natural remedy that again, has no side effects and is safe to use is ginger capsules. Ginger has a settling effect on the stomach. These capsules

are available in most health food stores.

3. Dramamine, Marezine, and Bonine are the old stand-by, over the counter anti-histamines. Dramamine in particular can make you very, very drowsy. You can miss some good times if you are sleeping the days away, however, it is better than being sick.

4. For a prescription drug, ask your physician for Transderm Scop. This is only sold as a prescription, and can have some side effects. It does have some restrictions and is not safe for everyone. Transderm Scop comes in the form of a medicated patch that is worn behind the ear for three days at a stretch.

Avoid reading and going below when you are underway. The fresh breeze can help, and also remember to look at the horizon instead of the waves passing next to the boat. Good luck, and let us hear from you if there are any other miracle cures around.

Provisions for the Cruise

Most charter companies in and around the Virgin Islands offer the charter party a choice of provisioning programs or other options.

The original concept was designed to cope with the lack of supermarkets. But in recent years, both in the U.S. and British Virgin Islands, the selection of goods has increased tremendously. Therefore, your provisioning options are as follows:

A) Allow the charter company to provision for you from a pre-selected plan, to save on sailing time. The main plans are full provisioning, which includes 3 meals a day, or the popular split program, which eliminates some evening meals so you can eat ashore. If you are considering this, ask the charter company for a sample menu.

B) Provision yourself from one of the local markets or delicatessens. This is a good idea if you have specific dietary needs, but it is time-consuming, and when analyzing costs, taxi fares and sailing time should be considered. However, many of the local markets have a surprisingly sophisticated array of products.

C) Have an independent provisioning company prepare your provisions in advance and have them delivered to the boat or swing by and pick them up. Provisioning lists can be faxed or emailed in advance, allowing you the luxury of choosing your provisioning from home.

Restocking Along the Way

However you provision your vessel you will probably wish to augment your supply at some point along the cruise. Major items are available in Road Town, Nanny Cay, Sopers Hole, Cane Garden Bay, Trellis Bay, Maya Cove and East End in Tortola. Provisioning is available in Virgin Gorda Yacht Harbour, the Bitter End, and Leverick Bay in Virgin Gorda. In the U.S. Virgins you will be able to provision in Cruz Bay, Redhook, Charlotte Amalie, and in Christiansted, St. Croix.

Cruising
Information

Cruising Information

Charts
Paper Charts

It is possible to navigate through the U.S. and British Virgin Islands with a single paper chart, NOS 25640. Many of the charter companies have duplicated this chart in one form or another as a handout for each charter group. If you're chartering, be sure to ask your charter company in advance which charts they'll provide you, when you'll receive them, and whether the charts are yours to keep. Then take a careful look at the areas you intend to cruise and order any additional chart coverage you may want.

Your own charts will allow you to plan your trip in advance and will also serve as a nice memento of your trip. Complete paper chart coverage of the Virgin Islands will range from about $50.00 to several hundred dollars, especially if you include electronic charts which are now very popular. Charts can be hard to obtain in the Virgin Islands, so taking your own charts is the best way to be sure you have the coverage you're comfortable with.

The following paper charts cover the Virgin Islands and surrounding areas, and they are available from larger chart agents in the U.S., Canada and Europe

Caribbean Yachting Charts
  (These charts are cross referenced in our anchorage sections).
CYC-Series 1 - Puerto Rico and the Virgin Islands, Fajardo to Anegada

C-11	-	St. Thomas to Anguilla
C-12	-	Anegada to Virgin Gorda
C-12A	-	Virgin Gorda - North Sound
C-13	-	Tortola to Virgin Gorda
C-13A	-	Tortola-Road Harbour
C-14	-	St. John to Tortola
C-14A	-	St. John-Coral Bay
C-15	-	St. Thomas - St. John - Pillsbury Sound
C-16	-	St. Thomas

C-16A	-	St. Thomas
	-	Charlotte Amalie
C-17	-	St. Croix
C-17A	-	Christiansted Harbour

Imray

A13	-	SE Coast of Puerto Rico
A131	-	Isla de Culebra and Isla de Culabea
A23	-	The Virgin Islands, St. Croix
A231	-	St. Thomas to Virgin Gorda
A232	-	Tortola to Anegada
A233	-	A231 & A232 (two sides)
A234	-	St. Croix NE Coast

Chart Kit

Reg. 10	-	U.S. and British Virgin Islands and Puerto Rico

U.S. National Oceanographic Service (NOAA)

25640	-	Puerto Rico and the Virgin Islands
25641	-	Virgin Gorda to St. Thomas; St. Croix
25644	-	St. Croix, Frederiksted Road and Pier
25645	-	St. Croix, Christiansted Harbour
25649	-	Charlotte Amalie
25647	-	Pillsbury Sound

U.S National Imagery and Mapping Agency (former DMA)

25600	-	Anegada Passage
25609	-	St. Thomas to Anegada
25610	-	Approaches to Gorda Sound
25611	-	Road Harbour and approaches

British Admiralty

485	-	St. Croix
2005	-	Road Harbour to Capella Islands
2006	-	Anegada BVI to St. Thomas USVI
2008	-	NE Virgin Gorda to Anegada
2020	-	Road Harbor Tortola and N Sd Virgin Gorda
2183	-	St. Thomas Harbor

Relaxing on the nets   *Simon Scott*

Chart Kit
Caribbean Leisure Folio – The Virgin Islands
SC5640 Includes 12 paper charts in a thick
plastic sleeve

Maptech-CYC – 11.1 Virgin Islands –
Includes 8 paper charts and CD of digital
charts with software in a thick plastic sleeve

Electronic Charts

Used in combination with GPS and paper
charts, electronic charts have become
extremely popular in the Caribbean, though
they remain hard to purchase in the islands.
The following electronic charts cover the
Virgin Islands (and beyond) and are available from selected chart agents and marine
electronic dealers in the U.S., Canada and
Europe.

Maptech CYC companion CD charts

C-Map – NAC501 Cuba to Trinidad

Garmin – US030 Southeast Caribbean

Passport World Charts --
10/ Caribbean Sea
Virgin Islands -
Grenada

Caribbean Yachting Charts
— The References at the Bottom of the Pages

We have cross-referenced all of our sketch charts for the U.S. and British Virgin Islands this year with the Caribbean Yachting Charts — Series 1 — St. Thomas to Anguilla. You will note at the bottom of the anchorage pages a number such as "C 14" which denotes the Caribbean Yachting Chart that the anchorage discussed appears on. The charts have been recently resurveyed and use WGS 84 map datum for the GPS waypoints. We think you will find these charts very accurate and easy to read. The charts are available from our website, our toll free number, or by using the order form at the back of the book.

Navigation

Pilotage through unknown waters is one of the major concerns of the cruising yachtsman. However, in the Virgins, where there is very little tide rise and fall and only minimal current to worry about, pilotage is extremely simple.

Since the weather is so warm, we don't experience any fog and you can always see the island for which you are heading.

Reefs and shoals are not a major problem as they are well marked and, provided time is taken to study the pertinent charts on a daily basis, your cruise around the island will be most enjoyable.

The islands themselves are high and volcanic, rising steeply from the crystal clear water. In many cases, it is possible to position your bow almost on the beach, providing you have a stern anchor set.

Since the island chain is close together, you will have no difficulty in distinguishing them. Using the contour marks on the charts you will usually be able to pinpoint your location without the use of navigation tools.

Equipment

Every cruising yacht should be equipped with the basic tools of navigation — parallel rules, triangles, dividers, plotters, etc. However, it should be noted that in order to navigate throughout the islands, the only equipment needed is a compass, chart, pencil and leadline or fathometer. Those wishing to brush up on navigational skills will find ample opportunity, although celestial observations are often difficult because of the proximity of the islands.

Reef Reading

There is no dark secret attached to the ability to read the reef. It is merely the ability to distinguish water color. Experience is, of course, the best teacher; however, with a few practical hints, even the novice will be able to feel his way to an anchorage within a few days.

It is important to have the sun overhead in order to distinguish reef areas. That is why most charter companies insist that the boats be at anchor by 1600 hours. Do not attempt to negotiate a reef-fringed entrance with the sun in your eyes, and always have someone on the bow keeping an eye on the water in front of the boat.

Deep water of 50 feet and over will be "inky" blue. This can be lighter if the bottom is white sand.

A light green or turquoise would indicate a depth of 15-25 feet. If the bottom has rocks or coral, these will change the color to a brownish shade.

Water of 10 feet and under will show as a very pale shade of green if there is a sandy bottom, or a light brown if rocks and coral are present.

CAUTION: There have been several incidents of people diving off of their vessels not realizing how shallow the water was and sustaining serious damage to their heads, back or neck. Be sure you check the water depth prior to the performing the graceful dive.

Right of Way and Night Sailing

A general rule of thumb is to stay out of everyone's way. There are times, however, when this is impossible and, in such instances, power boats should give way to boats under sail. This being the case, it is important in close quarters to hold your course so that the other skipper can take appropriate action to avoid you, without having to double-guess your actions.

If you are crossing ferry traffic, it is prudent to keep a weather eye on approaching vessels and make every effort to stay well clear.

Freighters trading between the islands are underway at night, and sometimes do not use their running lights. Don't sail at night!

Cruising Etiquette

During your cruise through the Virgins, please remember that there are a limited number of places on the smaller islands capable of dealing with garbage.

Check first before carrying it ashore — don't throw it over the side, even if it means keeping it a couple of days in a plastic bag. Always carry any refuse back to your boat, rather than leaving it on the beach.

Many of the beaches throughout the Virgins are private property and the cruising yachtsman must exercise care to respect any notice indicating such restrictions.

Navy Vessels and Cruise Ships

When approaching a navy vessel or cruise ship, Coast Guard regulations state that you must slow your vessel to 5 knots within 500 yards and maintain a 200 yard distance at all times.

Cane Garden Bay   *Simon Scott*

GPS — Global Positioning Satellite

Although the Virgin Islands are mostly line of sight navigation it is still quite helpful to have a GPS system aboard your vessel for occasional reference. It is certainly valuable when making passages to destinations outside of the Virgin Islands or for those very occasional days when the weather may somewhat obstruct your view of prominent landmarks.

GPS is a fantastic aid to navigation, but it should be used in conjunction with visual sightings and depth readings. It can be quite helpful for getting you near a harbor entrance, but it is not accurate enough to take you into the harbor. There have been reports of navigators finding themselves a couple of miles away from where they expected in places where our GPS showed good correspondence. Occasional errors are a possibility.

The latitudes and longitudes we give in our guide are courtesy of Nautical Publications, publishers of the Caribbean Yachting Charts that we cross reference in our guides. They are taken from the series 1 — Virgin Islands — St. Thomas to Sombrero and use WGS 84 map datum. To order a set of charts please refer to the order form in the back of the book.

GPS Waypoint	Location	Latitude (north)	Longitude (west)	Page
149	Great Harbour Jost Van Dyke	18°26.0 north	64°45.0 west	pg. 96
139	Road Harbour Tortola	18°24.8 north	64°36.2 west	pg. 124
138	Brandywine Bay Tortola	18°24.5 north	64°35.0 west	pg. 124
133	Beef Island Bluff	18°25.3 north	64°30.9 west	pg. 144
144	Water Point Norman Island	18°19.3 north	64°37.5 west	pg. 166 and 169
142	Rock Hole Peter Island	18°21.4 north	64°37.0 west	pg. 175
137	Deadman's Bay Peter Island	18°22.0 north	64°34.6 west	pg. 137
136	Cooper Island	18°23.5 north	64°31.0 west	pg. 180
134	Round Rock (north)	18°24.1 north	64°28.2 west	pg. 180
135	Round Rock (south)	18°23.3 north	64°27.1 west	pg. 180
132	The Baths Virgin Gorda	18°26.0 north	64°27.0 west	pg. 186
125	Mountain Point Virgin Gorda	18°30.4 north	64°25.2 west	pg. 186 and 194

GPS Waypoint	Location	Latitude (north)	Longitude (west)	Page
131	St. Thomas Bay Virgin Gorda	18°27.2 north	64°26.9 west	pg. 186
124	Mosquito Rock Virgin Gorda	18°31.3 north	64°23.1 west	pg. 194 and 205
121	Setting Point Anegada	18°42.4 north	64°24.5 west	pg.205 and 207
122	Horseshoe Reef Anegada	18°32.2 north	64°15.0 west	pg. 205
123	Pajaros Point Virgin Gorda	18°30.5 north	64°18.7 west	pg. 205
162	Charlotte Amalie St. Thomas	18°18.6 north	64°55.6 west	pg. 217 and 218
161	Packet Rock	18°17.6 north	64°53.4 west	pg. 217
165	Middle Passage Western St. Thomas	18°21.5 north	64°50.7 west	pg. 217
153	Jersey Bay St. Thomas	18°18.2 north	64°51.3 west	pg. 217 and 231
154	Maria Bluff St. John	18°18.5 north	64°47.7 west	pg. 240
151	Durloe Cays St. John	18°21.5 north	64°47.8 west	pg. 240 and 252
146	Ram Head St. John	18°17.8 north	64°42.2 west	pg. 240
145	Red Point St. John	18°19.4 north	64°40.3 west	pg. 240 and 258
171	Christiansted St. Croix	17°46.0 north	64°41.9 west	pg. 259 and 261
172	Green Cay St. Croix	17°46.6 north	64°40.1 west	pg. 259 and 272
173	Salt River St. Croix	17°47.8 north	64°45.0 west	pg. 259

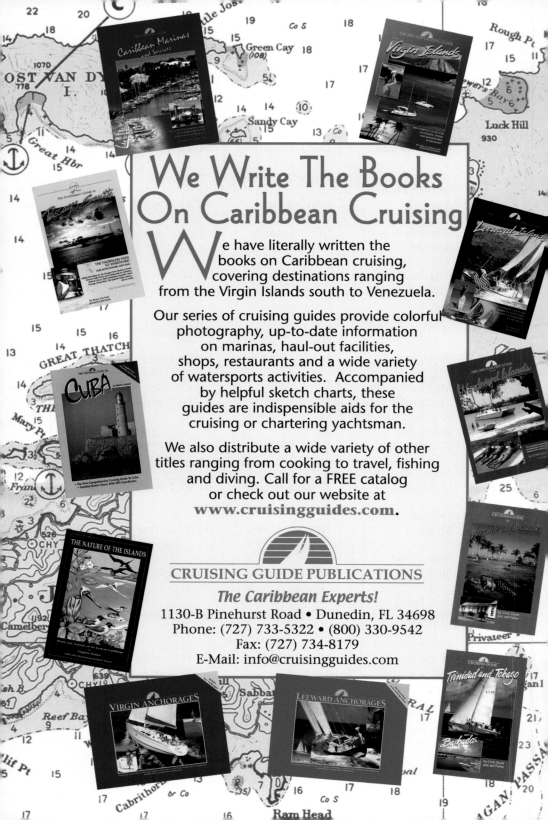

The Buoyage System of the Virgin Islands

In an international effort to standardize buoyage systems, the (IALA) International Association of Lighthouse Authorities has agreed that, in order to meet conflicting requirements, there will be two systems in use throughout the world. These are to be called systems A and B, respectively. The rules for the two systems were so similar that the "IALA" Executive Committee felt able to combine the two sets of rules into one, known as the "IALA Maritime Buoyage System."

This single set of rules allows lighthouse authorities the choice of using red to port or red to starboard on a regional basis, the two regions being known as region A and region B.

The latter system, system B, is used in North and South America and throughout the waters of the Caribbean. In system B the color red is used to mark the starboard side of the channel when approaching from seaward.

In this respect, it should be noted that the respective buoyage systems for both U.S. and British Virgins are the same.

Red right Returning!
The lateral 'system B' as seen entering from seaward.

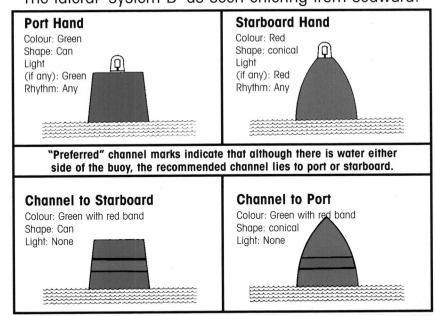

Port Hand
Colour: Green
Shape: Can
Light
(if any): Green
Rhythm: Any

Starboard Hand
Colour: Red
Shape: conical
Light
(if any): Red
Rhythm: Any

"Preferred" channel marks indicate that although there is water either side of the buoy, the recommended channel lies to port or starboard.

Channel to Starboard
Colour: Green with red band
Shape: Can
Light: None

Channel to Port
Colour: Green with red band
Shape: conical
Light: None

For regular V.I. information updates see our website: www.cruisingguides.com

Virgin Weather

Located in the northeast trade wind belt, the Virgin Islands are blessed with almost perfect weather the year round. The seas from the north are broken by the island chain, which provides the seafarer with ideal sailing conditions.

Weather Forecasts

Unlike that of most other parts of the world, the weather in the Virgin Islands is extremely stable. Forecasts are broadcast daily on most of the local stations:

St. Thomas:

WIVI 99.5 FM (Forecasts at 0730, 0830, 1530, 1630 with hourly updates); WVWI 1000 AM (Forecasts hourly); WSTA 1340 AM; Radio Antilles 830 AM

St. Croix: WSTX 970 AM

Tortola: ZBVI — 780 AM

Puerto Rico: WOJO 1030 AM (English speaking all day at 6 minutes past the hour)

NOAA Weather is broadcasted throughout the day on WX 3 or 4 or 6 on your VHF radio.

Tides

The tidal range throughout the Virgin Islands is about 12 inches, depending upon the time of year. You will probably be unaware of any fluctuation. However, you cannot rely upon the rising tide to float you off the odd sandbar. Currents in certain areas can reach 1-2 knots, namely through Pillsbury Sound between St. Thomas and St. John, the Durloe Cays in St. John, and in the narrows between St. John and Tortola.

Ground Swells

During the winter months of November through April, any significant weather in the North Atlantic will produce heavy swells along the entire north coast of the Virgins several days later. These ground seas have little effect on vessels under sail, but can turn a normally tranquil anchorage into pounding surf. Most anchorages exposed to the north are prone to this phenomenon—choose your anchorage accordingly.

Winds

Owing to the northeast trade winds, the wind direction throughout the Virgins is dominated by the movements of the Bermuda High. During the winter months of November to January, the prevailing wind is from the northeast at 15-20 knots. The fabled Christmas Winds can produce 25-30 knots for several days at a time. By February, the winds start to move around to the east, and by June, they are blowing out of the southeast at 10-15 knots.

During September to October, the trade winds are weakest, and the weather can be less settled. Although these months are considered hurricane season, Hurricane Hugo was the first to hit in 50-odd years. By

A.J Blake

November, the high pressure system around Bermuda starts to stabilize and 15-20 knot breezes become the norm.

Rain

While late summer to fall is considered rainy season, rain squalls can come at any time of year. Be aware of approaching squalls by watching the sky and clouds to windward.

If a dark squall is approaching, it probably has considerable wind velocity on the squall line, and the prudent skipper should shorten sail beforehand.

It also will give the crew a chance to arm themselves with soap and enjoy a fresh water shower.

Winter Storms and Hurricanes

Despite recent hurricanes, the Virgin Islands have fewer storms than does the Long Island Sound in New York. When the islands do experience a tropical storm or depression, it is usually in the early development of the storm center, and the storms usually do not reach full intensity until they are north of the area. Should a storm approach the islands, remember that they travel very slowly; consequently, with the communication systems used today, sailors can be assured of at least 48 hours' warning.

Communication

Telephone Service

AREA CODES

British Virgin Islands	.284
U.S. Virgin Islands	.340
Puerto Rico	.787

The U.S. Virgin Islands (area code 340) and Puerto Rico (area code 787) are on the same system as the U.S. Calls can be made at pay phones, as on the mainland, either collect, or with a telephone card or credit card.

The British Virgin Islands, area code 284, are serviced by Cable and Wireless. They can be accessed from the U.S. by using the prefix of 1 plus area code plus seven digit number. You can also use your credit card, or call collect. Several pay telephones are available throughout the islands for use with U.S. coins and BVI telephone cards. Major credit cards can be used to make international calls. To call the U.S. with a credit card, dial 1-800-call USA. BVI telephone

A.J Blake

cards may be purchased in many shops throughout the islands in denominations of ten to twenty dollars. Fax and email services are available at the Cable and Wireless office located at Wickham's Cay I. Dial "0" for an operator and 119 for local information.

VHF

Almost every boat sailing the Virgins will be equipped with a VHF radio. Apart from single side band for offshore communications, VHF is used for all local traffic.

The channels vary from boat to boat, but the most commonly used frequencies are listed below.

Channel 16: Standby and international distress frequency
Channel 12: Portside operations (Charter company to yacht)
Channel 6: Ship-to-ship, safety
Channel 24, 85, and 87: W.A.H. Virgin Islands Radio
Channel 68: Ship-to-ship communications
Channel 22A: Coast Guard
Channel 3, 4, 6: Weather
Channel 16 is used as a calling frequency, but the operator must switch to a second channel once contact has been established in order to keep channel 16 open.

Anchoring in coral is
STRICTLY PROHIBITED
in both the U.S. and B.V.I.

Cellular Telephones

For Virgin Island yachtsmen who need to keep in touch, cellular telephone service is now available. Cellular phones can be used for everything from checking in with the office, the family, or for local applications like ordering more provisions and making dinner reservations. Installed on many bareboat charter fleets as well as crewed yachts, this offers the yachtsman the choice of using a telephone for more privacy, or the radio.

You can rent cellular phones in the Virgins or bring your own from home. The service is provided by Boatphone in the BVI and most of the usual cell phone companies in the USVI, but check with your provider to make sure you will have service. Information is available from your charter company regarding the availability and operation of cellular phones. All that is required is a major credit card.

Cell phone services in the British Virgin Islands will allow you to roam with your cell phone from home. With the right band, European cell phones will also work.

Making Dinner Reservations

Where telephone service is non-existent, many restaurants stand by the radio on VHF channel 16 and will then have you switch to another working channel to complete your request. It is frowned upon by the local licensing authority to use the VHF Channel 12 for reservations.

Radio Procedure

Before attempting to make a VHF radio call, think it through. Understand the procedure and the limitations of the equipment you are using.

The call should begin with two repetitions of the station or vessel being called, followed by the name of your yacht, followed by the word "over." It is important to terminate with the "over" as the other party will then key his mike and reply.

Example:"...Moorings, Moorings, this is the vessel Bodacious ZJL 172, over..."

If you get no response, repeat the call. If there is still no response, try again in 5 minutes. When contact is to be terminated, the party will sign off: "...This is Bodacious, ZJL 172 clear with Moorings..."

EMERGENCY
U.S. COAST GUARD:
787-729-6770
VISAR: 999 or 911 or 767 (SOS)

Distress Calls

In case of a real, life threatening emergency, you use VHF Channel 16, key your mike and repeat the following: "...Mayday, Mayday, Mayday. This is the vessel Bodacious, over..."

Repeat three times until contact is made. Then give your location and the nature of your problem. It is important to state only the pertinent information and not to cloud the situation with emotion.

When stating your location is it critical to give both the name of the harbor if applicable and the island to avoid confusion. There is a Great Harbour in both Peter Island and Jost Van Dyke and a Little Harbour in both Peter Island and Jost Van Dyke!

- Stay calm; don't panic.
- Don't allow anyone to use the radio unless they are familiar with the procedure and the problem.

VISAR and the Coast Guard monitors the VHF radio 24 hours per day.

Customs and Immigration

Since the Virgin Islands are divided between the U.S. and Britain, you may be crossing international boundaries during your cruise. Therefore it is necessary to clear customs when entering and leaving each respective territory. Failure to observe this formality could result in substantial fines or even the loss of your vessel.

U.S. Customs and Immigration at the waterfront in Charlotte Amalie (tel: 340-774-6755) are open from 8am-noon and 1pm-4:30 pm Monday through Saturday. Sunday they are open from 10am to 6pm.

De Loose Mongoose   *Julian Putley*

In Cruz Bay, St. John Customs and Immigration (tel: 340-776-6397) are open from 7am to 5:30pm seven days a week. In Christiansted, St. Croix at Gallows Bay, Customs and Immigration are open from 8:00am – 4:30pm Monday through Friday. Vessels arriving on Saturdays and Sundays must contact the customs at the airport 340-778-0216.

To clear in to the B.V.I. proceed to the nearest B.V.I. port of entry for inbound clearance. Often, if your stay is short and of a known duration, you will be permitted to clear in and out at the same time.

When clearing in it is necessary to have in your possession the ship's papers and passports for all passengers and crew members as well as your clearance from the last port. All crew members must be present for clearance. It is also recommended that you wear proper attire when making your clearance.In the B.V.I. as of January 1, 2007, passports will be required of all U.S. and Canadian citizens to enter the British Virgin Islands. Passports will also be required to enter back into the U.S. Virgin Islands from the British Virgin Islands or other foreign countries.

All other nationalities must have a current passport. If you have questions regarding the need for visas contact your nearest British Embassy or telephone the B.V.I. Immigration Department at 284-494-3471.

- All crew members are to present themselves for clearance.
- Yachts dropping passengers off must first clear customs and immigration.
- All private yachts will be given no more than 30 days entry. Extensions will incur a fee.
- Late fees, in addition to customs charges are as much as $8 per vessel and higher on Sundays and public holidays.

Port Clearance

For vessels in the United States Virgin Islands over 300 tons gross weight, and any vessel carrying paying passengers or paid crew in and out of U.S. waters are now required to submit an advance Notice of Arrival/Departure (NOA/D) to the U.S. Coast Guard before calling at or departing from U.S. ports.

This notice must be filed electronically to the (NMVC) National Vessel Movement Center website at www.nvmc.uscg.gov, who can answer questions and provide downloadable forms.

For more information call:

U.S. Coast Guard regulation and related questions: 202-372-1244

Late fees may be charged for after hours arrivals or for arrivals on holidays."

Marinas catering to megayachts often offer clearance services to assist in the clearance procedures. Check with the marina offices in advance.

Locations of Customs

St. Thomas:	Wharfside at the ferry dock - Charlotte Amalie
St. John:	Waterfront at Cruz Bay.
St.Croix:	Gallows Bay at Christiansted.
Tortola:	Road town at the Government Dock. West End ferry dock.
Virgin Gorda:	Government Dock.
Jost Van Dyke:	Government Dock, Great Harbour.

Dougal Thorton

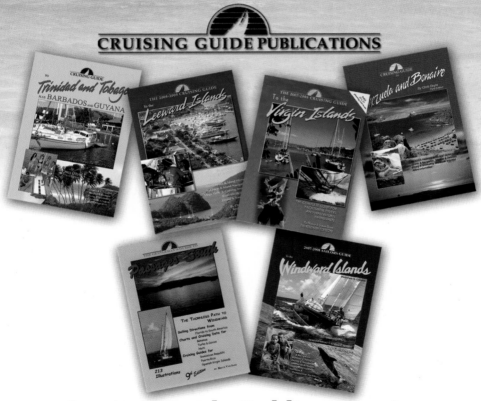

B.V.I. Cruising Permits

For yachts cruising in BVI waters there is a daily tax payable at the time of clearance or at the commencement of charter. Cruising vessels, dive boats, day charter, and sport fishing boats should contact customs for the required fees at 284-494-3701.

The rates are as follows:

December 1 – April 30:

A. Non recorded boats: $4.00 per person per day.

Recorded boats: $2.00 per person per day

May 1 – November 30

B. Recorded boats: $.75 per person per day

Non-recorded boats: $4.00 per person per day.

BVI National Parks Trust Permit

In order to use the moorings provided in the marine parks in the BVI, it is necessary to purchase a National Parks Trust permit. Charterers may purchase these permits through their charter company, and visiting private yachts may purchase permits through customs when clearing. The fees are nominal and go directly to the Parks Trust for the installation and maintenance of the buoys.

Fishing Permits in the B.V.I.

It is illegal for a non-resident to remove any marine organism from the waters of the British Virgin Islands without first obtaining a recreational fishing permit. Call the Fisheries Department at 494-5681.

Anchoring in coral is **STRICTLY PROHIBITED** in both the U.S. and B.V.I.

Water Safety

The waters of the Virgin Islands are essentially a benign area. When people think of tropical waters, man-eating sharks, barracuda and giant moray eels come to mind. The truth of the matter is that more injuries are sustained by cuts from coral or by stepping on sea urchin spines, than by encounters with underwater predators. (See Medical Information section at the back of the book.)

Jet Skis

It is against B.V.I. law to import jet skis. If you have a jet ski aboard you must declare it at customs when entering the B.V.I. Jet skis can be rented from local rental shops in certain locations.

Jet Skis are forbidden in the National Park Service waters in St. John and St. Croix.

Sharks

There are many large sharks around the waters of the Virgins, but they remain largely in deep water. It is highly unlikely that you will ever see a shark during your cruise.

Barracuda

You will, without doubt, see numerous barracuda of various sizes while snorkeling the reefs. They are curious fish and are likely to stay almost motionless in the water watching your movements. They will not bother you, and it is best to show them the same courtesy.

Moray Eels

These creatures are shy by nature and make their homes in rocks and crevices in the reef. They will protect themselves from perceived danger, so do not reach into caves or crevices unless you can see inside.

Coral

Exercise extreme caution around all coral as cuts and scratches can become infected quickly. Familiarize yourself with the various types of coral and remember to stay well clear of the fire coral. To preserve the reefs, do not touch the coral, with your fins, your hands or anything. Take only pictures, leave only bubbles.

Sea Urchins

These black, spiny creatures are found in abundance throughout the islands. They can be seen on sandy bottoms and on reefs and rocks. If you stand on one or inadvertently place your hand on one, it is likely that one or more of the spines will pierce your skin and break off. Do not try to dig the spines out of your skin. (See Medical Information chapter)

Don'ts

If you observe the following basic rules on water safety, you will add to your enjoyment of the cruise:

1. Don't swim at night.
2. Don't swim alone.
3. Don't swim in heavy surf.
4. Don't dump refuse in the water — it is illegal and attracts sharks.
5. Don't wear jewelry when swimming or diving.
6. Don't reach into crevices or caves.
7. Don't spear a fish and leave it bleeding in the water or in a bag at your waist.
8. Take no marine life without a permit!
9. Don't touch or anchor in coral under any circumstances.

BVI BEACH SAFETY FLAGS

Red & Yellow Flags - mark areas of water that are patrolled by Lifeguards. These are the safest places to swim.

Black & White Chequered Flags - mean an area of water that has been marked out for use by craft, for example wind surfing, surf boards or dinghies. For your safety do not swim in this zoned area.

Red Flags - these indicate danger. *Never swim when the Red Flag is flying.* At the Baths, Devils Bay & Spring Bay the Red Flag also indicates that the Yachts are prohibited from using the mooring field.

Yellow Flags - these indicate that you should take caution: weak swimmers are discouraged from entering the water. At the Baths, Devils Bay & Spring Bay the Red Flag also indicates that the Yachts should take caution when using the mooring field.

Purple Flags - indicate a marine life warning, for example Jelly Fish. The purple flag may also be flown with Yellow or Red Flags.

For More Information Visit: www.bvidef.org

Anchoring

Many sailors visiting the Virgin Islands have all sorts of sailing experience, both inshore and offshore; however, it is interesting to note that many have little experience anchoring.

Since you will be subjected to the constant trade breezes on a heavy displacement-type vessel, follow these suggestions for safe, hassle-free anchoring:

1. Pick your anchorage and arrive there early enough in the afternoon to assure both good light and a choice of spots. Bear in mind that during the peak season, December to April, some of the more popular spots become crowded.

2. Before doing anything else, work out a system of communication between the person on the helm and the crew member dropping the anchor. Remember that your engine will be running and therefore you will be unable to communicate verbally. Hand signals are needed and should be worked out beforehand.

3. Furl the sails and generally make the boat shipshape before entering the anchorage. Also shorten the dinghy painter to prevent its being sucked into the prop.

4. Pick your spot. Make sure you will have enough room to fall back on the anchor without lying too close to the yacht anchored behind, once you have laid out 5-to-1 scope. Sand makes the best holding ground. Do not anchor on coral.

5. Motor up to the desired spot slowly, ensuring that you are head to the wind. Stop the boat exactly where you wish the anchor to lay. Take note of the depth.

6. Once the vessel has lost all forward way, lower the anchor to the bottom.

7. Let the wind slowly push the vessel back. Don't try to reverse. Pay out adequate scope as the vessel moves aft. Don't worry about being broadside to the wind.

8. When the desired amount of scope has been paid out, snub the rope and allow the wind to straighten out the vessel.

9. Put the engine into reverse and increase throttle to 1500 rpm. This should set the anchor and the anchor rope should start to tighten. If you notice it "s k i p - ping," pay out more scope. Once you are satisfied that the anchor is set, take the engine out of gear. The vessel should spring forward.

10. Put on your snorkel gear and visually check your work. This is the best way to ensure a good night's sleep. If the anchor is lying on its side or caught in coral, or if the rope is caught around a coral head, avoid incurring additional damage to the coral and reset it. Better now than later.

11. Check your position relative to other vessels and/or landmarks. Is there enough room between you and the boats around you? If swinging room is tight or if you are expecting squalls during the night, you might think about laying out a second anchor at 45 degrees to the first. This can be accomplished best with the dinghy.

If the hook doesn't set the first time, don't feel embarrassed! There is not a skipper afloat who hasn't encountered this problem. It is due not to your technique, but to the nature of the seabed. Discuss the situation with your crew, pick it up and try again.

THE OTHER ALTERNATIVE

Tired of straining the old back? Tired of waking up all night worrying about your anchor dragging, thinking that THIS is supposed to be a vacation? WELL, now there is an alternative... Located throughout the British Virgin Islands at most popular anchorages there are professionally maintained moorings available for overnight use. The small fee for the mooring use is well worth the good night's sleep it affords.

Here are a few tips on picking up and leaving a mooring...

1. As in anchoring, approach the mooring area slowly with your dinghy pulled on a short line.
2. Have a crew member ready with a boat hook at the bow to direct you and to pick up the mooring pennant.
3. Approach the mooring buoy slowly from the direction that keeps the bow of your boat into the wind.
4. You may find that at idle speed by shifting alternately from forward to neutral you can coast to the buoy, then shift into reverse for a second to stop the boat as the crew member lifts the pennant on board and attaches it to the bow cleat.
5. Please do not be embarrassed if you miss picking up the pennant for the first time. It happens to all of us at sometime. Just circle around and make another approach. Please do not extend the length of the pennant.
6. To leave the mooring with your dinghy once again on a short line simply let go the pennant and set off for your next destination. Take care not to run over the mooring buoy and pennant as you leave.

These helpful hints are brought to you by Moor-Seacure Ltd.-the premier mooring company in the BVI. And remember, "If it doesn't say MOOR-SEACURE, it probably ISN'T!"

Moor-Seacure moorings are available at these and other fine locations...

Moorings

Throughout the BVI in various anchorages you will find moorings available for you to use for a nightly fee. Most moorings will have the name of the restaurant or establishment where you should pay your fee, or in some anchorages someone will come in a small boat in the late afternoon – early evening to collect the fee. This fee usually must be paid in cash and the person collecting the fees can give you a receipt if you ask for one. You should confirm that the mooring you are using is either a Moor Seacure mooring or is professionally maintained.

In the BVI, National Parks Trust moorings are available for daytime use with a permit that can be purchased at the same time as your cruising permit. In the USVI National Parks, moorings are provided for a nightly fee. Please see details in the Diving, Snorkeling, and Marine Parks section.

PUBLIC HOLIDAYS

Although the observance of public holidays will make little difference to you when sailing, it is prudent to plan your cruise so that you are not needing shore based facilities during the following holidays:

MONTH	U.S. VIRGIN ISLANDS	BRITISH VIRGIN ISLANDS
January	New Year's Day Three Kings' Day (Observed) Martin Luther King's Birthday	New Year's Day
February	Presidents' Day	
March	Transfer Day	Commonwealth Day
April	Holy Thursday Good Friday Easter Monday Children's Carnival Parade Adults' Carnival Parade	Good Friday Easter Monday
May	Memorial Day	Whit Monday
June	Organic Act Day	Sovereigns Birthday
July	Emancipation Day (West Indies) Independence Day Supplication Day	Territory Day
August		Festival Monday Festival Tuesday Festival Wednesday
September	Labor Day	
October	Columbus Day Local Thanksgiving Day	St. Ursula's Day
November	Liberty Day Thanksgiving Day	Birthday of Heir to the Throne
December	Christmas Day Christmas Second Day	Christmas Day Boxing Day

Should any holiday fall upon a Sunday, the Monday following shall be a legal holiday.

VISAR (VIRGIN ISLANDS SEARCH & RESCUE, LTD.)

VISAR (Virgin Islands Search and Rescue Ltd.) is a nonprofit organization that provides an invaluable and often lifesaving service to sailors voyaging in the British Virgin Islands.

Based in Road Town, Tortola, and Virgin Gorda Yacht Harbour, VISAR generally responds to medical emergencies or other cases where life or limb are endangered. The organization will also assist in communications to calls for help of a commercial nature and will put anyone in need of assistance with commercial towing operations, salvors or mechanics.

VISAR can be reached in the following ways:

- By VHF Radio Channel 16 — hail VISAR and relay the nature of your emergency.
- By telephone (either cellular or land line) - dial 767 (SOS) or 999 or 911 or 494-4357 (494-help).

In either case you will be put in touch with a VISAR coordinator who will be able to assist you. Once this initial contact has been established, make every effort possible to ensure that lines of communication (either VHF radio or phone) are kept open.

In emergency situations requiring assistance, VISAR recommends that you have the following information available:

- Location is most important. (Be accurate — e.g.: there is a Great Harbour on both Peter Island and Jost Van Dyke and several Long Bays through out the islands. You must be specific.)
- State the exact nature of your distress, such as fire, suspected heart attack, or other similar emergency.
- State the name of your vessel.
- Speak slowly and clearly.
- Remain as calm as possible. Panic can only make the situation worse.
- Listen carefully to what is said. In an international community like the islands, you are likely to speak to a responder that may be other than English speaking.

An accent can make it very difficult to understand, and consequently listening carefully as you talk is extremely important.

VISAR is largely supported by membership dues. These range from $25 for an individual to $1,000 for a life member. For further information, contact: VISAR, P.O. Box 3042, Road Town, Tortola, B.V.I.; phone: (284) 494-4357; email: visar@surfbvi.com On the web go to www.visar.org.

Tropical Fish Poisoning

Ciguatera, also known as tropical fish poisoning, is a disease which can affect people who have eaten certain varieties of tropical fish.

The results of such poisoning can be very serious and, although seldom resulting in death, can cause severe discomfort. Victims of ciguatera poisoning are often ill for weeks and some symptoms may persist for months.

Ciguatera occurs only in tropical waters and in the Atlantic area, predominantly in the waters of south Florida and the islands of the Caribbean.

One problem with fish poisoning is that it is impossible to differentiate between toxic and nontoxic fish. The fish itself is not affected by the toxins and therefore appears quite normal and edible. The toxins cannot be tasted and washing, cooking or freezing will not render them harmless.

Many tales exist throughout the Caribbean on how to tell toxic from nontoxic fish, including cooking silver coins with the fish and if the coin turns black, it is toxic. Another is that flies will not land on a piece of toxic fish. While such homespun ideas are interesting bits of Caribbean folklore, they do not work and should not be relied upon.

Symptoms of Ciguatera

In most cases, the symptoms will appear within three to ten hours after eating the toxic fish. The first signs are nausea, vomiting, diarrhea and stomach cramps.

Later, the patient may also start to suffer from a wide variety of neurological ailments, including pains in the joints and muscles, weakness in the arms and legs, and/or a tingling sensation in the feet and hands. A tingling sensation around the lips, nose and tongue is also common.

At the onset of any of the above symptoms, the patient should ask him- or herself, "Have I eaten any fish today?" If the answer is "yes," seek medical attention.

Types of Fish Carrying Ciguatera

The fish most likely to carry the toxins are the larger predatory fish associated with coral reefs. These include barracudas, grouper, snapper, jacks and parrot fish. It should be noted that only certain species in each family are associated with the toxins. Therefore, it is a good idea to check with a local fisherman before eating your catch.

The fish that are considered safe are offshore fish such as tuna, wahoo, swordfish, marlin, and dolphin. Others include sailfish, Spanish mackerel, small king mackerel and yellowtail snapper.

Jim Scheiner

FISH TRAPS

Throughout the Virgin Islands, you will become aware of plastic bottles floating low in the water. These are used by local fishermen to mark their fish traps.

There are usually two bottles or floats as shown. The upwind one is typically submerged, thereby making it extremely difficult to see until the last minute. Since the floats will trail downwind from the trap, the ideal approach is to pass downwind of the second float.

If you do not see the floats, it is quite likely that the line connecting them together will foul your rudder or prop shaft. If you pick up the line in your prop or prop shaft, your engine will probably stall when moved into gear. If this happens, a crew member might have to nip over the side with a sharp knife in hand to cut everything loose.

If it does become necessary to cut a fishing line, every effort should be made to retie the trap to the float in order to preserve the traps — as well as the livelihood of the local fishing industry.

Diving, Snorkeling & Marine Parks

Chikuzen   Jim Scheiner

National Marine Parks
British Virgin Islands

Visitors come to the Virgin Islands to savor the magnificence of the area's natural resources — the steady, gentle trade winds, glorious sunshine, crystalline waters, the splendor of the coral reefs and abundant sea life. This is a fragile area, however, which must be protected if it is to be enjoyed for many years to come.

The anchors of the charter boats have taken their toll in broken coral, destroying the incredible beauty below the sea that once housed many different forms of sea life. In an effort to defend the reefs against the carelessness of yachtsmen, the National Parks Trust has taken a firm stand and has installed mooring buoys developed by Dr. John Halas of the Key Largo National Marine Sanctuary. This mooring system is being used worldwide to protect reefs and prevent damage from anchors. It calls for a stainless steel pin cemented into the bedrock and a polypropylene line attached to a surface buoy. The system is very strong and extremely effective in eliminating damage when used properly.

Marine Park Regulations:

- Do not damage, alter or remove any marine plant, animal or historic artifact.
- All fishing — including spearfishing —is strictly prohibited. Lobstering and collecting live shells are also illegal.
- Use correct garbage disposal points; do not litter the area. Water balloons are prohibited.
- Water skiing and jet skiing are prohibited in all park areas.
- No anchoring in the restricted area in and around the Wreck of the Rhone. When the mooring system is full, vessels should utilize the Salt Island Settlement anchorage and arrive by tender, using the dinghy mooring system provided.

Mooring Usage Regulations:

- Vessels must legally have met BVI Customs and Immigration requirements, and have in their possession valid clearance forms andcruising permits.
- The buoys of the reef protection system are color-coded:
  Red: Non-diving, day use only.
  Yellow: Commercial dive vessels only.
  White: Non-commercial vessels for dive use only on first-come, first served basis (90-minute timelimit).
  Blue: Dinghies only.
  Large Yellow: Commercial vessels, or day sailing boats or vessels over 55' in length.
- Vessels must attach to the buoy pennant, making sure to avoid chafing of the pennant against the vessel. If the configuration provided is not compatible with your vessel, an extension line must be attached to the pennant eye.
- All buoys are used at user's risk. While the moorings are the property of the B.V.I. Government and are managed by the B.V.I. National Parks Trust, neither bears the responsibility for any loss or injury resulting from the use of the system. **Charterers may purchase permits through their charter companies, and visit ing private yachts may purchase permits through customs. The fees are nominal and go directly to the Parks Trust for the installation and maintenance of the buoys.**

The British Virgin Islands National Parks Trust Maintains Moorings On The Following Islands

- Norman
- Pelican
- The Indians
- Peter Island
- Dead Chest
- Salt Island
- Cooper
- Ginger
- Guana
- George Dog
- Great Dog
- Cockroach
- Tortola
- Virgin Gorda

NATIONAL PARKS TRUST
MOORING BUOYS IN THE BVI

For day use only with National Parks Permit

Norman Island
1. Angel Fish
2. The Caves
3. Ring Dove Rock
4. Black Forest
5. Santa Monica Rock
6. Water Point
7. Spyglass Wall
8. Brown Pants
9. Pelican Island &
   The Indians

Peter Island
10. Carrot Rock
11. Shark Point
12. Black Tip
13. Rhone Anchor
14. Fearless
15. Great Harbour

Dead Chest
16. Painted Walls
17. Coral Gardens
18. Blonde Rock

Salt Island
19. The Rhone
20. Rhone Reef

Cooper Island
21. Dry Rocks East & West
22. Haulover Bay
23. Mary L.
24. Incannes Bay
25. Cistern Point
26. Thumb Rock
27. Markoe Point

28. Devil's Kitchen
29. Carvel Rock

Ginger Island
30. Ginger Steps
31. Alice in Wonderland
32. Ginger Patch
33. Alices's Backside

Virgin Gorda
34. Fallen Jerusalem
35. The Baths
36. Fisher's Rocks

The Dogs
37. Great Dog South
38. George Dog
39. Bronco Billy
40. Cockroach Island
41. The Chimneys
42. Wall to Wall
43. Joes Cave
44. Flintstones
45. Dolphin Rocks
46. Seal Dogs
47. Mountain Point
48. Cow's Mouth
49. Paul's Grotto

Necker Island
50. The Invisibles

Scrub Island
51. Scrub Island
    Point
52. Scrub Island
    West

Great Camanoe
53. Diamond Reef

Guana Island
54. Monkey Point
55. The Chikuzen

Tortola
56. Brewers Bay
57. Green Cay
58. Great Tobago
59. Great Thatch

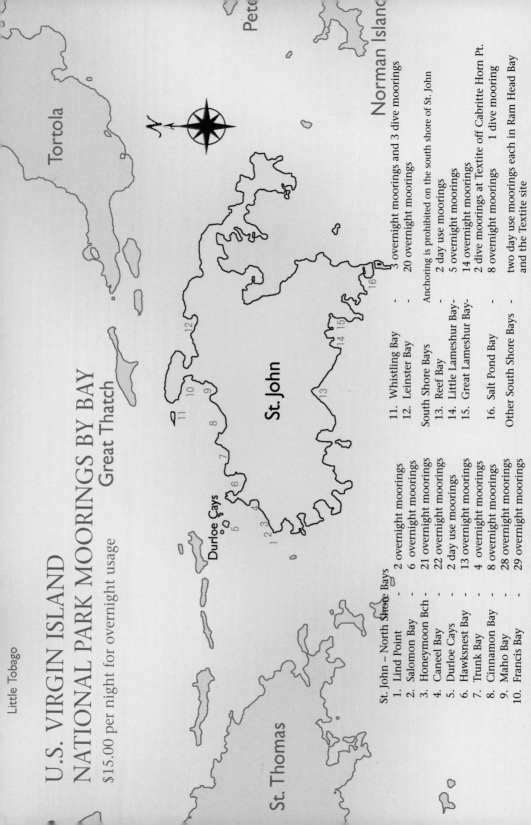

U.S. VIRGIN ISLAND
NATIONAL PARK MOORINGS BY BAY

$15.00 per night for overnight usage

Little Tobago

Tortola

Peter

Great Thatch

Norman Island

St. Thomas

St. John

Durloe Cays

St. John – North Shore Bays

1. Lind Point - 2 overnight moorings
2. Salomon Bay - 6 overnight moorings
3. Honeymoon Bch - 21 overnight moorings
4. Caneel Bay - 22 overnight moorings
5. Durloe Cays - 2 day use moorings
6. Hawksnest Bay - 13 overnight moorings
7. Trunk Bay - 4 overnight moorings
8. Cinnamon Bay - 8 overnight moorings
9. Maho Bay - 28 overnight moorings
10. Francis Bay - 29 overnight moorings

11. Whistling Bay - 3 overnight moorings and 3 dive moorings
12. Leinster Bay - 20 overnight moorings

South Shore Bays - Anchoring is prohibited on the south shore of St. John
13. Reef Bay - 2 day use moorings
14. Little Lameshur Bay- 5 overnight moorings
15. Great Lameshur Bay- 14 overnight moorings
16. Salt Pond Bay - 2 dive moorings at Textite off Cabritte Horn Pt.
                      8 overnight moorings   1 dive mooring
Other South Shore Bays - two day use moorings each in Ram Head Bay
                          and the Textite site

THE VIRGIN ISLANDS CORAL REEF
NATIONAL MONUMENT

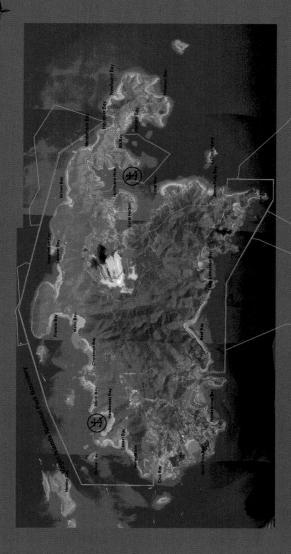

Virgin Islands Coral Reef National Monument Boundary

Virgin Islands National Park Boundary

Newfound Bay
Haulover Bay
Hansen Bay
Privateer Bay
Mennebeck Bay
Hurricane Hole
Bill Bay
Coral Bay
Long Point
Brown Bay
Leinster Bay
Coral Harbor
Johnson Bay Bay
Waterlemon Cay
Francis Bay
Maho Bay
Cinnamon Bay
Reef Bay
Trunk Bay
Hawksnest Bay
Cruz Bay
Caneel Bay
Dittes Cay
Rendezvous Bay
Enighed
Cruz Bay
Great Cruz Bay
Henley Cay

Aerial Photo Source:
1999 NOAA/NOS/NCAA/
Biogeography Program
NOAA Aerial Photos
Map Developed at
Virgin Isalnds
Biosphere Reserve Center
7/4/2004
Christy Loomis

N

Virgin Islands National Park

Virgin Islands Coral Reef National Monument

1000   0   1000   2000 Meters

1   0   1   2 Miles

Virgin Islands National Park, St. John, US Virgin Islands

By Carol Bareuther

Coral reefs reflecting sapphire seas, pristine beaches rimmed with palm trees and lush green hills unmarred by resorts or residences. The paradisiacal beauty of the Virgin Islands National Park is like a movie scene that makes you want to jump in and instantly become immersed. But slow down. To really appreciate the charms of this southernmost U.S. park, you have to add some new lingo to your vocabulary. "Limin'", meaning to "hang around idly", as defined by the late Virgin Islands historian and park ranger, Lito Valls, is a verb best carried out by forgetting time, setting aside the to-do list and enjoying your surroundings in a lazily, leisurely, limin' sort of way.

About the Park

The Virgin Islands National Park covers 9,485 acres of the U.S. Virgin Island of St. John, or roughly two-thirds, and another 13,000 acres of adjoining submerged lands and waters. What makes the park unique is its mix of history, natural assets and breathtaking beauty that are wonderfully accessible.

Long before Christopher Columbus arrived, Amerindians migrating north by canoe from South America made St. John their home. An extensive archeological dig at Cinnamon Bay has unearthed artifacts dating to 710 B.C. that give clues these ancient people lived off the sea, practiced agriculture and made pottery. During his second voyage in 1493, Columbus did name the numerous cluster of islands of which St. John is part, calling them "Las Once Mil Virgines," after the 11,000 virgin followers of St. Ursula. However, no permanent European settlements were founded until the 1720's by the Danes who were lured by the prospect of cultivating sugar cane.

Forests were cut down all over St. John for sugar plantations, farms, and estates during the 1700's and 1800's. Trees and

shrubs, imported to provide food or medicines, invaded the native forests, and by the early 1900's, no sizable original stands were left. Animals, too, like the weasel-like mongoose, was introduced to control the rat population, but unfortunately the mongoose likes to eat the eggs of ground-nesting birds and sea turtles too. With much of St. John's natural resources managed by the park, the tropical forest and native wildlife are protected. Natural assets include over 800 species of plants including the teyer palm, which is St. John's only native palm tree; the bay rum tree, whose aromatic leaves once provided the oil for the world-famous bay rum cologne; and rare, brilliantly colored wild orchids. St. John is a sanctuary for animals as diverse as corals, sea turtles and reef fish; insect- and fish-eating bats; frogs; gecko, angle, and iguana lizards; and, of course, birds. More than 30 species of tropical birds breed on the island. They include the bananaquit, the black, parrot-like smooth-billed Ani, and two species of Caribbean hummingbirds.

Following emancipation of slaves in 1848, St. John's population plummeted to less than 1,000 people. The United States purchased the islands in 1917, and by the 1950's the tourism industry took root as word spread of the picture postcard beauty of this Caribbean paradise. In 1956, Laurence Rockefeller purchased land and transferred it to the Federal Government to be designated a national park. Today the park works closely with local and Caribbean-wide conservation-minded interests to preserve the area's natural and cultural resources. In recognition of the significance of its natural resources, the park also is a part of the international network of biosphere reserves.

Marine Scene

Secluded coves, dazzling beaches and wondrous coral reefs have lured pleasure boaters to park waters. In addition, the Virgin Islands rank as one of the Caribbean's premier diving and snorkeling locations. Several dive shops rent snorkel and scuba gear and run trips to offshore reefs. Park waters are open to sports fisherman with hand-held rods, and bone fishing along the flats by Leinster Bay is excellent.

Over the last two decades, however, the sheer number of visiting boats has accelerated damage to sea grass beds and coral reefs due to anchor damage. To protect these natural resources, the park has installed 182 moorings – 154 on the North Shore and 28 on the South Shore, and established protected zones around several of the more sensitive sea grass and reef areas. Starting in 2002, the park implemented a fee for the overnight use of these moorings. To pay the mooring fee on the mooring several "iron rangers", (small kiosks) are located in several of the bays. Envelopes are provided for enclosing the fee, with a place to note your vessel's name and the date. Rangers patrol the bays regularly to insure compliance.

Anchor Zone

Park regulations require vessels 17 to 60 feet to pick up a mooring if one is available. However, there is an anchoring zone in the park, designated by four GPS coordinates, where anchoring is permitted. Vessels 60 to 125 feet, who are prohibited from using moorings are encouraged to use this anchor zone. Please see the diagram and coordinates on page 243.

Jim Scheiner

There is no reservation system for moorings, but one may be developed in the future. Moorings are in high demand from December to March, while September and October usage is low because of the threat of hurricanes. Boaters may only stay in park waters for a maximum of 30 nights in a 12 month period and no longer than seven consecutive nights in one bay.

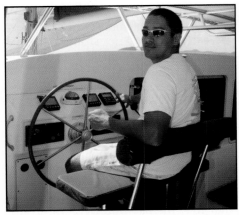

Using the National Park Mooring System

Park moorings are safe, easy to use and identified as white balls with blue stripes. Moorings are fixed to the sea bottom with either a sand screw or a stainless steel eyebolt, which is cemented directly into coral pavement. To pick up a mooring, grab the floating mooring line, or painter, and tie it to a short bowline on the vessel. Don't raft boats together or set anchors while on a mooring. All moorings are checked and maintained by Park Service personnel, however please do report any safety defects to a park ranger so they can be promptly repaired. The moorings are not designed for rough weather use. In high wind or heavy sea conditions, it is recommended that vessels anchor in a protected bay.

Bay-by-Bay Guide North Shore

Cruz Bay: Snug on the western side of St. John and less than an hour's sail from St. Thomas, this is the island's main town. The Customs & Immigration Office is here, a mandatory stop for cruisers coming in from the nearby British Virgin Islands. There are limited moorings and anchoring space in Cruz Bay harbor and the park's finger pier does impose a 15-minute limit.

Cruz Bay is limited to vessels under 60 feet for a period of three hours only because of the high influx of boaters needing access, and the local services and ferries.

Steps from the pier, the park headquar-ters is a great place to preview exhibits and videos about the park, talk with rangers and obtain pamphlets on hiking trails, interpretative programs and mooring how-to's as well as reminders for mariners for using the park waters. Around Cruz Bay itself, there are provisioning opportunities at several nearby stores, a post office, bank, several cyber-cafés at Connections and the Quiet Mon Pub, shops, car rental, medical care and pharmacies, and dining options ranging from casual burgers to white tablecloth chic. Boater's services include gas and water from the Caneel Shipyard, next to the park bulkhead. On the opposite end of the island, there are also provisioning, dining and marine repair facilities – although on a smaller and more laidback scale – in Coral Bay.

Lind Point: Named for the site of a makeshift fort built by the British to help the Danes defend themselves against the French, this spit of land is easily visible from the 21 NPS mooring buoys to the north, near a clearly visible coral reef.

Salomon Bay – 21 overnight moorings: This tiny strip of beach is popular with day sailors. Twenty-one NPS moorings are provided in the sandy area outside the swim area. Contrary to local lore, this is not a nude beach. A one-mile trail leads from the beach into Cruz Bay.

Honeymoon Bay: A favorite destination of day sail companies, this bay can get crowded during the daytime. Pick up a mooring either in Caneel Bay or Salomon Bay outside the swim area to access the beach.

Caneel Bay: - 22 overnight moorings: Home to the Rockefeller built resort of the same name and play-ground for the rich and famous, the beach, hotel bar and dining facilities are permitted but non-guests must register in the main lobby. You may tie up dinghies at the resort's dock only long enough to load and unload passengers.

Durloe Cays: Don't anchor here, instead moor on any of the buoys located off the southeast corner of Henley Cay, one of the three small uninhabited islands that make up the Durloe Cays. Snorkeling is great over Henley Cay's surrounding reef, but currents can be strong.

Hawksnest Bay – 13 overnight moorings: Filming site for the Four Seasons, starring Alan Alda, and a favorite destina-

Courtesy of Virgin Islands National Park

tion of locals, this bay boasts three beaches. Tie up to mooring buoys located along the eastern shoreline, and access the beaches through marked dinghy channels. There's an emergency use telephone next to the parking lot behind the middle beach. Other facilities include bathrooms, shelters and picnic tables.

Trunk Bay – 4 overnight moorings: The renowned self-guided 225-yard long underwater snorkel trail makes this by far the most popular beach among visitors.

Fifteen underwater plaques identify the corals and fish that inhabit these waters. Rental snorkeling gear is available; an information kiosk, shop, snack bar and changing facilities are located here as well. Access the trail and beach via a dinghy channel that leads to an anchoring area past the swim buoys. Just north of the bay, beware of Johnson's Reef, a treacherous stretch of reef marked by yellow marker buoys.

Cinnamon Bay- 8 overnight moorings: This is the site of the National Park campground, which includes a museum in the Old Customs House down by the beach, shore side amphitheater where park rangers host evening campfire programs, and a self-guided nature trail that has well-preserved plantation ruins, tropical flora and fauna. Facilities also include a cafeteria, store and water sports concession. Moor on buoys to the west end of the beach or, if occupied, anchor between Little Cinnamon and the moorings. There's wonderful snorkeling around Cinnamon Cay and the nearby fringing reef.

Maho and Francis Bays – 28 overnight moorings: protection from the roly-poly swells makes these bays ideal for overnight stays. The private Maho Bay campground is here, with dining, commissary and taxi services available. There's a dinghy channel at the south end of Francis Bay, while at the north end is a trail leading to a salt pond where bird watching is excellent in the winter. In the water, watch for sea turtles that frequently feed on the sea grass.

Leinster Bay – 20 overnight moorings: Head to Waterlemon Cay, which dots this bay, for spectacular snorkeling or hike the trail along the beach to the Annaberg plantation ruins perched on an overlooking hill. Use the dinghy channel at the western end of the bay to access the Annaberg ruins. There is a public trash bin here.

DIVING & SNORKELING

South Shore

Reef Bay: Watch out for the reef protecting both sides of this bay on the way into the inner bay mooring area. Do not use the reserved "concession mooring" (white with no stripe). Explore the extensive sugar plantation factory ruins just behind the beach or take off on a 2.2 mile uphill hike past the petroglyph rock carvings and on to Centerline Road. Twice weekly, rangers lead hikes down Reef Bay Trail – past the mysterious petroglyph rock carvings and the island's last working sugar mill – and provide boat service back to the VINP headquarters in Cruz Bay.

Little and Great Lameshur Bay - 5 and 14 overnight moorings: Preservation of marine resources here is a high priority since this is the core area of the Biosphere Reserve. Long-term research programs on coral reefs, sea grass beds, and fish populations are underway, hence anchoring is not permitted. You will find mooring buoys on the eastern side of the bays. At Great Lameshur there is a park service dock along with a field station laboratory. Dock usage is restricted to passenger loading and off-loading. The house and radio tower above Little Lameshur is a ranger residence and office.

Saltpond Bay - 8 overnight moorings: This sheltered bay is a good overnight spot. Carefully navigate through either side of the bay to avoid the reef in the middle. Moorings are available and no anchoring is permitted. Trailheads to Drunk Bay (0.2 miles) and Ram's Head (1.0 miles) begin at the south end of the beach.

Safety Information

Park Rangers monitor VHF channel 16 on boat patrol or may be contacted during the day directly by telephone at 340-776-6201. For assistance after hours please call the Virgin Islands Police at 340-693-8880. For safe boating, use NOAA nautical charts 25641 and 25647, which show navigational aids and hazardous areas, such as coral reefs, in detail. Watch out for unmarked reefs and other boats and swimmers. Divers and snorkelers are required to fly a standard diver's flag; stay at least 100 feet away from them. If you plan to visit the British Virgin Islands, take your passport (U.S. citizens are required to have passports to enter the BVI as of 2007). Follow island customs and courteously greet others with "good day!"

Park Activities

The Cruz Bay Visitor Center is a short walk from the public ferry dock and is open daily from 8 am to 4:40 pm. The center contains exhibits, a park video, brochures, maps, and books. Park rangers can help you plan your visit, which may include island hikes, historical tours, snorkeling, cultural craft demonstrations, and evening campground programs. Advance registration and transportation fees are required for some park activities; schedules are available at the Center's information desk.

Throughout the year, the park plays host to two to three day events. A commemoration of Black History Month is held at the Annaberg Sugar Plantation the latter part of February and includes crafts, storytelling, and cooking demonstrations. St. John's Carnival on July fourth includes parades and island cultural activities during the week prior. The park presents interpretive programs during the winter season at Cinnamon Bay campground. From January through April, the non-profit Friends of the National Park offer seminars with topics ranging from outdoors photography to archeology, natural his-

tory and traditional West Indian cooking. Hurricane season extends from June through November. The park provides ongoing information for visitors including where to go in the event of a serious storm.

Park Rules & Regulations

This section is very important for boaters visiting the National Park to read and understand before visiting the Park waters.

Vessels & Water Operations:

*Vessels with a length overall greater than 210 feet are prohibited from anchoring or mooring within Park waters.

*Commercial vessels with a length overall of greater than 125 feet are prohibited from anchoring or mooring within Park waters.

*Private vessels with a length overall between 125 and 210 feet shall only anchor in sand seaward of mooring areas and at depths greater than 50 feet in Francis Bay shoreward of a line from Mary Point to America Point.

*Vessels with a length overall between 60 and 125 feet shall anchor in north shore bays, in sand at least 200 feet seaward of mooring fields only if there are no moorings available.

*Vessels less than 26 feet length overall may access NPS beaches where channels have been designated by a red and green buoy to drop-off or pick-up passengers.

*Motorized vessels or vessels under sail shall not enter or anchor in areas identified as Boat Exclusion Areas.

Anchoring and Mooring

*Anchoring is prohibited within beach access channels marked by red and green buoys.

*Vessels less than or equal to 16 feet length overall may anchor within park waters on the south side of St. John. The only exception is that anchoring is permitted for the specific purpose of fishing for Blue Runner in the area due south of Cabritte Horn Point extending to Virgin Islands Coral Reef National Monument boundary. Vessels over 16 feet length overall must use NPS provided moorings on the south side of St. John.

*Vessels with a length overall of 60 feet or less are required to use NPS moorings if available; if moorings in a specific bay are fully occupied, vessels may anchor 200 feet seaward of mooring fields except for the south side. However, commercial day charter vessels and those vessels not staying overnight, may only anchor in Salomon Bay which is adjacent to Honeymoon Beach and Cinnamon Bay adjacent to Little Cinnamon Beach.

*Setting of anchors is prohibited while on NPS moorings. Vessels using NPS moorings may not use additional ground tackle.

* Rafting of vessels is prohibited while on moorings provided by the NPS.

Private Vessel Size Limits for St. John National Park

Length on Deck	North Shore	South Shore
16ft or less	May anchor only in sand and not within 200ft of a mooring field	May anchor only in sand and not within 200ft of a mooring field
17 to 60ft	Must use moorings if available	Must use moorings if available
61 to 125ft	Prohibited from using moorings —must anchor in sand 200ft seaward of mooring field	Prohibited from mooring or anchoring
126 to 210ft	Prohibited from using moorings - must anchor in sand at Francis Bay 200 ft. seaward of mooring field (at depths greater than 50 ft.) and shoreward of a line drawn from Mary Point to America Point.	Prohibited from mooring or anchoring
Greater than 210ft	Prohibited from mooring or anchoring	Prohibited from mooring or anchoring

*Securing vessels to moorings using stern cleats is prohibited.

*NPS moorings shall be vacated if sustained winds exceed 40 mph.

*NPS moorings shall not be modified by any user.

*Vessels anchoring or mooring within park waters may not exceed 30 nights in a calendar year and no more than seven consecutive nights in one bay.

*The National Park water area in Cruz Bay Creek in the vicinity of the boat ramp is authorized for only vessels 60 feet or less to anchor no longer than three hours, to utilize local public services.

*Recreational kite surfing is prohibited in boat exclusion areas and moorings areas. Commercial kite surfing activities are prohibited within park waters.

*Operating a vessel in excess of five mph or creating a wake in mooring fields or within 200 feet of a mooring field is prohibited.

*Trash being disposed of from vessels may not exceed two 10-gallon bags and must fit inside NPS trash containers identified for vessel trash in Cruz Bay, Francis Bay, Leinster Bay, Salt Pond and Little Lameshur Bay.

*Each vessel is required to pay an overnight fee of $15.00 per night when mooring or anchoring in the park between 5:00pm and 7:00am. Failure to pay the overnight fee is prohibited.

*Coral is very fragile and easily damaged by anchors, human touch, feet and flippers. Coral damaged by one person can take hundreds of years to re-grow. Remember, "If it's not sand, don't stand." Coral and other sea life can also cause injury to people when touched.

*It is illegal to dump litter in park waters or on land. Dispose of litter in designated receptacles throughout the Park.

*No dumping of waste from vessels, use your storage tanks.

*Water skiing and jet skiing are not permitted in Park waters.

*Kayaks, dinghies, rafts or any other motored or rowed vessels must stay outside demarcated swim areas. Boats 26 feet or less may access the beach using channels marked by red and green buoys, but may not anchor in this channel. Boats may pick up NPS moorings.

*Boat anchoring is prohibited in Park waters on the south shore and boats must use moorings provided. This includes all the bays from Cocolobo Point to Ram Head and the new Coral Reef Monument.

*Boats are limited to 30 nights per calendar year in Park waters. Moorings are provided on a first-come, first-served basis.

*Boats 125 feet to 210 feet (length on deck) may anchor only in Francis Bay, in sand, and must be in depths greater than 50 feet.

*Fishing is allowed outside of swim areas, but not in Trunk/Jumbie Bay. Spear guns are prohibited anywhere in Park waters.

*Caribbean spiny lobster catch is limited to two per person per day and the season is October 1 – March 30. Whelk must be larger than 2.5" and take is limited to one gallon per person per day, and 3/8" lip thickness.

*Collecting plants and animals – dead or alive – or inanimate objects, including cultural artifacts, coral, shells, and sand is prohibited. Metal detectors are not allowed anywhere in the Park.

*Camping is allowed only at Cinnamon Bay Campground.

*Fires are permitted only on grills at designated picnic areas.

*Feeding marine and terrestrial wildlife is prohibited and may be dangerous to you.

*Pets are not allowed on Park beaches, in the campground or in picnic areas, but may be walked – leashed – on trails.

*Glass bottles are not permitted on Park beaches.

Contact For More Information

It is highly recommended you look at these websites before boating in the Park to get any updates to the current information, and to familiar-ize yourselves with the Park rules and regulations. The National Park Service offers a wealth of fascinating information on the underwater sea life and above water flora and fauna.

Virgin Islands National Park
1300 Cruz Bay Creek
Saint John, V.I. 00830
Tel: 340-776-6201
Email: virg@us-national-parks.net
Internet: www.nps.gov/viis
www.virgin.islands.national-park.com
Friends of the VI National Park:
www.friendsvinp.org
Mooring & Anchoring Guide for the Virgin Islands National Park:
www.usviinfo.com/infousvi/npmooring

Divers on beach *Jim Scheiner*

Diving the Virgin Islands

The Virgin Islands are one of the best sailing and cruising areas in the world. They are also recognized as one of the top dive destinations.

The wreck of the R.M.S. Rhone has become synonymous with the B.V.I. in dive circles, regarded by many as the best wreck dive of the Western Hemisphere.

Superb reefs for both snorkeling and diving are found in and around most of the anchorages. The U.S. Virgin Islands have a series of underwater parks: Trunk Bay, St. John, Buck Island, St. Croix, Coki Beach, St. Thomas. In the British Virgin Islands, the island of Anegada has over 300 documented shipwrecks.

Servicing the needs of the visiting yachtsmen, many professional dive shops and dive tour operators have set up businesses, providing complete services from equipment rental and air tank refills, to tours and instruction.

For the non-diver, a resort course will enable you to explore the underwater world with the aid of an instructor. Full certification courses are available from the individual dive shop operators conveniently located throughout the islands.

The rules and regulations of the marine parks of both the U.S. and British Virgins are similar.

Diving in the British Virgin Islands

Dive operators of the Virgin Islands, through a cooperative effort, have pooled information to give you these brief but picturesque descriptions of 20 of their favorite locations:

Painted Walls — Long canyons, a cave, a sponge-encrusted tunnel, barracudas, rock beauties, angelfish and a variety of pelagic fish make the Painted Walls an exciting and picturesque dive with 28 to 50-foot depths.

The Rhone — Just about everyone in diving has heard of the classical wreck, the RMS Rhone. Even those

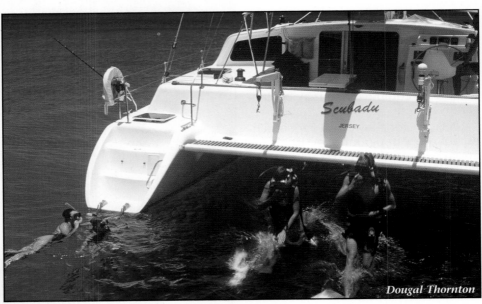

Dougal Thornton

DIVING & SNORKELING

who have not visited the B.V.I. have seen the Rhone in Columbia Pictures' treasure diving epic, *"The Deep."* An ocean steamer, 310 feet in length, this magnificent vessel sank off Salt Island during an extremely violent hurricane in 1867. After 117 years of silent slumber in 20-80 feet of water, this great ship remains remarkably intact with much of her decking, rigging, steam engine and propeller still visible. Gilded with colorful sponges and flourishing corals, the Rhone is perhaps the most impressive shipwreck in the entire Caribbean.

Rhone Reef — Two coral-encrusted caves are located in less than 25 feet of water at Rhone Reef, Salt Island. A variety of hard and soft corals, fish, turtles and the occasional shark can be found here. Due to its proximity to the Rhone, it is a protected area.

Great Harbour — Directly across the channel from Road Town Harbour lies a large, protected bay on the north side of Peter Island. At the center of this bay is a shallow coral reef less than 20 yards offshore, beginning in 8 feet of water. Loaded with colorful sponges and a marvelous array of small marine life, the reef slopes gently to approximately 18 feet, then drops vertically to a depth of 40 feet.

Indians — The Indians are four large rock formations that rise from the ocean floor to a height of about 90 feet. Deepest depth is 50 feet on the westward side. The Indians have just about everything for the snorkeler as well as the scuba diver; brain, finger, star and elkhorn corals are abundant, as are gorgonians and sea fans.

Caves — The caves at Norman Island can provide many hours of fun for snorkelers. There is a large variety of subjects for the underwater photographer such as schools of dwarf herring or fry. These fish provide food

Jim Scheiner

for the many pelicans in the area. The reef in front of the shallow caves slopes downward to a depth of 40 feet.

Angelfish Reef — One of the best sightseeing dives is a sloping reef located off the western point of Norman Island. Depths here range from 10–90 feet. The high point of your dive will be a visit to the bottom of the channel where a large colony of angelfish resides. There is plenty of fish action at this particular site because of the swiftly flowing currents in the nearby channel and the close proximity to the open sea.

Cooper Island — The southeastern shore of Cooper Island, called Markoe Point, is a sheer rock wall that plunges some 70 feet to the ocean floor. Nurse sharks are frequently encountered lying on sandy floors at the base of small canyons formed by the rugged walls of the island.

Scrub Island — The south side of Scrub Island is a splendid reef with depths of up to 60 feet.

Little Camanoe — The northeastern tip of Little Camanoe offers a 30-foot reef dive. The coral overhangs in this area are exceptionally good. Caution: ground seas.

Seal Dog Rock — Plenty of pelagic fish. Depth of 80 feet. Caution: may have a current. This dive is recommended for experienced divers.

George Dog — The rocky point in the anchorage at George Dog is an easy 25-30 foot dive for beginning divers.

Invisibles — (East of Necker Island) Spectacular soaring peaks from 4-70 feet from surface. Flashing schools of every kind of fish, sleeping nurse sharks and all forms of sea life abound.

Visibles — (Southwest underwater pinnacle off Cockroach Island) Caves, canyons, resident 8-foot green moray and nurse shark. Depths to 70 feet. Spawning area for many species of jacks, snappers, groupers.

Chimney — (West Bay of Great Dog) Winding canyon goes to a colorful underwater arch. Many coral heads with an unbelievable variety of small sea creatures.

Joe's Cave — (West Dog Island) Cathedral-effect cave with schooling glassy-eyed sweepers. Clouds of silversides overshadow a variety of eels, pelagic fish and other species, with an occasional school of bulky, splashing tarpon.

Van Ryan's Rock — (Off Collison Point, Virgin Gorda) Huge lobsters, turtles, and plenty of fish among brilliant corals and swaying sea fans.

Ginger Island — Mushroom coral heads 15–20 feet high, great visibility. Graduated shelves ending at 70–90 feet in a huge sand patch. Pet the stingrays and play with huge jewfish.

Southside of Great Dog Island — Reef runs east and west, 100 yards of island coral, butterfly fish. Exciting dive locations, each more unusual than the next. Expect to see just about anything!

Anegada Reef — Graveyard of some 300 documented shipwrecks dating from the 1600s to the present. Spanish galleons and English privateers with uncountable treasure.

The Chikuzen — This 245-foot ship was sunk in 1981 and provides a fantastic home for all varieties of fish, including big rays and horse-eye jacks. The depth here is feet. Located about 5 m Camanoe Island.

Diving In The U. S. Virgin Islands

Cartenser Sr. — (Off St. Thomas, near Buck Island) A spectacular dive on the intact, coral-encrusted hull of a World War I cargo ship in 50-foot depths. Tours easily arranged.

Cow and Calf — Two rocks between Christmas Cove and Jersey Bay, 5 feet below the surface. The lee side of the western rock provides intricate arches, ledges and caves. Many angelfish and beautiful coral.

Christmas Cove — Good beginner's dive on the northwest side of Fish Cay in 40 feet of water. Swim amongst the coral heads. Plenty of fish.

Dog Rock — For advanced divers

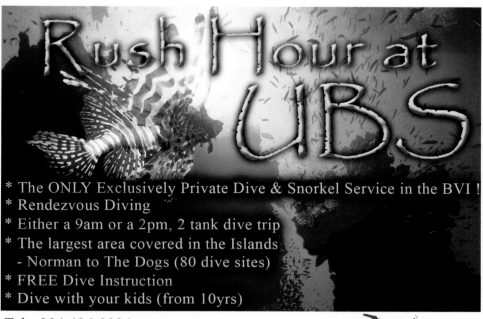

ne northwestern side of Dog and in 40-50 foot depths. Rock and coral ledges and caves. Caution: This one can be rough.

Coki Beach — A good place to snorkel off the beach. Coral ledges.

Little Saint James — A 40-foot dive on the lee side has some deep ledges to explore, sheltering various schools of fish.

Twin Barges — Located off Limetree Beach lie two wrecks sunk approximately in the 1940s. Although visibility is limited outside the wrecks, the clarity improves inside the ships' chambers.

Carvel Rock — Off of the northern side of this rock, near St. John, in depths to 90 feet, big schools of pelagic fish pass through colorful, sponge-encrusted caves.

Thatch Cay — Divers at the Tunnels here explore 8 different arches and tunnels.

Scotch Bank — Off St. Croix, this popular dive spot is a favorite for spotting stingrays and manta rays.

Long Reef — A 6-mile-long reef which provides dives at depths from 30–50 feet. A forest of coral, including pillar and elkhorn colonies.

Salt River — This area has 2 distinct walls. The East Wall plunges from depths of 50-100 feet, revealing many caves and caverns. The West Wall peaks at 30 feet and tumbles to 125 feet. The colors of the sponges grasping the crevices and pillars are awesome.

Buck Island — Off St. Croix, this national monument features abundant tropical fish and a jungle of huge staghorn and elkhorn coral. An absolute must for anyone visiting St. Croix.

Frederiksted Pier—(St. Croix) 30-foot-deep pilings offer splendid diving day or night. The pilings provide a home for bright sponges and algae, as well as sea horses, crabs and octopus.

Cane Bay, Davis Bay and Salt River — All have walls of coral from 20 feet to over 1000 feet. Several anchors have been discovered along the wall. One of the most-photographed anchors is nestled in sand at 60 feet on the Northstar Wall.

Simon Scott

The Royal Mail Steamer Rhone

On the morning of October 29, 1867, the R.M.S. Rhone was at anchor outside of Great Harbour, Peter Island. The Rhone, under the command of Captain Robert F. Wooley, had left Southampton on October 2, 1867, and was taking on cargo and stores for the return crossing.

The R.M.S. Conway, commanded by Captain Hammock, lay alongside.

The stillness of the tropical day was undisturbed as the sun blazed down from a clear sky upon calm seas. As the morning wore on, the barometer began to fall, hinting the weather might deteriorate. The seas, however, remained untroubled. Although the captains alerted themselves, work was allowed to continue. Captain Wooley hailed Captain Hammock that he did not like the look of the weather and, as the hurricane season was over, it must be a northerly brewing. Wooley felt they should shift to the northern anchorage of Road Harbour, Tortola.

About 11am., the barometer suddenly fell to 27.95 degrees. The sky darkened, and with a mighty roar a fearful hurricane blew from the north/northwest. The howling wind whistled through the shrouds and tore at the rigging. With engines going at full speed, the ships rode the storm.

At noon there came a lull in the storm. The Conway weighed anchor and headed toward the northern anchorage of Road Harbour. As she steamed across the Sir Francis Drake Channel, she was hit by the second blast of the hurricane. Her funnel and masts were blown away, and she was driven onto the island of Tortola.

The Rhone tried to weigh anchor during the lull, but the shackle of the cable caught in the hawse pipe and parted, dropping the 3,000-pound anchor and some 300 feet of chain. With engines running at full speed, she steamed seaward in order to seek sea room to weather the second onslaught. She had negotiated most of the rocky channel and was rounding the last point when the hurricane, blowing from the south-southeast, struck, forcing her onto the rocks at Salt Island where she heeled over, broke in two, and sank instantly, taking most of her company with her.

—Courtesy of R.M.S. Rhone by George and Luana Marler

DIVING & SNORKELING

81

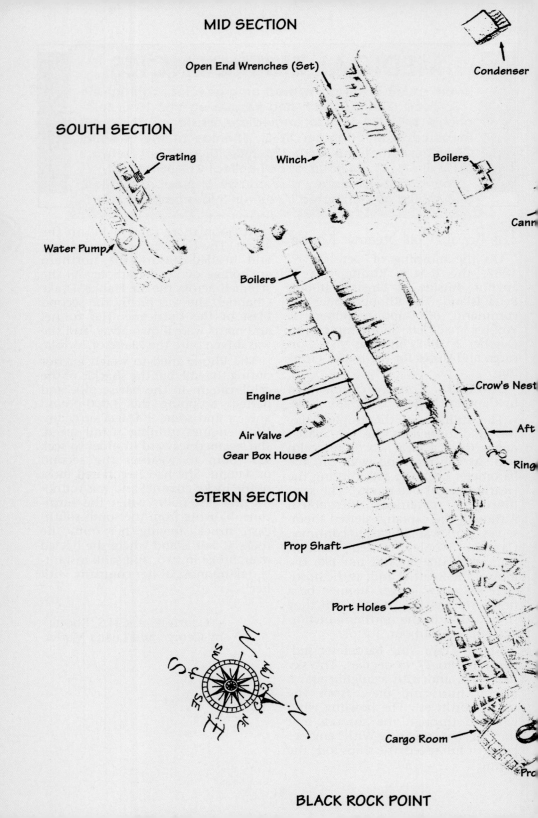

MID SECTION

Condenser

Open End Wrenches (Set)

SOUTH SECTION

Grating

Winch

Boilers

Cann

Water Pump

Boilers

Crow's Nest

Engine

Air Valve

Aft

Gear Box House

Ring

STERN SECTION

Prop Shaft

Port Holes

Cargo Room

Pro

BLACK ROCK POINT

Hatch

BOW SECTION

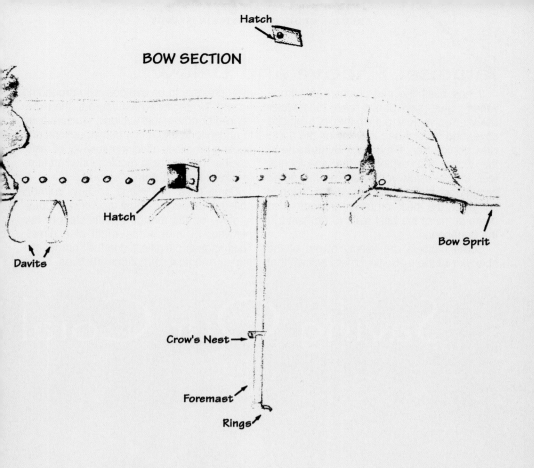

Hatch

Bow Sprit

Davits

Crow's Nest

Foremast

Rings

R.M.S. RHONE NATIONAL PARK
No Spearfishing, Linefishing, Taking of
Coral or Shells, or Anchoring in the Wreck.
GOVERNMENT OF THE BRITISH VIRGIN ISLANDS

This is a diagram to the Rhone
as it is positioned underwater.

LEE BAY

Paradise: Above and Below

It has been the perfect day; 15kt trade winds, blue sky above and bluer-water below. You've just pulled into a secluded cove, had a meal and lazy lay on the deck. How do you top off this day? By jumping in the water and exploring the spectacular reefs that lie below your keel. The very same conditions that make the Virgin Islands some of the best cruising grounds also make some of the best reefs to be found in the Caribbean.

Some cruisers are keenly aware of the splendor of the reefs, yet others believe that reefs are only to be avoided as a grounding hazard. No matter which you are, the experienced or novice reef explorer, cruisers need to understand that many of their actions and boating practices affect the survival of reefs, whether they put on a mask snorkel and fins to take a look, or not.

Coral reefs are made of tiny animals called coral polyps. Most grow tremendously slow, on the rate of a millimeters or two per year (1 mm = the width of a dime). Their shapes are reflected in their name, giving us magical formations such as "Brain

Saving Our Coral

Corals", "Pillar corals", "Lettuce corals", "Small and Massive Star corals"; yet these names hide the fact that these structures are colonies of animals that are centuries old. As Columbus and his ships sailed these waters, the reefs that we see today were already beginning to take shape.

For a novice, the first look underwater is often defies description. The structures of the reef, the coral colonies, crate a three-dimensional mosaic, often rising up from the bottom. Some corals appear hard and daunting, and others appear soft and sway in the water currents. This interpretation is accurate as there are both "hard" and "soft" corals; the main difference is soft corals animals don't create the hard skeleton that forms the foundation of the "hard corals". Soft corals have a less rigid, more flexible skeleton, thereby allowing them to bend in the water currents.

Corals, especially hard corals, may look like rocks, lumps passively sitting on the bottom. Yet, corals actively feed, and defend themselves against predators. The polyp of a coral is made up of a ring of tentacles. These tentacles have stinging cells called nematocysts. These harpoon-like structures are ultra-fast, and efficient at both killing small food items (called zoo-plankton) that drift into the coral's tentacle reach, and defending the coral against predators (called corallivores). Although some fish, worms and even snails will eat corals, the nematocysts are a major deterrent for most marine life, and even humans that venture too close to corals. For example, "Fire Coral" acquires its name from the painful sting felt by those that come in contact with this mustard-colored coral. However, snorkelers and divers should realize that touching any coral, whether a painful sting is felt or not, should be avoided to prevent damage to the coral (breakage) and the human.(scrapes, abrasions and cuts).

Of course corals are not the only animals on the reef. Sponges of spectacular color, shapes and sizes are abundant. Worms, with feather respiratory structures, with names like "Plume worms", and "Christmas Tree worms" can be readily seen. Shrimp and crabs hide in the reef cracks and crevices. Then there are the more obscure animals like tunicates, zoanthids, and anemones. They all combine to make up the magical mix of coral reef critters.

And then there are the fish. In all colors of the rainbow and amazing shapes and sized. Some dart and scurry about. Others gather in large schools sometimes above the reef, sometimes within reef channels or among the reef structure itself. Fish need the reef and the structure it provides for shelter (called habitat). Without that structure, they've no where to live, rest or feed. The fish need the reef.

Observation Tip:

Watching the fish interact with the reef can provide endless enjoyment. Observing a cleaning station is one of the reef's secret treasures. Watch for a fish to stop swimming, and begin hovering motionless above one spot on the reef. It might be over a coral head, or over a sponge. Then watch this fish to see if another small fish (a goby, wrasse, or even a shrimp) moves around on the fish "cleaning" particles. Sometimes you can see the fish open its' mouth, or gills and the cleaner will move inside to perform the cleaning service.

Observation Tip: when snorkeling an area dominated by sea fans, notice the "orientation" of the fans in relation to the current. Sea fans will grow in an orientation perpendicular to the prevailing current. This allows maximum water flow through the fan/animal providing good feeding opportunities.

Observation Tip: Realize, any coral you contact will be stinging you with nematocysts, shooting a small, hollow dagger into your flesh, and injecting you with a toxin designed to stun. ("Fire coral" is just toxic-enough for us to feel! The best advise: don't touch any coral; hard coral or soft. Fire coral or other type. You won't get stung or cut by the coral and coral won't be damaged by you.

Coral: the amazing solar powered animal!

When snorkeling around a coral reef most are awestruck by the intricate coral formations. But just how does coral grow? To answer that, we need to understand that although
corals are animals, they are also part plant. Living within the thin layer of tissue that covers the coral skeleton are millions of single-celled plants called zooxanthellae. These plants
play a vital role for the reef building corals by providing energy and assisting in the secre-
tion of skeleton. The relationship between the coral animal and the small plants within their
skin is so critical, that without the plants, coral reefs would not exist the way we see them
today. They need the extra energy and benefits the internal-plants provide.

What do the corals do for humans?

Snorkeling and diving on reefs provide life-long memories that will enhance any cruising adventure. But did you realize that corals provided more than just gorgeous scenery?
Reefs provide numerous valuable functions for humans that affect our lives daily, even if we
live far from the tropics. For example reefs help protect our shorelines from waves and ero-
sion. They help create those gorgeous sandy beaches. Without the reefs, the fish would
have no-place to live. Reefs provided habitat for fish that support shore birds like pelicans.
Mangroves and seagrass beds found associated with coral reefs are tremendous nurseries
for countless organisms, from both the land and the sea.

Reefs also provide a source of chemicals that are used to make medicines of the future.
Bio-prospecting is the field that investigates animals including many marine animals like
corals, sponges, and animals called tunicates as sources of drugs to fight cancer and other
life-threatening illnesses. Reports estimate one million plants and animals live in or on coral
reefs and their associated communities (mangroves, seagrass beds, algal plains...), yet
scientists have identified only about 10%. It would be very sad to lose animals and plants
that may provide the cure for some of the world's deadliest diseases.

Threats to coral reefs

As you snorkel and dive around your favorite reef, remember that corals are very slow
growing animals that have fairly specific requirements to survive. They need clean, clear,
tropical waters, with the right amount of salt (called salinity), the right amount of nutrients,
and food. They can't get out of the way of physical contact, and their primary defense is
their stinging nematocysts. Physical contacts with reefs from direct contact by a diver,
snorkeler, boat anchor or chain can scrape off coral tissue, or break the colony. And
changes in water temperature, salinity, nutrient levels, clarity, or pollution (solid or liquid
waste) can harm coral reefs by altering the environment in which they live.

Dr. Caroline Rogers, USGS.

What can/must you do while cruising to protect coral reefs?

Ten things you can do to protect the coral reefs.

(adapted from article by William Stelzer)

1. Realize that coral reefs are systems of slow-growing animals that have taken many centuries to develop into what we see today. They are not rocks and standing on them or kicking them will cause substantial damage. Corals have very limited ability to recover from damages, or heal physical scars. And breaking off a piece of coral is usually fatal, killing hundreds of years of growth.

2. Don't drop anchors or anchor chains on corals. Know what is below before you drop your anchor. If you aren't sure that you are over sand jump in the water with a mask to take a look. Dropping anchors and chains on coral crushes, pulverizes and dislodges the corals from the bottom. This destructive practice can b e easily avoided by a) using a mooring to secure your boat, or b) snorkeling to see what lies below your keel before you drop the hook.

3. Don't touch, kick or stand on coral. Don't drag dive equipment or cameras across it. Don't kick sand on it. Fins, cameras, dive gauges, and regulator second stages can crush coral polyps, or break of entire sections of coral. Sand kicked up by fins, feet or boat engines can smother corals, depriving them of sunlight and food they require for growth and life. And while small contacts may not be life-threatening, the additional stress may prove too much and become fatal. Abrasions also provide locations for infections in the coral, or places for invasion by marine micro-organisms.

4. Don't drive boats into reefs. While running aground is a nightmare for the cruiser, it is also fatal for the reef. Know where you are cruising. Pay attention to charts and navigation and limit distractions. Don't leave the helm while operating a boat and don't (or limit) cruising at night.

5. Don't pump-out holding tanks/bilges and don't add chemicals to these places. Pollutants in the form of sewage and oils are harmful to reefs. Nutrients in the sewage promote algal growth that out-compete coral for space on the reefs. (This is also why you should avoid urinating while snorkeling or diving. Use your boat's marine heads, that is why they are there.) Chemicals that are put into holding tanks and bilges are harmful to reefs and can interfere with the treatment of these wastes when they are properly pumped-out on shore.

6. Know where and how you can fish. Many cruisers love trolling and fishing, but before doing so, make certain you are in compliance with local regulations (either US or British).

7. Catch only what you will eat. Once you are aware and in compliance with fishing regulations, catch only what you will eat. Local reef fisheries are over-exploited, and fish play an important role in the ecology of the reef.

8. Take only pictures, leave only bubbles and footprints. Collecting shells and coral/live rock is illegal in the British and US Virgin Islands, even the "dead" rubble on shorelines. Shells, even ones that appear "empty" are illegal to collect. Photography or sketching is a non-destructive way to turn these finds into lasting memories.

9. Littering kills. Cruisers love Caribbean trade winds, but care must be taken so articles don't blow off the boat into the water. Towels and wet clothes will blow off safety lines, sinking to entangle in the reef. Solid waste such as cups, napkins and plates that blow overboard are unsightly and destructive to marine life. Plastics smother reefs and harm turtles. Use proper trash facilities for solid waste, and don't let towels or trash blow off your boat into the water.

10. Avoid fuel spills. Use extreme care when fueling you boat and dingy. If you do spill gas, don't use any dispersants such as detergents or soap. This causes oils to sink to the bottom and smother corals. Oil spills are an environmental and safety hazard, and legal violation. The best way to avoid spills is to pay close attention whenever handling or transferring fuels.

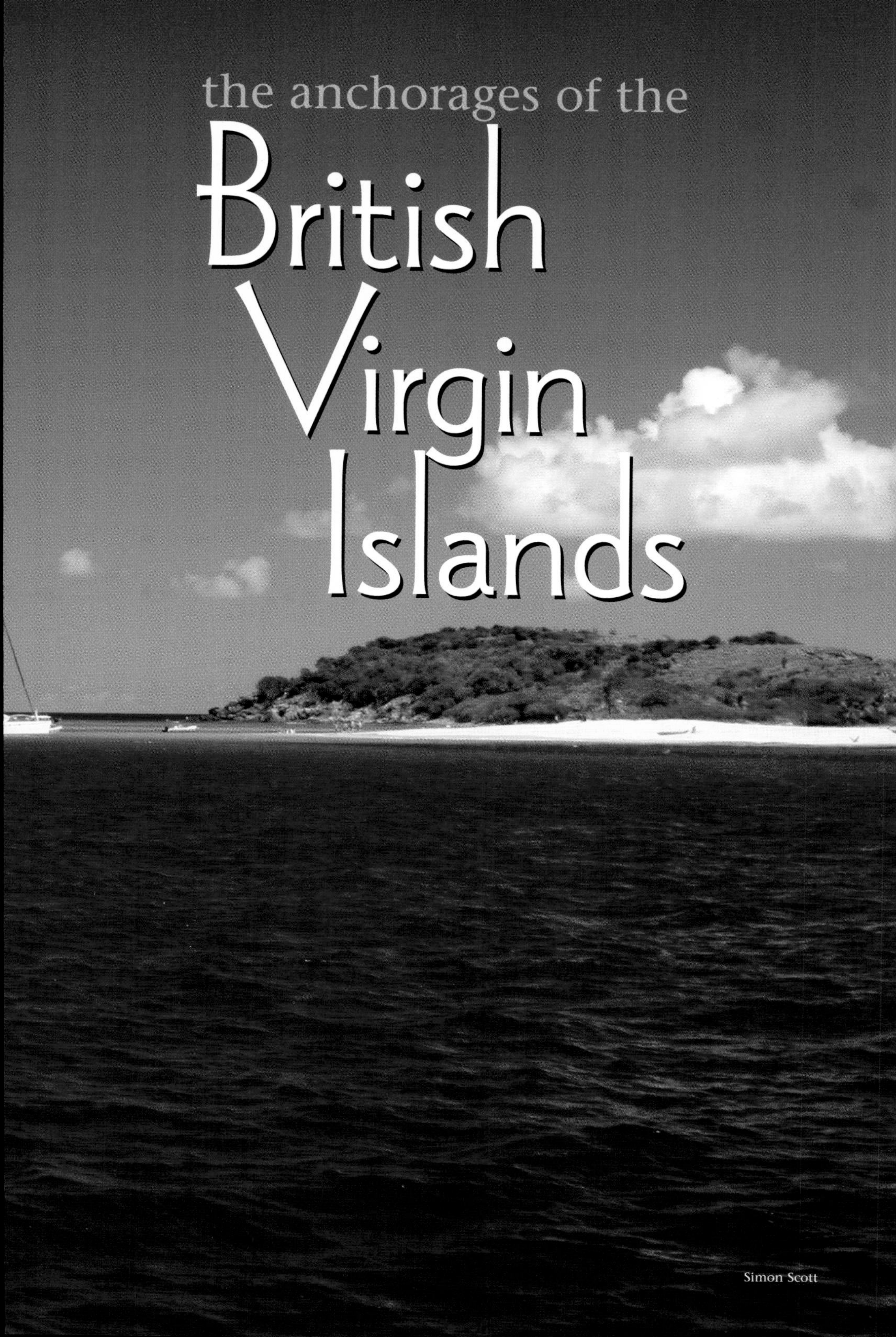

the anchorages of the

British
Virgin
Islands

Simon Scott

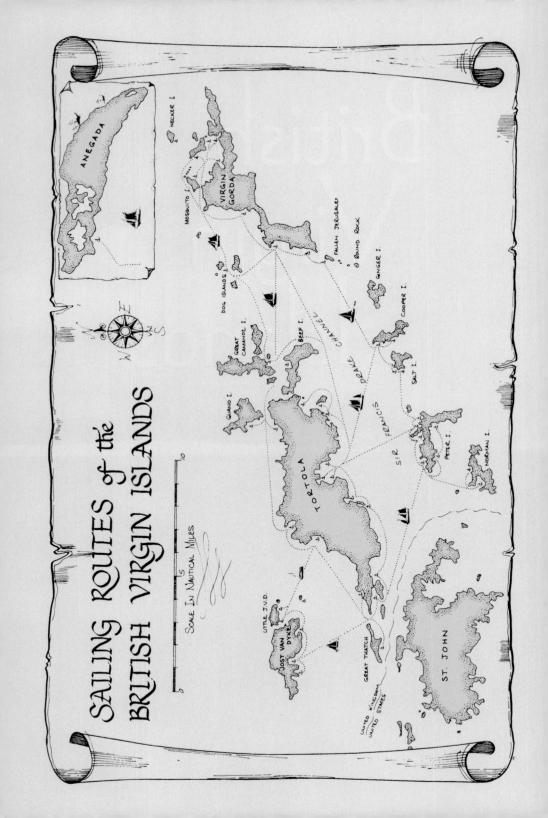

SAILING ROUTES of the BRITISH VIRGIN ISLANDS

SCALE IN NAUTICAL MILES

ANEGADA

HECKER I.

MOSQUITO I.

VIRGIN GORDA

FALLEN JERUSALEM

ROUND ROCK

GINGER I.

DOG ISLANDS

GREAT CAMANOE I.

BEEF I.

COOPER I.

GUANO I.

DRAKE CHANNEL

SALT I.

TORTOLA

SIR FRANCIS

PETER I.

NORMAN I.

LITTLE J.V.D.

JOST VAN DYKE

GREAT THATCH

UNITED KINGDOM
UNITED STATES

ST. JOHN

Message from Premier Honourable Ralph T. O'Neal, OBE

Dear Yachtsmen:

It is a pleasure for me to welcome you to the beautiful British Virgin Islands, also known as Nature's Little Secrets.

As you cruise around our beautiful islands, I know that you will be enchanted by the breath-taking scenic views of our rolling emerald mountains, blue-turquoise waters and white sandy beaches.

My Government is committed to protecting and preserving our environment and we expect our visitors to do likewise. Government recently published, in conjunction with The Moorings, a 56-page Marine Awareness Guide to raise awareness on the importance of protecting our resources for the people of this Territory and for visitors like you who sail around these islands.

The Guide features marine habitats, marine species, marine-related laws, conservation practices, potentially dangerous marine organisms and storm preparation and safety measures. I therefore encourage you to obtain a copy and learn more about the BVI's marine environment.

I invite you to be good stewards and join us in our efforts as we preserve and protect our marine environment for generations to come.

Welcome to our lovely islands and I wish you a fun-filled time.

Ralph T. O'Neal, OBE
Premier and Minister of Tourism

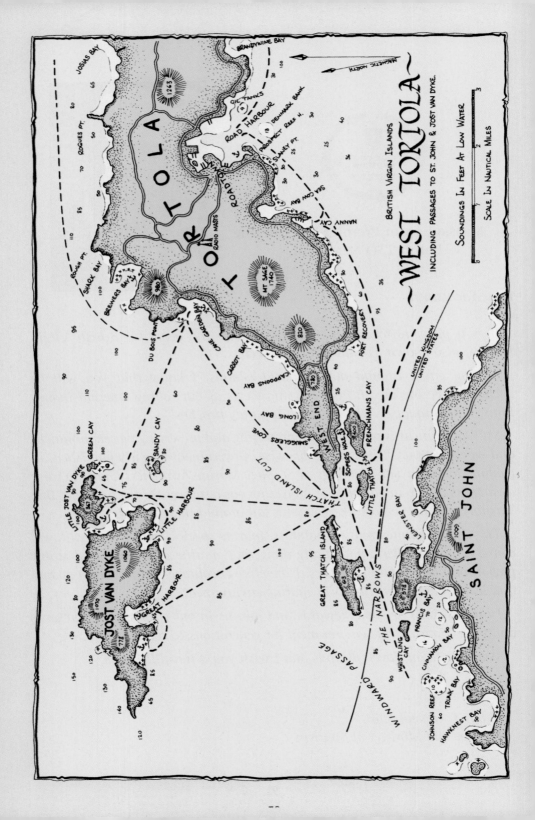

TORTOLA panorama

Jim Scheiner

Simon Scott

Jost Van Dyke

A large, high island, Jost Van Dyke lies to the north of Tortola and becomes visible to yachtsmen sailing from St. Thomas upon entering Pillsbury Sound. With a population of under 225, the island remains relatively unspoiled. The largest settlement is Great Harbour, which is also a port of entry into the BVI.

Named after a Dutch pirate, the island is known as the birthplace of Dr. John Lettsome, born on Little Jost Van Dyke in 1744. Dr. Lettsome later returned to his native England and founded the London Medical Society of the Royal Humane Society. Known for his good sense of humor, Dr. Lettsome wrote the following:

I, John Lettsome,

Blisters, bleeds and sweats 'em

If, after that, they please to die

I, John Lettsome.

While visiting Jost Van Dyke visit the JVD 32 island sloop. The Jost Van Dykes Preservation Society has undertaken the building of a traditional island sloop designed by local residents who have sailed these traditional wooden vessels in days gone by. They are also assisting in the construction of the wooden sloop along with high school students who will be taught lessons on boatbuilding. Ask anyone for directions to the sloop behind Foxy's. This is only one part of the mission of the Jost Van Dykes Preservation Society who are honoring the islands maritime heritage. You can check the progress of the sloop project at www.jvdps.org and read about the many other projects they are working on in order to preserve the history of the islands, and if you feel inclined, you may help them out with a donation.

White Bay

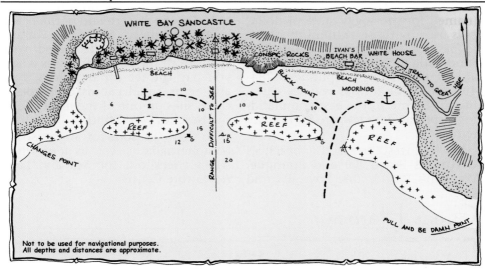

Not to be used for navigational purposes.
All depths and distances are approximate.

White Bay is the westernmost harbor on the south side of the island. Aptly named for its beautiful stretch of white sandy beach, White Bay is an excellent anchorage under normal sea conditions. During the winter months, however, ground swells can make it an untenable anchorage, suitable for day stops only.

Navigation

White Bay is a relatively small anchorage with very little swinging room once inside the reef; however, there is room for several boats if anchored properly. Although there are three entrances through the reef, it is recommended that you make your approach between the middle of the two reefs, leaving the red buoy to starboard and the green to port. You may also enter the eastern most channel marked by privately maintained red and green markers.

Anchoring and Mooring

The middle channel will take 10 – 12 feet draft. Once inside the reef, anchor to port or starboard in approximately 7 – 10 feet of water with a sandy bottom. Do not anchor in the channel or block it, and stay well clear of the shoal spot just off the black rocks to starboard of the channel entrance.

The eastern most entrance is usually marked with a set of red and green buoys, however, as they are privately maintained there is a chance that one or both may be missing. As of May 2008, there was one buoy missing. Once you are inside the reef you may pick up a mooring and pay the fee at Ivan's Stress-Free Bar. Keep an eye on the black rocks. If anchoring, make sure there is enough swinging room between your vessel and those on moorings. Take care not to drop your anchor on coral!

Ashore

White Bay Sandcastle is a small delightful resort that serves breakfast, lunch and four course gourmet dinners with reservations. The Soggy Dollar Bar is a great spot to swim ashore for a Painkiller and to while away the afternoon under a palm

Painkiller, a delicious but rum drink was originally [serv]ed at the Soggy Dollar Bar [nam]ed for the soggy state of dollar bi[lls] used by those swimming ashore to pay for their drinks). White Bay Sandcastle monitors VHF 16 and can also be reached by telephone at 284-495-9888. The houses you see clinging to the hill to the east commanding a spectacular view, are for holiday rentals.

To the west down the beach is Gertrude's Beach Bar and Boutique, Wendell's World, One Love Bar and Grill, Jewel's Snack Shack, and the White Bay Superette, a small market where you can pick up a few essentials. On the eastern end of the beach is Ivan Chinnery's Stress Free Bar and Restaurant lavishly decorated with shells from the beach. Ivan's is where you pay the fee for moorings. Ivan also rents small cabins or prepared camp sites on one of the most exquisite beaches you'll find.

To rent all sorts of water sports paraphernalia as well as four wheel ATV's check out the Sea and Land Adventure Centre.

Great Harbour

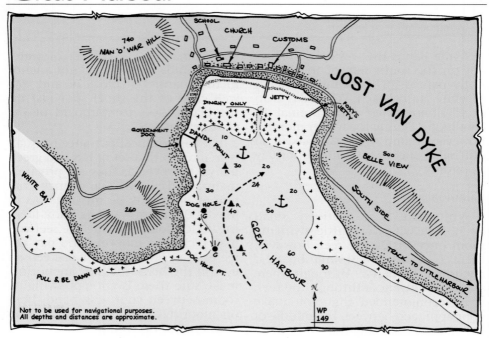

Not to be used for navigational purposes.
All depths and distances are approximate.

WP 149

This normally sheltered harbor at the foot of 1000 foot high peaks, Great Harbour is a port of entry in the BVI and is the largest settlement on the island.

Navigation

On your port side upon entering are three lit red and green buoys designating a channel for official government business only. This channel carries a depth of about 12 feet. Most boats, however, head down the middle of the harbor giving the shorelines on either side a reasonable berth. There is a large reef extending out 300 yards from the inner shoreline, be sure to drop anchor before you reach it.

Foxy's

where friends are met... and memories made

You will be delighted to find
• Good Company
• Special Drinks • Good Food
• Memorabilia — all in the most natural tropical setting you can imagine as well as being spontaneously entertained by FOXY himself !!!!

Great Harbour
Jost Van Dyke

major credit cards accepted
284 495-9258

Lunch & Dinner — 7 Days a Week
Our Famous BBQ — Fri & Sat nights
LIVE BANDS —
Thurs, Fri & Sat nights

vhf ch.16

Dougal Thornton

ANCHORAGES OF THE BRITISH VIRGIN ISLANDS

Caribbean Yacht Chart C14 97

Sidney's Peace & Love   *Simon Scott*

Anchoring

Anchor anywhere outside the reef in 15 – 30 feet of water. It can be difficult to get your anchor to hold, but once well set you should be okay. It would be a good idea to put your snorkel on and check your anchor visually to avoid a middle of the night anchor drill!

Ashore

Take the dinghy ashore through the break in the reef and head directly for the dock, in order to avoid shallow coral heads. The customs officer for Jost Van Dyke will clear vessels in or out of British waters for both customs and immigration. The office for customs and the police are

located just at the base of the government dock. Across from the police station at the base of the dock is a dumpster for garbage disposal.

Great Harbour has a worldwide reputation for having great beach parties. It is amazing the countries and places you will see someone with a Foxy's t-shirt strolling by! The atmosphere is casual with flip-flops and shorts welcome everywhere.

Down the beach to the west is Rudy's Mariners Inn with five rooms, a bar and restaurant that features fresh seafood and live entertainment along with Rudy's Superette for necessities. The Jost Van Dyke Health Service is situated near Rudy's. Continuing towards the police sta-

Simon Scott

Great Harbour Jost Van Dyke Police Station

Simon Scott

tion is Jost Van Dyke Scuba, and Corsairs Restaurant and Bar. Corsairs serve breakfast, lunch and dinner starting at 8:30 am. The open air restaurant faces the beach – it is fun and casual, serving northern Italian dishes and TexMex with a Caribbean flair. Ask Vinny for a pirate punch or a voodoo juice, to name two of their potent specialty drinks. Next down the beach is Ali Baba's restaurant - great for local food and it is open for breakfast, lunch and dinner with a Monday night pig roast. Wendell's World is on the beach near the Jost Van Dyke grocery store, the Ice Cream Parlor, and Tropical Kisses, selling casual, tropical clothing.

On the road perpendicular to the beach you will find Nature's Basket with locally grown fresh fruits and vegetables and Christine's Bakery with her delectable fresh baked bread. Further up the road, the ice house can replenish the ice aboard.

Around the corner next to the fire department is a small gas station.On the eastern end of the beach visit JVD Water Sports and BVI Eco Tours for tours off the beaten track.

Tucked into the corner on the far eastern end of the beach is Foxy's dock in front of the restaurant. Foxy and his wife, Tessa, just celebrated the fortieth anniversary of the opening of Foxy's beach bar! It has grown in popularity and now is legendary. Foxy's has become famous over the years amongst charterers and cruisers alike, as the locations for many wild and wonderful parties where the music and dancing in the sand go on until the wee hours. Stop in at their extensive gift shop, the Foxhole, and sport your own Foxy t-shirt. On rare occasions you may catch Foxy singing calypso or playing his guitar – he is the one with the twinkle in his eye! Foxy's monitors VHF 16 or can be reached at 284-495-9258.

Little Harbour

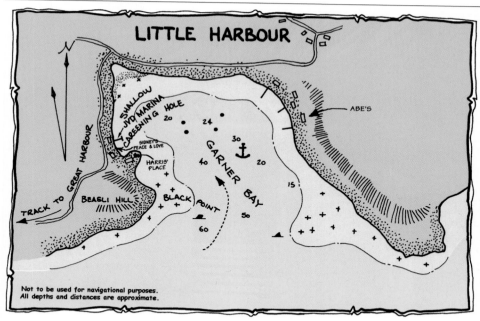

LITTLE HARBOUR

SHALLOW
JVD MARINA
CAREENING HOLE
20
24
30
20
SIDNEY'S
PEACE & LOVE
HARRIS'
PLACE
GARNER BAY
40
20
15
TRACK TO GREAT HARBOUR
BEASLI HILL
BLACK POINT
50
60
ABE'S

Not to be used for navigational purposes.
All depths and distances are approximate.

Little Harbour, or Garner Bay, as it is sometimes called, lies to the east of Great Harbour. Once used as a careenage for island sloops, the harbor now caters to charter parties, with three restaurants ashore.

Navigation

The entrance to Little Harbour is straightforward and deep. There is a shoal area to port when entering, but the channel is wide and clear and marked with a red buoy to starboard and a green one to port.

Anchoring and Mooring

The traditional anchorage is off the western end of the bay in 12 feet of water, but in recent years boats have been anchoring all over the bay.

Pick up one of the moorings and pay for it at Harris's Place ashore on the western end of the beach, or on the eastern side, pay for the moorings at Abe's. For anchoring, the shore is rocky along the east side, but

the bottom is clean, hard sand. Insure that your anchor is well set with sufficient scope, as parts of the harbor are very deep.

Ashore

On the western end of the bay is the Little Harbour Marina, where you may purchase fuel - both gasoline and diesel as well as water and ice. There are three restaurants in the bay. On the eastern side is Abe's By the Sea, serving lunch and dinner with reservations. Abe's also has a little grocery store where you can buy ice and some provisions for the boat. Inflatable dinghies are available for rent next door to Abe's.

The western side of Little Harbour is home to Sidney's Peace and Love and Harris's Place. Sidney's is open at 9am for breakfast, lunch and dinner with live music on Monday and Saturday nights. Harris's can provide you with ice, fax and phone and a brand new dock with electricity. They

ANCHORAGES OF THE BRITISH VIRGIN ISLANDS

Simon Scott

are open from 11 to 11 daily. Monday nights Harris's have live entertainment and all you can eat lobster and the other nights they offer a barbeque. All of the restaurants monitor VHF 16.

For those who enjoy hiking, there is a small track that takes you about 1000 feet up the mountain. For those ambitious enough to make the climb, the views are spectacular – bring your camera!

Sandy Cay, Green Cay, Little Jost Van Dyke

Little Jost Van Dyke & Diamond Cay

There is a delightful small anchorage on the southeastern end of Little Jost Van Dyke. Entrance to the Little Jost Van Dyke anchorage from the south presents no hazards though it

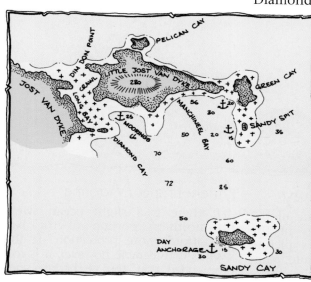

is prudent to watch the water depth.

Anchoring & Mooring

As you approach Foxy's Taboo restaurant and marina you will see the 10 moorings in the bay. Although they are not marked you may pick one up and pay for it at the bar.

You can also anchor in 15 – 25 feet of water. Make sure you are far enough away to avoid swinging into the moorings. The bottom is sandy and provides excellent holding. If the wind is out of the south, the anchorage becomes very sloppy and during northerly ground swells the surge can be excessive.

There is no passage between Jost Van Dyke and Little Jost Van Dyke, but good snorkeling exists along the south side of Little Jost.

Ashore

Foxy's Taboo, a charming restaurant with a marina, is just north of Diamond Rock on Jost Van Dyke facing east towards Green Cay and Sandy Spit. This is a fun spot with an open air bar and dining area. The food is excellent and the atmosphere is breezy and light. The marina has depths of 8 to 20 feet and several slips. For marina and dining information Foxy's Taboo monitors VHF 16. There are no facilities for garbage disposal here, so please hang on to it until you are somewhere that has garbage bins.

A good place for a refreshing dip is the "Bubbly Pool", a natural pool surrounded by rocks at the ocean's edge. At high tide, waves tumble in through the holes in the rocks creating a bubbling salt water pool. Ask for directions at the restaurant.

Bubbly Pool   *Julian Putley*

Tortola

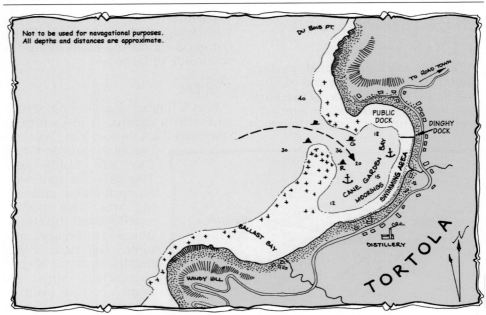

Not to be used for navagational purposes.
All depths and distances are approximate.

Cane Garden Bay

Regarded by many as one of the more beautiful anchorages in the B.V.I., Cane Garden Bay is picture postcard material, with a white, palm fringed beach stretching the entire length of the bay. When approaching from the west, you will sail past Smugglers Cove, Belmont, Long Bay and Carrot Bay before reaching Cane Garden Bay. If you have any doubt, line up the south side of Jost Van Dyke directly under the peak of Tobago, and this range will bring you to the entrance.

Navigation

There are two reefs at the entrance to Cane Garden Bay. Entering boats should favor the northern end of the bay. The reef is marked by two sets of buoys, which simplify the entrance appreciably. Leave the red buoy to starboard when entering. Once clear of the reef, you'll have plenty of room to anchor or pick up a mooring.

Anchoring & Mooring

If there is a slight ocean swell, the northern portion of the bay will afford more protection. If the swell is considerable however, it is recommended that you reschedule your cruise to return a few days later when it has subsided and no longer rolly.

When anchoring, keep clear of the buoys designating the swimming area. The bottom affords excellent holding in 15 – 25 feet of water. Moorings buoys are available. The mooring balls identify the name of the establishment where the fee should be paid.

Owing to the mountains, the wind tends to change directions, so check your swinging room in relation to other vessels, particularly if you are anchored and they are on a mooring. You will tend to swing much further on an anchor than a mooring.

Caribbean Yacht Chart C14

Cane Garden Bay   Simon Scott

Ashore

The public dinghy dock has been renovated and now is lighted, with side boards to tie up to and a railing to hang on to on your way back from the beach bars. A dock attendant with a dinghy is on duty most nights to assist. You will find the dinghy dock in the middle of the bay by the rocks.

On the far eastern side of the bay is the Cane Garden Bay public dock where you can tie up to fill your water and fuel tanks. However, there are no overnight facilities at this dock. Be sure to check the depth at the dock before moving your boat there.

Cane Garden Bay is lined by several terrific beach bars for the choosing. You can usually hear the live music from the anchorage and jump in your dinghy and head for shore to rock the night away. There is almost always live entertainment nightly at one establishment or another. Check ashore to find where the music will be on any given night.

Next to the dinghy dock is Quito's Gazebo serving lunch and dinner. Quito performs alone and with his band, The Edge, several nights a week. Quito's is a favorite amongst both visitors and locals. The place is jamming when the band is playing!

Just west of Quito's on the beach is Al Henley's Big Banana Paradise Club open from 7am serving delicious

breakfast, lunch, dinner and drinks at the bar inside, or on the deck outside.

Rhymer's Beach Bar and Restaurant further west along the beach is the pink building. Rhymer's serves break-

Courtesy of HIHO

fast, lunch and dinner daily with live entertainment on special occasions. Ice, telephones, showers, and a small market stocking most necessities, are available on the premises.

Still going west along the beach is Stanley's Welcome Bar, open from 10am to 10pm serving lunch, and dinner with reservations. Stanley's was one of the original restaurants in Cane Garden Bay and was famous for the palm tree with a tire swing until, unfortunately the tree was lost in a storm.

Pleasure Boats handles small boat rentals from the beach, with kayaks, pedal boats, motorboats and windsurfers. Cane Garden Bay is an excellent place to hone your kayaking or windsurfing skills.

On the beach past Stanley's, nestled in the almond trees, is Myett's Garden & Grille Restaurant. The restaurant is open for breakfast, lunch and dinner daily with reservations. A charming location, Myett's offers dining in their garden grill serving lobster, fish, steak, chicken and burgers, while viewing the bay and the sunset. There is live music most nights featuring calypso, fungi and reggae music. During the busy season they have a breakfast bar with fresh baked goodies and specialty coffee and teas. The latest news headlines are printed off the internet along with a current daily weather report.

Check out Olivia's new expanded gift shop full of all kinds of goodies, including Cane Garden Bay t-shirts. An ATM is available if you need cash. Upstairs are some lovely guest rooms if you need to get off the boat, or want to stay a few extra days. For a really relaxing vacation, try their spa for a massage or facial. The communications center is complete with telephones, fax and computers with high speed internet connections.

Cane Garden Bay

Simon Scott

At the far end of the beach is De Wedding open from 11am serving lunch and dinner with reservations. Their specialty is fresh seafood.

The Elm Bar and Gift Shop are open daily until 7pm, 5pm on Sundays. Check to see if they have live music on Sunday afternoon from 2pm.

Supplies can be purchased from a well-stocked branch of Bobby's Market on the road behind the beach, or at Callwood's Grocery Store, Rhymer's, and a few other local shops.

Mr. Callwood's rum distillery affords visiting yachts a glimpse back into history. White and gold rum is still produced from the cane grown on the hillsides and bears the label Arundel from the name of the estate purchased by the Callwood family in the late 1800's. It is recommended that you ask permission prior to wandering through the distillery, and the purchase of a bottle or two is expected.

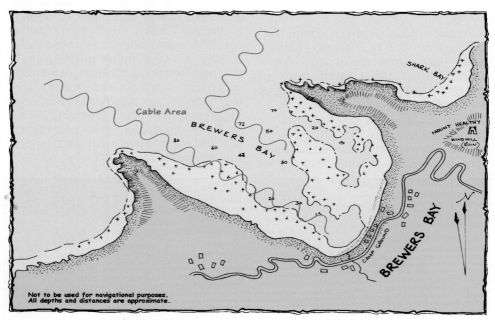

Not to be used for navigational purposes.
All depths and distances are approximate.

Brewers Bay

Without question, Brewers Bay, on the northern side of Tortola is one of the most beautiful bays in the Virgin Islands. Unfortunately, however, it is not used as an anchorage due to underwater cables. It is also vulnerable to northerly ground swells owing to the northern exposure and is prohibited as an anchorage by most charter companies.

If you are in a dinghy or a shallow powerboat it is worth a visit providing the seas are flat. You will need good light to read the bottom and to avoid coral heads and reef.

There is a reef that fringes the southwest shoreline and another in the center of the bay. You can work yourself up to the beach if you are careful.

Ashore

While the snorkeling is excellent, time should also be taken to explore ashore. For those interested in a shore walk, it would be worthwhile walking up the road to the east, toward Mount Healthy to see the ruins

Brewers Bay Julian Putley

of Tortola's only remaining wind-mill. Only the base of the original mill has survived the passing years, along with the broken remains of the old distillery buildings.

Brewers Bay Campground is located on the beach at Brewers Bay.

Soper's Hole

West End is shown on the charts as Soper's Hole, a protected harbor lying between Frenchman's Cay and Tortola. It is a port of entry for vessels arriving and departing British waters, and a ferry stop between the British and United States Virgin Islands.

Navigation

Whether you enter Soper's Hole between Frenchman's Cay and Little Thatch or Steele Point and Great Thatch, you will be in deep water at all times. A current of up to three knots depending on the tidal flow, can be expected. If you are sailing in, then you should cut the points of either Frenchman's Cay or Steele Point as close as is possible, mindful of the depth.

The government dock is located on the northern shore, near the channel markers for the ferries, but yachtsmen are advised not to tie up while clearing customs because of the movement of the ferries. Rather, it is recommended to pick up a mooring and bring the dinghy into the dinghy dock just to the east of the ferry dock.

Anchoring & Mooring

The harbor is so deep in places that yachts will find themselves in 60 – 70 feet of water. The best place to anchor

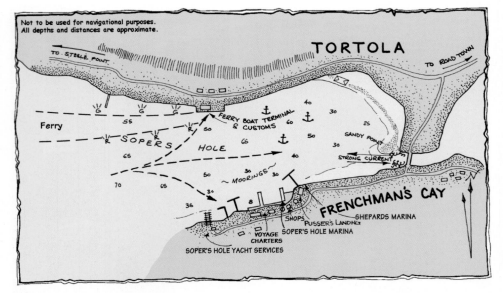

is in the northeast corner near VI Shipwrights, where the water depth is 20 – 35 feet on a sandy bottom.

There are moorings off of Shepherds Marina and you will find a shallow dinghy passage behind the sandbar between Frenchman's Cay and Tortola suitable for dinghies only.

There are also moorings off of the Soper's Hole Wharf & Marina in the southeast section of the bay, which are maintained regularly by Moor Seacure. These moorings may be picked up and paid for at the Soper's Hole Wharf & Marina office ashore.

Moorings are available in the vicinity of Soper's Hole Yacht Services and are marked accordingly. Be advised not to anchor in the way of the slipway as they need ample room to operate the railway and maneuver vessels during adverse wind conditions.

Soper's Hole Yacht Services has a KMI SeaLift that can haul almost any kind of vessel up to a 14 foot draft including mono hulls and catamarans. The yard offers fuel, water, showers, provisioning and wifi. Security is provided around the clock. They are open Monday through Friday from 8am to 4pm and monitor VHF channel 16.

Ashore

The West End customs office is located in the building on the ferry dock and is open Monday through Friday from 8:30am to 4:30pm. For clearance outside of those hours overtime fees will apply. Some supplies are available from Zelma's Courtesy Grocery & Snack Bar, and ice from the Rocky Willow Bar & Restaurant across from the customs building. Taxis are available in abundance when the ferries arrive.

On the southeast side of the harbor is the Soper's Hole Marina, providing dockage for vessels up to 150 feet with a 20 foot draft. Both slips and moorings are available along with several charming air-conditioned rooms. This is the base of the Voyage Yacht Charters fleet who manage the marina.

At the marina you can fill up on fuel, water and ice and dispose of your garbage. Free wifi is provided for marina guests. There is a First Caribbean Bank ATM located on the premises. The marina monitors VHF 16 or can be reached at 284-495-4589.

ANCHORAGES OF THE BRITISH VIRGIN ISLANDS

Jim Scheiner

The two story Pusser's Landing features waterfront dining with two restaurants and bars, an outdoor terrace and the Pusser's Company Store. Downstairs, the restaurant offers a more casual ambiance, with an open air bar, on the deck dining and the Company Store which carries Pusser's special line of nautical and tropical clothing, watches, luggage, nautical accessories and even cigars.

Pusser's Seashell and Beach Store is a fun store with everything beach for sale, from gift items to hats, t-shirts, beachwear, towels and more. You won't leave without buying something! Pusser's is open seven days a week and monitors VHF 16.

For provisioning, try the Harbour Market which is located at the base of Sheppards Marina. Normal opening hours are 8:00am to 6:30pm. Harbour Market offers a large variety of provisions, gourmet foods, liquor, beer and wine. Credit cards are accepted. At Sopers Hole Yacht Services you will find another market called Ample Hamper 2.

Culture Classic Boutique and Arawak sell casual clothing and swim wear. BVI Apparel Factory Outlet sells souvenirs and t-shirts. Zenaida has some fascinating jewelry, accessories and sarongs. Latitude 18 is now on the waterfront next to Voyage Charters with clothing, sunglasses and BVI Yacht Club gear for the whole family. Hucksters is a small, unique gift shop with many interesting items and prints. Caribbean Jewelers sell jewelry, arts and crafts and have a Cyber Café for those with withdrawal anxiety from email.

A popular destination after a long day of sailing and sunning is the Ice Cream Parlor followed by a visit to Serenity Spa for a massage, or facials, manicures and pedicures.

Bluewater Divers is located on the waterfront with tank rentals, dive

Simon Scott

Sopers Hole Marina   *Simon Scott*

trips, and a shop with clothing and gift items. For powerboat rentals, water taxi services, day charters and island trips visit Sheppard Boat Rentals.

D' Best Cup features a variety of coffee drinks, ice cream, smoothies, pastries, beer, wine, sandwiches and snacks. They also have a variety of gift items.

Near to West End is the Frenchman's Cay Hotel overlooking the Sir Francis Drake Channel. Breakfast, lunch and dinner are served and the pool and tennis courts are available to diners. The restaurant is open Tuesday through Sunday for breakfast, lunch and dinner and their bar is open from 11am daily. The view is spectacular and diners are invited to use the pool.

Located near the ferry dock, the popular Jolly Roger Inn, perched next to the sea provides views of all the activity in the harbor. The Inn serves breakfast, lunch and dinner, as well as a late night menu including pizza.

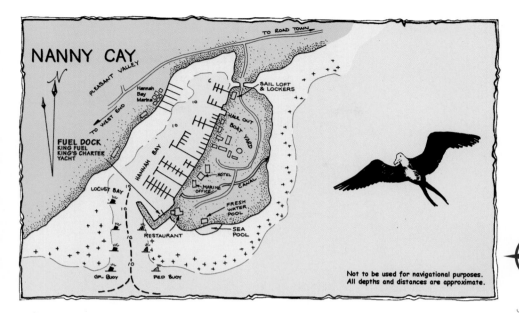

Not to be used for navigational purposes. All depths and distances are approximate.

Nanny Cay

Approaching Nanny Cay from the West End of Tortola, the first landmark will be the masts of the boats hauled out in the boatyard and at the dock. Nanny Cay is a peninsula jutting out from the south coast of Tortola, behind which is the Nanny Cay Marine Centre, a full service marina and boatyard offering a 70 ton lift capable of lifting boats of up to 70 feet.

Navigation

Head for the southern most point of Nanny Cay (the Peg Leg Landing restaurant is an easy landmark), until you see the red and green lighted entrance pilings. On the port side when entering there are two green buoys, the first one is lit but not the second. On the starboard side when entering use the breakwater as the outside limit of the channel. The breakwater is marked with four red lights. Yachts with a draft of ten feet or less will be able to use the channel. Yachts with a draft of over ten feet should call the marina first for instructions.

The inner harbor has shoal water on the western shore and is marked with a series of green buoys – do not go too far to the west. There is no anchoring permitted due to the lack of space and there are no moorings available.

Ashore

The marina is often full necessitating a call to check on the availability of a slip. You may call the marina on VHF channel 16 (switching to VHF 68) or by telephone at 284-494-2512.

Nanny Cay Marine Centre offers a wide range of services including the marina, the boatyard, hotel, restaurants and everything else a yachtie could need or want. The marina can accommodate yachts up to 140 feet long, 12 feet draft, and 33 feet wide. Amenities available within the marina complex include showers, water, laundromat, ice and fuel. Provisions may be purchased from the Gourmet Chandler and storage lockers may be rented through the marina. An ATM is planned for the near future.

Bluewater Divers, based in Nanny Cay for over twenty years, operate a

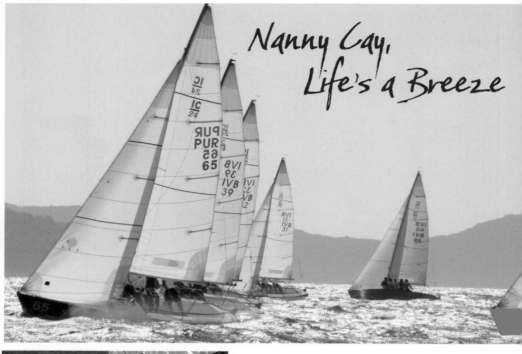

Nanny Cay, Life's a Breeze

Nanny Cay is more than a marina, it's a unique sailing community. Stroll down the jetties or hang out in the bars and restaurants and the talk is all boats.

We've everything you need to keep your boat seaworthy; a chandlery, sail loft, maintenance contractors and a fully working boatyard complete with two travel lifts.

While your boat is well looked after so are you, with a great range of shops, the Genaker Café and Peg Leg's Landing Bar and Restaurant on the beach.

And if you want to take some shore leave the Nanny Cay Hotel provides a welcome berth with internet, cable TV, a gym and spa.

In fact, you can even make Nanny Cay your home from home with a townhouse in Nanny Cay Village. Ownership guarantees your own mooring, so you can be on the deck of your boat from the deck of your house in a couple of minutes. Some homes are available for short and long term rental, built to very high standards and are luxuriously furnished.

To find out more just visit our website www.nannycay.com Phone 284 494 2512 Fax 284 494 3288 E-mail info@nannycay.com The breeze is waiting.

Nanny Cay Marina   *Mauricio Handler*

dive shop and conduct diving tours daily. Nanny Cay is their main base of operations. BVI Marine Management is based at this marina for mechanical repairs, refrigeration, welding and 24 hour chase boat service. Johnny's Maritime Services, a complete yacht management and maintenance company with many years experience, is also located on the dock.

Nanny Cay Chandlery is open from 8am to 5pm daily except on Saturday when they close at noon. Sundays they are closed. BVI Painters and Yacht Restoration Marine Services (shipwrights) complement the boatyard along with Antilles Yachts who arrange yacht deliveries and management. For electronics, see Island Care Electronics. Check with BVI Yacht Sales to purchase a boat and have it surveyed by Caribbean Marine Surveyors, Marine Consultants and Surveyors, or West Indies Marine Surveyors. For those who hate to varnish call on Tony's Marine Varnishing. Quantum Sail Loft can repair your sails and they have an inventory of battens and sail hardware.

The Nanny Cay boatyard has two travel lifts; one with a capacity to haul mono-hulls up to 68 feet long and 10 foot draft. The other travel lift can accommodate catamarans up to 32

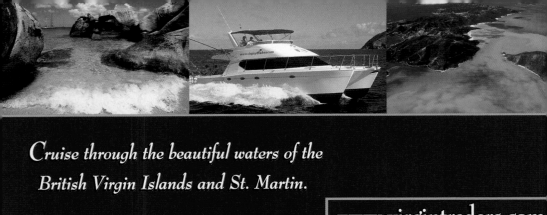

feet wide and 70 tons. Richardson's Rigging can take care of any rigging issues. Please note: customs and immigration services are no longer available at Nanny Cay Marine Centre. You must clear in at one of the other ports of entry.

For the shopper Arawak Boutique sell souvenirs and interesting gifts to bring home. Bamboushay creates pottery in every shape and size. They are located on the access road to the marina.

Two restaurants complement the marina. Genaker Café is open all day at the waterfront mall. Peg Leg Landing, a rather whimsical restaurant on the point, serves lunch and dinner and overlooks the Sir Francis Drake Channel. It's a great place to dine, with a view from every table.

The following charter companies and boat rentals are based at the Nanny Cay Marina: Catamaran Charters, Horizon Yacht Charters, Virgin Traders, Island Time, King Charters and Rob Swain Sailing School. HiHo on the southern shore of Nanny Cay offer surfboard and windsurfer rentals, as well as instructions. If you need to check your email, Coconut Telegraph Internet Service is at your service!

Nanny Cay Marine Centre viewed from the air. *Dougal Thornton*

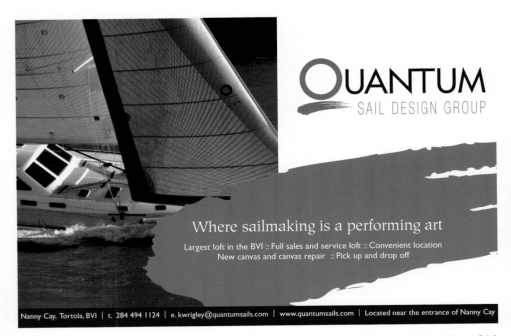

Jim Scheiner

Julian Putley

Sea Cow's Bay
Manuel Reef Marina

Navigation

From the Sir Francis Drake Channel you will see a lighted red buoy at the mouth of Sea Cow's Bay marking Manuel Reef. Boats entering Sea Cow's Bay should keep the red buoy on their starboard side and keep a heading of 340 degrees for a quarter of a mile to the Manuel Reef Marina. Tie up at the end of the t-dock, and if that is occupied, take any empty slip on the south side of the dock. The water depth at the dock is 9 feet. Manuel Reef Marina monitors VHF channel 16.

Ashore

Manuel Reef Marina is conveniently situated between Nanny Cay and Road Town. The marina offers electricity, water, and showers as well as yacht management services. Check out the Sports Bar and BVI Water Sports Centre located on the premises.

Not to be used for navigational purposes. All depths and distances are approximate.

MANUEL REEF MARINA

TORTOLA

Anchoring in coral is **STRICTLY PROHIBITED** in both the U.S. and B.V.I.

Caribbean Yacht Chart C14

Courtesy of seahawkpaints.com

ANCHORAGES OF THE BRITISH VIRGIN ISLANDS

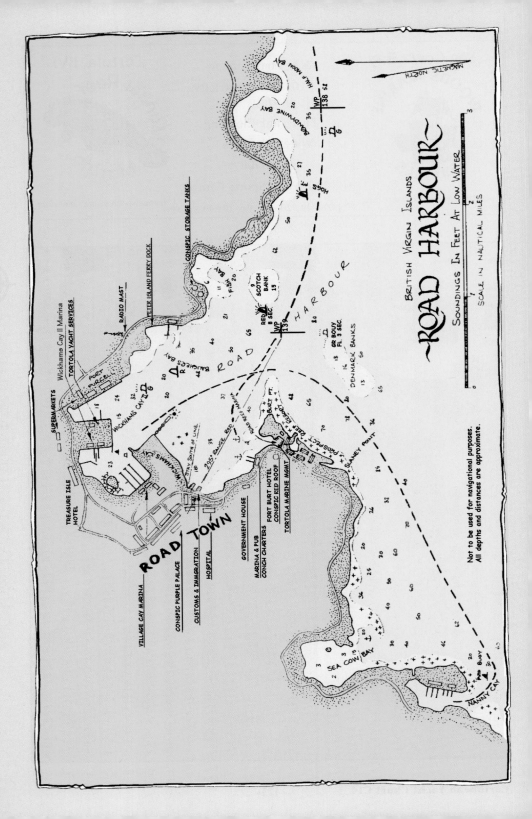

ROAD HARBOUR panorama

Wickhams Cay II & VILLAGE CAY

FL GREEN 3 SEC.

ROAD HARBOUR

ROAD REEF

ROAD REEF MARINA

DOLPHIN FL W 3 SEC

PORT PURCELL

Wickhams Cay II

CRUISE SHIP DOCK

SHOALS

GOV'T BUILDING

CUSTOMS & FERRY DOCK

INNER HARBOUR MARINA

VILLAGE CAY MARINA

FORT BURT MARINA

N

Road Harbour

Road Town, the capital of the British Virgin Islands, is the center of commerce, shipping and social activity. Over the past two decades, tremendous development has taken place to enable it to better cope with the steady influx of cruising and charter boats. Road Town can boast some of the most sophisticated nautical facilities in the Caribbean chain.

Navigation

Approaching Road Harbour from the west, your first landmarks will be the fuel tanks located by Fish Bay on the eastern side of the harbor. The other is the dome shaped roof of the Fort Burt Hotel, located high up on Burt Point, on the western side of the harbor entrance.

Locate the green sea buoy (FL green 3 seconds) marking the end of the reef, extending east from Burt Point and leave it to port. There is a red conical buoy (FL red 8 seconds) marking Scotch Bank on the eastern side of the harbor.

Road Reef Marina

Heading to Fort Burt Marina, turn to port when you are close to the Fort Burt Marina docks, keeping the docks close on your starboard side. You will be leaving Fort Burt Marina, Conch Charters and Smith's Ferry dock to starboard. There are a couple of shallow patches close to the road side beneath Fort Burt Hotel, so favor the port side of the channel as you enter the pool of Road Reef Marina.

Road Reef Marina is managed by Tortola Marine Management. Electricity, ice and water are available as well as wifi from the TMM office. The marina can accommodate vessels 60 feet in length, with a maximum

Caribbean Yacht Chart C13, C13a, C14

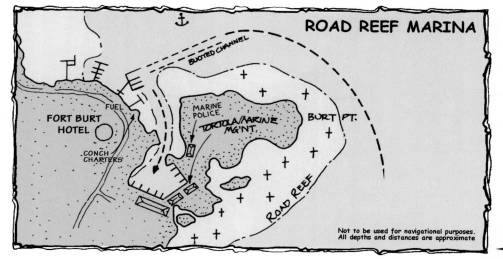

BUOYED CHANNEL

FUEL

FORT BURT
HOTEL

MARINE
POLICE

TORTOLA/MARINE
MG'NT.

BURT PT.

CONCH
CHARTERS

ROAD REEF

Not to be used for navigational purposes.
All depths and distances are approximate

draft of 7.5 feet. The beam size is unrestricted. The marina is open from 8am – 5pm daily and they monitor VHF 12 or can be called at 284-494-2751.

In the same complex that houses the marina office is the marine division of the British Virgin Island Police, the Royal BVI Yacht Club, VISAR Base Station, Doyle Sailmakers and Island Care Electronics. Road

Reef Plaza, next door to the marina has a variety of shops including a Riteway market that sells provisioning to the yachting community.

Fort Burt Marina

Once inside the buoys, it is advisable to head for the customs dock (approximately 292 degrees magnetic), until the Fort Burt jetty is abeam. This will bring you clear of the reef

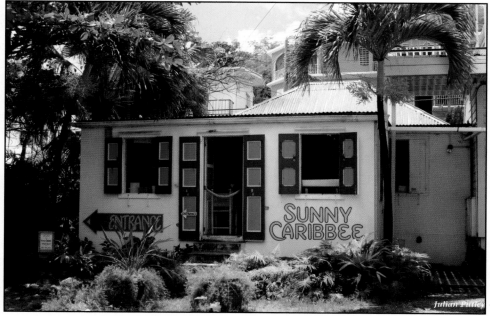

Julian Putley

Caribbean Yacht Chart C13, C13a, C14

127

ANCHORAGES OF THE BRITISH VIRGIN ISLANDS

Tortola BVI
Belize
The Grenadines

UNIQUELY TMM

"**Quality**
at your
Service"

*Corrine
TMM Tortola*

Most charter companies offer blue water & palm trees, but it takes the personalized care of people like Corrine to make your vacation a success. With a smile as warm as the Caribbean sun she'll bring your charter dreams to life.

Like Corrine, everyone at TMM is committed to your complete satisfaction. Our specialized three-location operation offers large company quality with small company service. A combination that is uniquely TMM.

TMM
Yacht Charters
since 1979

1.800.633.0155
www.sailtmm.com

catamarans • monohulls
motor yachts
ownership programs

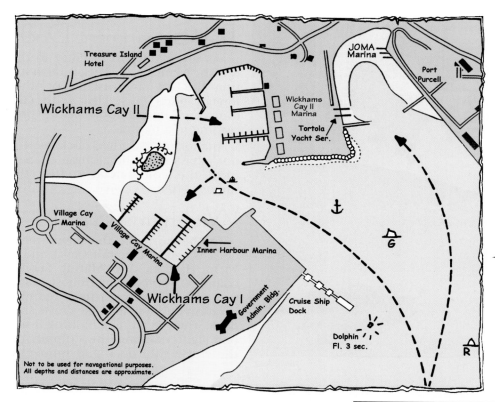

Not to be used for navagational purposes.
All depths and distances are approximate.

that extends to the north of the mangroves. Anchor to the northeast of the docks, about 300 feet out. Check the sketch chart for the location of sandbars and the anchorage.

Hundreds of sailors have found themselves aground on the sandbar that extends north of the mangroves because they rounded up too quickly. The situation is particularly embarrassing because of the proximity of the local pub, which overlooks the anchorage.

Fort Burt Marina accepts transient boats and offers gas, diesel, water and ice as well as telephone, TV cable hook-ups and, of course, electricity. Pull alongside and check for slip availability with the dockmaster. Next to the Fort Burt Marina near the Pub is Tradewind Yachting Services, retailers of marine batteries, outboards, and they sell, repair, and certify life rafts.

The Pub is perched at the water's edge with a dinghy dock. It is open Monday through Saturday from 7am to 10pm; Sundays they open for happy hour from 5pm. Dress is casual. On Thursday and Friday nights during the season there is entertainment and the Pub rocks!

Julian Putley

Caribbean Yacht Chart C13, C13a, C14

The Government Dock

As the main port of entry to the British Islands, all vessels arriving from the U.S. Virgin Islands or other foreign ports must clear with customs and immigration before proceeding to a marina.

Anchor off the town dock, as it is not advisable to lie alongside; apart from the commercial traffic, the surge is often excessive.

Wickhams Cay I

To the north of the government dock is the Wickham's Cay I and II Yacht Harbour and Marine Service complex. Approaching from seaward, you will see the government administration building and the cruise ship dock. There is a quick flashing 3 second light marking the dolphin off the cruise ship dock and numerous

Simon Scott

Caribbean Yacht Chart C13, C13a, C14

Village Cay

Wickams Cay II

masts behind a stone breakwater. Leaving the cruise ship dock to port, head for the masts until you see the two breakwaters. Inside the breakwaters is a set of buoys marking the channel entrance. Leaving the red markers to starboard, proceed through the breakwater entrance (a width of 80 feet by 12 feet deep). There is one 9 foot shallow spot on the port side of the channel about 45 feet off the port breakwater. In the near future the channel and marina will be dredged to a depth of 16 feet. Hard to your port when entering is Village Cay Marina; hard to starboard is the Wickham's Cay II Marina. There are no mooring buoys in the basin.

Village Cay Marina

Village Cay Marina can accommodate over 100 yachts of up to 200 feet in length, 38 feet wide and 12 feet deep. The slips offer water, electricity, telephone, cable TV and internet.connections. Shower facilities, ice, provisioning, and garbage disposal are all conveniently available. You can even drop off laundry or do it yourself. When you've taken care of the things on the boat, have a drink or meal at the Village Cay Dockside breezy waterfront restaurant where you can view all the activity in the harbor.

To fill up on fuel and water, contact the dockmaster at VHF channel 16 (switching to the working channel 71) or telephone them at 284-494-2771 ext. 6. Fuel is located at the end of "A" dock. Village Cay can also assist with procuring propane.

Village Cay Marina is home to Sunshine Powerboat Rentals, Special Care Yacht Management, the Dock Master Deli, Oasis Spa & Salon, Jasanay Boutique, and Carilink (Money Grams).

The Marina Hotel offers air-conditioned rooms, all within short walking distance of the government administration building, banks, shopping and other conveniences of downtown Road Town.

Near the marina, the Cellars Deli offers custom provisioning services and a fine selection of wine, cheese, pate and numerous other goodies to

Dougal Thorton

ANCHORAGES OF THE BRITISH VIRGIN ISLANDS

tempt the palate. Behind Cellars Deli is Mill Mall which has a cyber café for those addicted to email, or just trying to keep in touch with the office or family. B & F Medical Complex (284-494-2196) can help with non-emergency medical needs. They are also located in Mill Mall, a short walk from the marina.

Columbus Centre houses the Charter Yacht Society, Shore Side Services, Girl Friday, DHL, Caribbean Connections and several shops. Within a few minutes walk of the marina are several banking institutions including First Caribbean Bank, Scotia Bank, the BVI Tourist Board, and numerous business offices, gift shops and restaurants.

At the southern end of the complex you will find The Moorings, Moorings Power and Moorings Crewed Yachts on docks A and B at the inner harbor. The Moorings Village is home to Charlie's restau-

A.J. Blake

The Inner Harbour

Inner Harbour Marina is nestled alongside Village Cay to the south. Yachts can pay for their stay by the hour, day or month. The services provided include water, electricity, and convenient walking distance to the shops of Road Town. North South Yacht Charters bases its operation at the marina and monitors VHF channel 16. Overlooking Road Harbour is the Captain's Table Café, a congenial restaurant offering excellent meals.

Wickham's Cay II

One of the Caribbean's most comprehensive marina facilities, Wickham's Cay II Marina is the base for several charter companies. The marina is home to The Moorings, Moorings Power, Moorings Crewed Yachts, Sunsail and Footloose. Dockage is also available for visiting yachts.

rant and bar (named for Charlie Cary, the founder of The Moorings). It is perched over the water at the base of "B" dock. Charlie's is open for lunch and dinner (until late) with an in house pizza oven and an upscale menu. It is casual; with no reservations required.

At the Moorings Village you will also find a boutique, a sales office for Moorings yachts, concierge services and a spa. If you need to cool down try the café for ice cream or a thirst quenching beverage from the coffee bar. In the near future, seven five star hotel rooms will be built over-looking the Sir Francis Drake Channel.

The Mariner Inn is the Wickham's Cay II hotel, with 32 recently renovated rooms overlooking the activity in the marina. The hotel offers all the amenities including wireless internet

CELEBRATING 40 YEARS IN THE BVIS

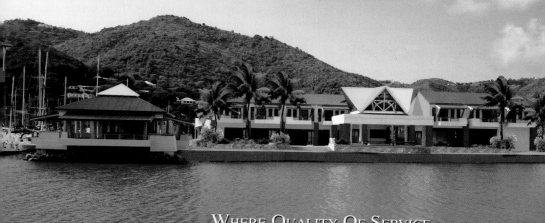

WHERE QUALITY OF SERVICE,
MEETS QUALITY OF LIFE.

In perfect timing with our 40th Anniversary, The Moorings is proud to open its multi-million dollar flagship base at Road Town, Tortola in the British Virgin Islands. The reception area opens onto a plaza area featuring retail shops, café and a new over the water bar and restaurant. Plus, you will find new hotel suites, a health spa and club style showers. This new 5-star base is home to the largest catamaran charter fleet in the world and a wide selection of custom monohulls. Visit the most trusted name in chartering to arrange your sailing vacation.

TheMoorings®
The Best Sailing Vacations In The World!

1969 - 2009

and air conditioning. The Mariner Inn Restaurant and Bar is open seven days a week serving breakfast, lunch and dinner. Guests staying in the hotel or in the marina are welcome to the restaurant and to use the swimming pool.

Transient yachts may go to "C" dock for overnight dockage, you may call Wickham's Cay Marina on VHF channel 12 for availability of dock space and docking instructions. Dockage is on finger piers and can accommodate vessels with a draft of 9 feet. Vessels up to 120 feet may tie up at the T dock when it is available. Amenities include water, ice, and electricity. Fuel (gasoline and diesel) and ice are sold at the bulkhead between dock "D" and "E".

Sunsail, chartering both bareboats and flotillas is located on the "D" dock. The Sunsail office is at the base of the dock. Behind the office are showers, an ATM machine, and

Renport (who rent DVDs, cell phones and other electronic gear). Last Stop Sports rent water toys and dive equipment. HIHO's shop sells casual, fun surf clothing. If you are interested in purchasing a Sunsail boat, the brokerage office is nearby.

Opposite the Wickham's Cay II Marina is Tortola Yacht Services, one of the foremost yacht care centers in the Caribbean and has been operating since 1965. This full service boatyard has a 70 ton Travelift, dry storage, Caribbean Refinishing (concentrating in Awlgrip application), yacht brokerage, and the well-stocked Golden Hind Chandlery.

Also associated with the boatyard is Caribbean Technology Watermakers, Wickham's Cay II Rigging, Marine Power Service for both engine and outboards, Cay Electronics, Bristol Boatworks who specialize in fine marine woodwork, and Island Yacht Management.

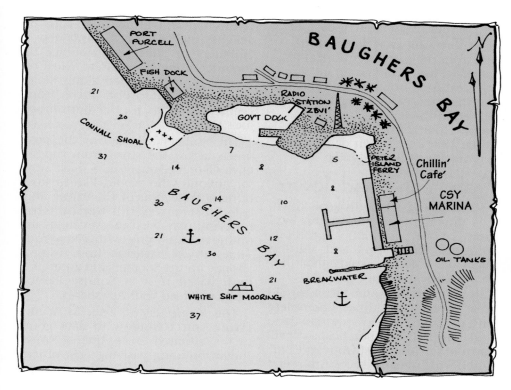

In the immediate vicinity are Nautool Machine, focusing on machining and welding, and Omega Caribbean Woodworkers.

Treasure Isle Hotel is a short walk across from the Wickham's Cay II Marina. It is one of Road Town's finer hotels, just renovated, offering air-conditioned rooms, a fresh water pool and garden-side dining.

TICO, located at the entrance to Wickham's Cay II, is a close walk from the Marina. They offer online ordering and delivery from a well rounded list of wines, liquor, beer, mineral water and juices. Stop by and stock up for the boat from their extensive beverage selection or order online before your trip and have it delivered to your boat when you arrive.

Across the main street from TICO is Riteway, a full-sized market. It is a perfect place for provisioning as they carry a wide range of Caribbean, American, and British products.

Baugher's Bay

On your starboard hand as you enter Road Harbour is the former CSY marina, the base for the Peter Island Resort ferry. At this time it is mainly a commercial marina. Based at the marina is BVI Marine Services who specialize in woodworking. This is also home to the Chillin' Café, a restaurant and bar situated on the second floor overlooking Road Harbour offering outdoor dining on the verandah or air conditioned comfort inside. They are open from 11am – 10pm Monday through Friday serving lunch and dinner with unique Caribbean fusion flavors.

To the north of the marina, near the ZBVI radio antenna, is a small government marina that is the base for the marine division of customs.

A short walk away to the north (left from the marina entrance) is Spaghetti Junction Restaurant serving great food from 6pm – 10:00pm and the Bat Cave Night Club, both located in the Beach Club Terrace. Happy Hour is from 5-7 daily and things heat up on their dance area and outside deck until late!

Ashore in Road Town

When going ashore in Road Town, it is important to observe the local dress code, which prohibits swimwear, brief attire and shirtless males. In order to avoid embarrassment, please cover up!

Road Town has some beautiful old West Indian buildings, complete with red tin roofs and Victorian dado work around the porches. A walk down Main Street east from Fort Burt Hotel, which guards the western end of the harbor, will reveal all sorts of delights tucked away behind newer buildings or squeezed shoulder to shoulder along Main Street. Most of the shops are clustered along Main Street and Waterfront Drive from Peebles Hospital to the bottom of Joe's Hill.

The Philatelic Bureau of the post office, across the street from the Sir Olva Georges Square, is a must stop for anyone who would like to take home a collection of the exotic and colorful stamps of this tropical territory. You may wish to get caught up on the news at home with a New York Times or a magazine from Esme's Shoppe on the Square. Find yourself a fresh baked treat at Sunrise Bakery while you read your newspaper.

The Virgin Island Folk Museum, giving you a window to days gone by, is situated in a quaint West Indian building past the post office.

Caribbean Yacht Chart C13, C13a, C14

Jim Scheiner

Caribbean Yacht Chart C13, C13a, C14

On the waterfront Capriccio di Mare offers breakfast, lunch and dinner from 8:00 am. They also serve a great cappuccino while you wait for the ferry arrival across the street and gaze at the boating activity in the harbor.

The ferry dock at the center of town on the waterfront houses customs and immigration, as well as a convient office of the B.V.I. Tourist Department. A taxi stand is right there making it convenient for the ferry passengers or anyone to get where they want to go.

Straddling the waterfront and Main Street you will find the Pusser's Company Store and Pub. This is a delightful, air-conditioned pub where you can cool down with a beer or lemonade and a deli sandwich or pizza. If you haven't tried a Pusser's Painkiller, this may be just the time! Friday nights the Pub is jamming at happy hour. The Pusser's Company Store, with tropical and nautical clothing for ladies and men, watches, luggage and nautical accessories attached to the Pub, leads to Main Street. Next door, Le Cabanon Café serves breakfast, lunch and dinner from 8am to 11pm. They tend to draw the late night crowd in their bar for a drink and a chat.

Further along the waterfront to the east is the Seaview Hotel and Maria's By the Sea, a restaurant which features local Caribbean cuisine and seafood overlooking Road Harbour.

The brightly colored Crafts Alive Market, right on the waterfront features local souvenirs of all kinds, including t-shirts, hats, baskets, shell work and more. Nearby Crafts Alive, an even better souvenir can be found at Columbian Emeralds! They offer a glittering selection of emeralds, diamonds, watches and jewelry at excellent prices.

Caribbean Yacht Chart C13, C13a, C14

Back on Main Street, hand-crafted silver and gold jewelry is a specialty of Samarkand. Shirt Shack on Chalwell Street has all kinds of t-shirts and casual cotton clothing.

Sunny Caribbee Spice Company and Art Gallery are located in a delightful old West Indian house. The shop carries specially packaged herbs and spices from the islands that make wonderful gifts for friends or yourself . The air-conditioned art gallery is next door with art treasures displayed for sale.

Little Denmark has a wide assortment of things from jewelry and watches to fishing gear and china. Next door is Serendipity with handicrafts, books and cards. Caribbean Arts offers custom framing with a selection of West Indian and local art and prints.

Don't miss the HIHO windsurfing shop with the HIHO brand of surf clothing next to the roundabout. You can also inquire about their windsurfer rentals, surf board rentals and island adventures.

Smith's Gore Real Estate is perched on a huge boulder across from Little Denmark. Further down Main Street is Her Majesty's Prison, an old and interesting edifice, and one we hope you will never have to see from the inside! St. George's Anglican Church is another lovely landmark worth a visit.

Continuing past the church on your left is Joe's Hill which leads up to Mount Sage or over to Cane Garden Bay. The panoramic view is breath taking at the top of the hill and the temperature is usually cool and breezy. If you are still feeling energetic, continue on Main Street past Sunday Morning Well, past the court house and high school to the J.R. Botanical Gardens across the street from the police station. It is a refreshing place to stop, away from the hustle and bustle of Road Town. The garden features a beautiful, exotic variety of lush, tropical plants.

Arriving in Road Harbour from the sea, you will see an old, purple Victorian building just above town. The Bougainvillea Clinic, affectionately known as the "purple palace" and a Road Town landmark, is world-renowned for its plastic and reconstructive surgery. The clinic also offers emergency and general care for visitors and can be contacted at 495-2181.

Many other shops and services, too numerous to mention, are waiting for you to discover in Road Town. Check with the Tourist Department, the Welcome Magazine or even the yellow pages of the phone book to find what you are looking for.

ANCHORAGES OF THE BRITISH VIRGIN ISLANDS

Brandywine Bay

This lovely curve of a bay with a stunning white sand beach is east of Road Town on the southern side of the island. It provides a comfortable overnight anchorage in the usual east/southeast moderate tradewinds, but it can have an uncomfortable surge if the wind moves around to the south.

Navigation

Brandywine Bay is tucked in behind a reef that extends out from both sides of the land. The opening between the two sections of reef is wide and safe for entry in the center between the reefs, with a depth of at least 10 feet. The entrance is easy enough to see in reasonable light.

Anchoring & Mooring

Brandywine Bay Restaurant, situated on the headland to the east of the bay, and overlooking the Sir Francis Drake channel, maintains 4 moorings in the center section of the bay for dinner guests. Please do not pick up any of the moorings in front of the waterfront apartments as they are private. The restaurant monitors VHF channel 16 after 2pm and is available by telephone at 284-495-2301 all day for reservations and instructions for mooring.

If you choose to anchor, select a spot in the center of the bay to the east or west of the line of moorings beware of the shoal water that extends from all shores. If there is a surge, usually caused by a southerly wind or generally very rough local conditions, you may want to use a stern anchor in order to keep the bow of your boat facing the entrance of Brandywine Bay.

Ashore

As you face the row of condominiums on the waters edge on the eastern side of the bay you will see the dinghy dock located about 50 yards to their right. Once ashore, follow the pathway to the left of the dock to where it meets the concrete road on the Brandywine Estate, and then it is just a short walk up the hill to the restaurant.

Simon Scott

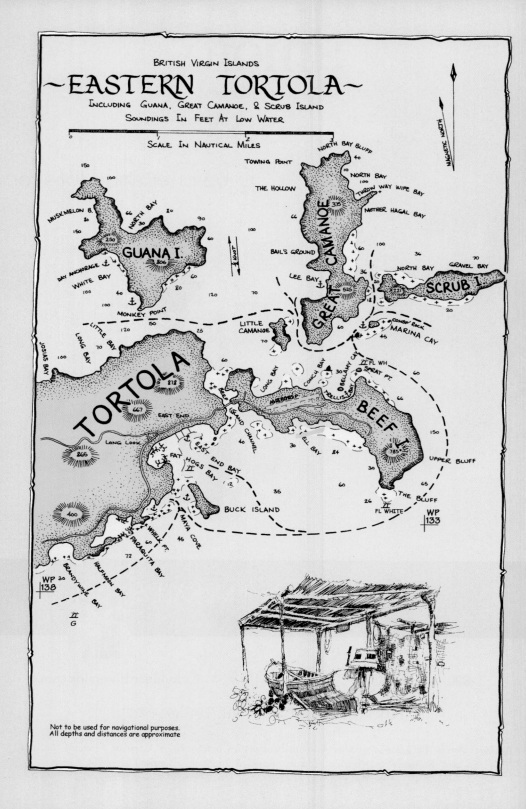

BRITISH VIRGIN ISLANDS
~EASTERN TORTOLA~
INCLUDING GUANA, GREAT CAMANOE, & SCRUB ISLAND
SOUNDINGS IN FEET AT LOW WATER

SCALE IN NAUTICAL MILES

MAGNETIC NORTH

TOWING POINT

THE HOLLOW

NORTH BAY BLUFF

NORTH BAY

THROW WAY WIFE BAY

MOTHER HAGAL BAY

GUANA I.

MUSKMELON B.

NORTH BAY

DAY ANCHORAGE

WHITE BAY

MONKEY POINT

BAIL'S GROUND

GREAT CAMANOE

LEE BAY

NORTH BAY

GRAVEL BAY

SCRUB I.

CONSP' ROCK

MARINA CAY

LITTLE BAY

LONG BAY

JOSIAS BAY

LITTLE CAMANOE

FL WH

SPRAT PT.

BELLANY CAY

CONCH BAY

TRELLIS

LONG BAY

TORTOLA

EAST END

LONG LOOK

BEEF GRAND CHANNEL

BEEF I.

FL BAY

UPPER BLUFF

FAT HOGS BAY

EAST END BAY

BUCK ISLAND

MAYA COVE

WHELK PT.

PARAGUITA BAY

HALF MOON BAY

BRANDYWINE CAY

THE BLUFF

FL WHITE

WP 133

WP 138

Not to be used for navigational purposes.
All depths and distances are approximate

Maya Cove

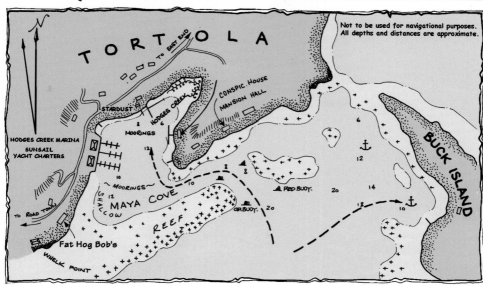

Not to be used for navigational purposes.
All depths and distances are approximate.

Maya Cove or Hodges Creek as it is shown on the charts is approximately a half mile west of Buck Island on the southeastern shore of Tortola. Sheltered by the reef, it is always cool and relatively free of bugs.

Navigation

When approaching Maya Cove from the west, it is well to remember that the reef extends from Whelk Point to the buoyed entrance at the northeastern end of the reef. Entry should be made only under power.

The buoys are easy to see and are located under a promontory of land approximately 75-100 feet high. The channel is marked with red and green buoys. Proceed through the center leaving the red buoy to starboard. Hodges Creek Marina monitors VHF channel 16.

Anchoring & Mooring

This bay can be very busy with the activity at Hodges Creek Marina. The main anchorage is to the south of the

channel. Don't go too far back into the Cove as it shoals off rapidly. Finding a spot to anchor is somewhat difficult without swinging into one of the permanently moored vessels. However, the holding ground is good if you can pick your spot.

Immediately in front of you when entering the Cove is the red roof of Hodges Creek Marina. This full service marina provides water, ice, and showers. Calamaya, the marina restaurant, serves a variety of Caribbean and Mediterranean cuisine for breakfast, lunch and dinner.

Sail Caribbean Divers (a PADI Gold Palm Five Star Resort) maintain their headquarters at the Hodges Creek Marina and offer dive tours and instruction. Nestled into the corner of the reef on the southern end of the Cove is Fat Hog Bob's Caribbean Barbecue. Go carefully in the dinghy as it is very shallow. Fat Hog Bob's has a fabulous view of the Sir Francis Drake Channel and the reef that protects Maya Cove.

Caribbean Yacht Chart C13, C13a, C14

Maya Cove & Buck Island   *Dougal Thornton*

Buck Island

There is a small anchorage in 7 to 10 feet of water on the western shore of Buck Island. Very few yachts anchor here. In certain sea conditions, it can be very rolly, but usually is quite comfortable.

Take care not to go too far toward the northwest tip of the island, as the bottom shoals rapidly. There is no passage between Buck Island and Tortola except by dinghy with the engine tilted up. As this is a privately owned island, going ashore is strictly prohibited.

Simon Scott

Caribbean Yacht Chart C13, C13a, C14

Fat Hog's and East End Bay

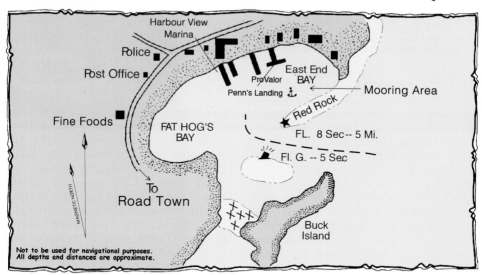

Harbour View
Marina

Police

Post Office

Fine Foods

FAT HOG'S
BAY

ProValor

East End
BAY

Penn's Landing

Mooring Area

Red Rock

FL. 8 Sec -- 5 Mi.

Fl. G. -- 5 Sec

To
Road Town

MAGNETIC NORTH

Buck
Island

Not to be used for navigational purposes.
All depths and distances are approximate.

ANCHORAGES OF THE BRITISH VIRGIN ISLANDS

Fat Hogs Bay and East End Bay are located north of Buck Island between Beef Island channel and Maya Cove. These beautiful, well-protected bays are conveniently situated in the middle of the cruising grounds and are perfect for overnight anchoring.

Navigation

Both anchorages are easily accessible from Sir Francis Drake channel by leaving Buck Island to port and going between the green can and Red Rock. There is a buoyed, unlit channel leading to Penn's Landing Marina or you may head directly to the Harbour View Marina.

Anchoring & Mooring

The average depth from Red Rock into East End Bay is about 9 feet with good holding ground and excellent protection behind the reef. You may pick up one of the white mooring buoys on the eastern side of the channel. Please do not anchor within the mooring area or obstruct the

channel by anchoring inside of it.

You may call ahead to Harbour View Marina or Penn's Landing on VHF channel 16.

Ashore

Three marinas line the bay, Harbour View Marine Center, James Young Marina and Penn's Landing.

The modern, well-maintained Harbour View Marine Centre has dockage for vessels from 50 to 80 feet in length in a depth of 10 feet. They are open from 8am to 6pm daily and monitor VHF channel 16. Amenities include ice, water, diesel fuel, showers and a few charming rooms for those wishing to get a break from the boat.

The Harbour View Marine Supply Chandlery is on the premises along with UBS Dive Center, Kenny T's gift shop and the Kong Ming Asian Terrace restaurant. UBS Dive Center offers individualized dive trips from a wide selection of sites, as well as rendezvous diving. The Kong Ming

Caribbean Yacht Chart C13, C13a, C14

Asian restaurant is on the second story overlooking the bay and captures the trade winds, making it a breezy place to have a meal and watch the activities in the bay. Conveniently located across the street from the marina is Emile's Restaurant and Cantina serving Mexican fare from 11am for lunch and dinner, with happy hour from 5 – 7pm.

Pro Valor Charters operate from both the Harbour View Marina and James Young Marina. The James Young Marina offers slips with most amenities including fuel and water. Also conveniently located here is the Ritebreeze market, a branch of Riteway market in Road Town. Facilities at Penn's Landing include water, ice, freshwater showers and overnight dockage. Moorings, maintained by Moor Seacure, can be paid for at Penn's Landing. The Eclipse Restaurant at Penn's Landing is open for lunch and dinner and offers casual seaside dining. The Sailor's Ketch Seafood Market supplies a wide variety of freshly caught local fish in addition to imported seafood.

The three nearby markets for stocking up on food supplies are Ritebreeze market at the Seaview Marina, Fine Foods Market, and the Parham Town General Store. The B & F Medical complex offers walk-in appointments as well as having a dispensary on the premises. First Caribbean Bank has an ATM located here for your convenience.

Fat Hogs Bay, East End

Simon Scott

Caribbean Yacht Chart C13, C13a, C14

Trellis Bay, Beef Island

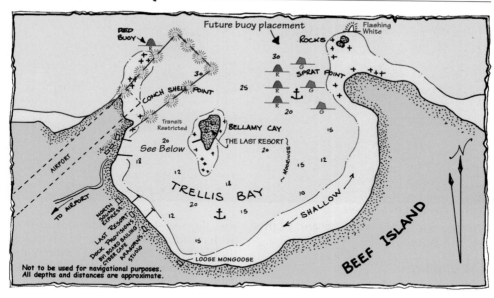

Not to be used for navigational purposes.
All depths and distances are approximate.

Located on the north shore of Beef Island, Trellis Bay was once a major anchorage in the British Virgin Islands with a hotel, large marine railway and jetty. The railway and hotel have since been abandoned, and the jetty is now used by the ferries servicing the surrounding islands and Virgin Gorda. The anchorage is well protected even in adverse weather conditions, and its proximity to the airport makes it convenient for embarking and disembarking passengers. As it is a short five minute walk to the beach bars lining the bay, it has become the unofficial departure

Important navigation information for vessels in Trellis Bay, Beef Island

When entering the anchorage at Trellis Bay, the easiest way is to leave Sprat Point to port and continue into the harbor keeping the red markers and Bellamy Cay to starboard. Pick up a mooring or anchor in the anchorage. The BVI Airport Authority is now requiring vessels with a height over 30 feet that are traveling into and out of the anchorage between Bellamy Cay and the airport runways to first call the "Beef Island Tower" on VHF channel 10. Boaters are then requested to state the name of their vessel, the height at the top of the mast and their intended course. In addition, off of the end of the runway is a rectangular area marked by yellow buoys. It is prohibited for any vessel over 8 feet in height to transit through these markers. This is a safety precaution as the airplanes that take off and land on this runway need to be sure there are no obstructions in their path. Vessels under 30 feet high are free to move around Trellis Bay without calling, except for the restricted area surrounded by yellow buoys.

Trellis Bay and BVI Airport   *Simon Scott*

lounge for those waiting for flights off the island.

Navigation

It is important to check with your charter company or with local businesses at Trellis Bay for the latest regulations before entering the bay on either side of Bellamy Cay.

Entering Trellis Bay from the north, stay to the east of Bellamy Cay, as the passage to the west of Bellamy Cay and east of Conch Shell Point is restricted because of the extension of the Beef Island International Airport. Leave the white flashing light marking the outside rock to port and enter Trellis Bay leaving the red buoys to starboard.

Anchoring & Mooring

Be advised the area to the west of Bellamy Cay is off limits. A good anchorage is available off the eastern and southern side of Bellamy Cay in 10 – 20 feet of water. Leave room for ferries to maneuver when arriving and departing the docks. The holding ground is excellent in some places, but poor in others. However, moorings are available throughout the anchorage and can be paid for at the Loose Mongoose. Beware of underwater obstructions in areas less than 10 feet deep (in the eastern and southern parts of the bay). The area south of Sprat Point is very shallow and should be avoided, even in the dinghy. It will soon be marked with a red buoy or marker at the end of the shoal.

Ashore

The community of Trellis Bay offers an interesting and fun combination of restaurants, water sports, entertainment, local artists and local crafts. And now organic fruits and vegetables are cultivated by Aragorn to sell to the anchored boats or they can be purchased at Aragorn's Studio. It is a short trip from Marina Cay if you want to visit this interesting enclave on your way to or from a day of sailing.

Check for the date of the Trellis Bay monthly full moon parties complete with dancing mocko jumbies (stilt dancers) and amazing fire balls created by artist Aragorn at the water's edge with dancing and live music. The moon is bright and lights up the bay, the breeze is cool and the activity on the beach is lively and not to be missed.

Full Moon Party Fire Ball - Trellis Bay

Courtesy of Aragorn Studios

Trellis Bay

Mauricio Handler

The Last Resort on Bellamy Cay, a tiny tropical island, is an absolute must on a cruise around the Virgins. The Last Resort has singing dogs and a donkey named Bottom. Bottom replaced the previous donkey named Vanilla, who went for a midnight swim during a full moon party and never returned. The meals are excellent as is the atmosphere. Happy

❂ TRELLIS BAY VILLAGE ❂

Art galleries, shops, cafes, beach bars, watersports, and connections to points beyond in a shoreside community.

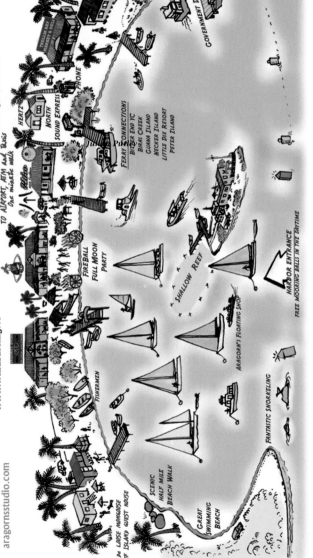

FIREBALL **FULL MOON** P A R T Y ! ⊛TRELLIS BAY⊛ VILLAGE

Plan your vacation around the moon!

A family friendly cultural party on the beach with a delicious West Indian buffet, traditional island music, Moko Jumbie dancers and Fire Sculptures.

284-495-2447 windsurfing.vi
284-495-1849 aragornsstudio.com

2009		2010	
Jan 10	Jul 7	Jan 30	Jul 25
Feb 9	Aug 5	Feb 28	Aug 24
Mar 10	Sep 4	Mar 29	Sep 23
Apr 9	Oct 4	Apr 28	Oct 22
May 8	Nov 2	May 27	Nov 21
Jun 7	Dec 2/31	Jun 26	Dec 21

hour is from 5-6pm daily with half priced drinks and bar snacks. Dinner is from 6:30 – 9:30 daily. Lunch is available during the season and on week ends. Call before heading out to confirm they are serving. You can also check your email here.

Live music is provided nightly by the singing chef and/or the "house" bank, and with Tony Snell himself making occasional guest appearances. The Last Resort monitors VHF channel 16.

Located on the beach on the south shore of Trellis Bay is the Beef Island Guest House with a bar and restaurant called De Loose Mongoose. Happy hour is daily from 5 – 7pm and on Sunday they provide a barbeque with live entertainment. De Loose Mongoose monitors channel 16 for restaurant reservations. The Beef Island Guest House also has a few rooms available.

Trellis Bay is a haven for artists and

local craftsmen. Aragorn's Studio, is the creation of Aragorn Dick-Read, who works in copper, ceramics and silkscreen. The studio is identified as the building with the thatched roof on the beach. Aragorn is famous for his copper sculptures and one of a kind wood-cut and hand-painted fish print t-shirts. Courses in pottery and crafts are taught in Aragorn's Studio. It is fascinating to go ashore and watch the artists and artisans at work. Keep an eye out for his boat laden with t-shirts, crafts, fresh bread and organic fruits as he stops at the boats in the anchorage.

Trellis Bay is home of Gli Gli, the largest Carib Indian dugout sailing canoe in the Caribbean. Gli Gli is available for day charters, providing a unique and historical sailing experience. More of the traditional West Indian vessels will be built in Trellis Bay, affording a unique opportunity for visitors to see the boats from earlier days.

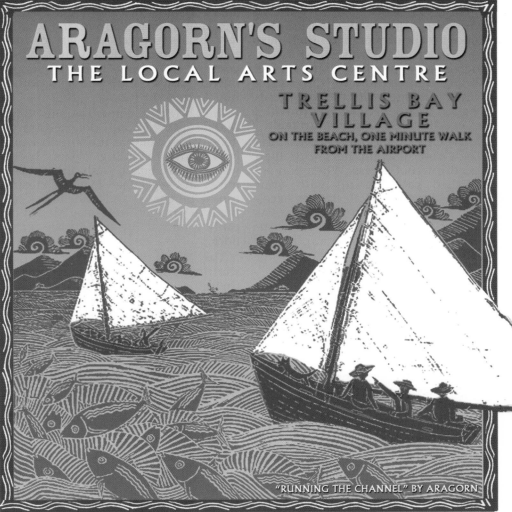

For those who wish to learn to windsurf, the BVI Boardsailing School is located on the beach next to Aragorn's. Windsurfing is an increasingly popular sport in the Virgin islands due to the steady winds combined with the consistently good weather. Trellis Bay provides an excellent learning environment.

The Cyber Café at BVI Boardsailing has a row of computers with high speed internet access. When you are finished catching up with your email, the Cyber Café makes excellent sandwiches and smoothies. As with all of the Trellis Bay establishments, it is close to the airport and makes a great place to wait for your flight.

D' Best Cup features a variety of espresso drinks, ice cream, smoothies, pastries, beer, wine, sandwiches and snacks. Check out their boutique/gift shop. This is a great place to grab a coffee or a smoothie, and a snack after checking in at the airport and also a last chance to purchase a gift for the folks back home, or a souvenir for yourself. Don't miss the HIHI shop, offering casual Caribbean island clothing, designed in Tortola.

The brightly colored Trellis Bay Market provides all the necessary items when you are running low on provisions, including cigars, beer, wine, liquor, bread, fresh and frozen meats and vegetables. Even ice cream can be purchased and rushed back to the boat's freezer. Trellis Bay Market is easily found at the base of the ferry dock.

The North Sound Express Ferry shuttles guests to North Sound from their dock in Trellis Bay. The Marina Cay Pusser's ferry picks up guests at the government dock. Near the Trellis Bay Market is the dock for the Last Resort ferry.

Eastern Tortola and The Camanoe Passage

When sailing around Tortola from the north side, several passages are available.

The passage between Monkey Point on the southern end of Guana and Tortola is plenty wide and free of hazards. The large rock on Monkey Point is your landmark. Once through, you may continue due east, leaving Little Camanoe to starboard, making the transit between Little Camanoe and Great Camanoe.

The latter should be negotiated in good light and then only under power. There is a small reef on the northeast tip of Little Camanoe and the seas are usually breaking, making it easy to identify. When the ground seas are up during the winter months, the surf breaks heavily on this reef.

The channel, though narrow, carries adequate depth and is free of reef and other hazards. Once clear of the channel, the entrance to Marina Cay to the northeast and Trellis Bay to the southeast are before you.

Anchorages & Moorings

All the anchorages listed below are recommended as daytime stops only. During the winter when the northerly ground seas are running, none of these are recommended even as comfortable lunch stops.

Camanoe Passage and Marina Cay

Simon Scott

Monkey Point, Guana Island   A.J. Blake

Tortola / Little Bay

Sailing east toward the cut between Guana Island and the eastern tip of Tortola, there are numerous white sandy beaches to the south. They are all exposed but when the weather is calm, we recommend Little Bay as a lunch stop only. If there is any surf activity apparent on the beach, do not anchor here. Use the anchorage at Monkey Point or continue further east through the cut. The bottom is sandy and holding is good in 15 feet of water.

Guana Island / Monkey Point

At the southern tip of Guana Island is a delightful anchorage known as Monkey Point. An excellent day anchorage, Monkey Point is situated on the western side of the rocky outcrop that marks the southern extremity of the island. There are several National Park moorings in place for those with a permit.

The small beach area and excellent snorkeling make this a great lunch stop. When there is a northerly swell running, the anchorage can be rolly.

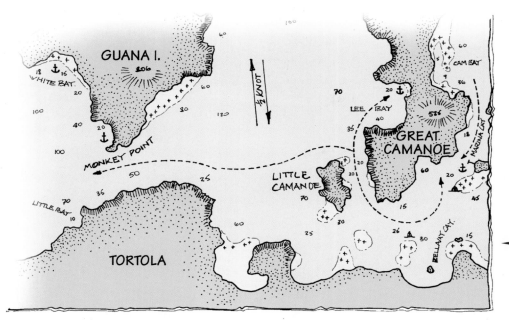

Guana Island / White Bay

Easily identified by the long stretch of white beach, White Bay is located on the southwest side of Guana. The anchorage, located at the northern end, is relatively deep (20 – 25 feet) and when anchoring be care-ful not to swing into the coral heads closer to the shore.

To the north of the anchorage you will notice the rock formation that looks like the head of a large Iguana for which the island was named. This is a private island and trespassing is prohibited.

Boat Building In The Virgins

Because of the scattered formation of the Virgin Islands, the inhabi-tants, by necessity, became expert boat builders, specializing in small, light craft that were ideal for these sheltered waters.

The unique skills that the West Indians learned from the 18th-century Navy have been preserved, virtually unchanged to the present day.

Camanoe Passage looking south   *Jim Scheiner*

Great Camanoe / Lee Bay

Although often ignored in favor of the more popular anchorages in this region, Lee Bay on the west coast of Camanoe, provides a quiet respite for those wishing more seclusion. The approaches to Lee Bay are clear and unobstructed. If you are transiting from the Marina Cay area, use the channel between Great and Little Camanoe. There are rocks on the northeast point of Little Camanoe that you will need to identify otherwise the channel is clear and easy to negotiate under power.

Lee Bay is well protected in most weather conditions and cooled by the breeze that flows over the saddle of land that provides a backdrop for Cam Bay on the other side of the hill. When a northerly sea condition is present during the winter months, and surf is breaking on the northern tip of Camanoe, the resulting ground swell can work its way into this anchorage. Depending on the prevailing conditions, a second anchor should be set or an alternate anchorage identified until the sea conditions return to normal.

Anchoring & Mooring

The best spot to anchor is located dead center, off the shoreline under the saddle of the hill in 15 feet of water. The holding ground is good and apart from the occasional low coral growth, the bottom is clear. Please be careful that you do not anchor in coral.

PUSSER'S® MARINA CAY ~
A TROPICAL JEWEL YOU WON'T FORGET

Sports Illustrated says, *"... for travelers wanting a simple place on an island yet unspoiled, where they can swim, snorkel, scuba dive, sail and fish. Those who have such a modest goal should look up the island called Marina Cay."*

The shallow, warm, waters of the lagoon make it ideal for snorkeling, especially for beginners, families and children.

At Marina Cay, you will find . . .

- Casual Dining on the beach.

- A full service fuel dock with ice and water.

- Quaint boutique hotel with 4 single rooms and 2 villas.

- Laundromat.

- Showers

The Pusser's Co. Store at Marina Cay

- A Pusser's Co. Store with a full line of Pusser's apparel, and a limited supply of condiments and grocery items.

- Snorkeling SCUBA and watersports.

Some Marina Cay History

Marina Cay was home to newlyweds Robb and Rodie White in the late 1930's. His best selling book of 1953, *Our Virgin Island,* chronicled their life on Marina Cay. It became a film starring Sidney Poitier and John Cassavetes, much of it filmed on the island. For 20 years after Robb White's departure for WWII, the island lay uninhabited, until our small hotel opened in 1960. His home is restored on the summit. A photographic essay on the restaurant's wall, from photos shot in the 1930's, recounts the White's poignant story.

Call us on Channel 16 or Tel: (284) 494-2174 ~ Fax: (284) 494-4775
www.pussers.com

Marina Cay is the official headquarters of the PUSSER'S® PYRATE SOCIETY

Marina Cay

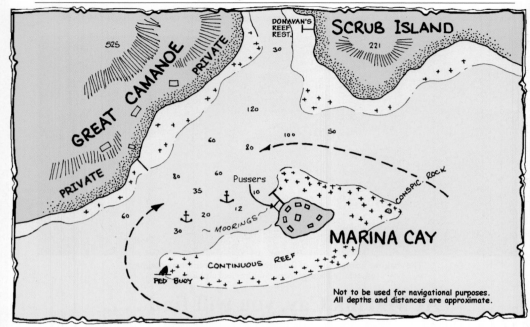

Not to be used for navigational purposes.
All depths and distances are approximate.

Marina Cay, nestled behind a reef and lying between the islands of Camanoe and Scrub, is easy to enter and provides the visiting yachtsman with good holding in an all weather anchorage. For those who have read Robb White's book *Our Virgin Island* it was Marina Cay that was the setting for the story.

Navigation

Approaching Marina Cay from the east, you have two choices. The recommended route is to go around the north end of the island. There is good water up to the large rock that marks the northeast end of the reef. Leave it to port and pass between Marina Cay and Scrub Island into the anchorage.

Alternatively, approaching from the west, you should favor the southern tip of Great Camanoe. There is a red marker at the southwest end of

the reef. Leaving it well to starboard, you will enter the anchorage. The reef extends south and west of Marina Cay and is highly visible in good light.

If the light is good, it is also possible to approach Marina Cay from the north between Scrub Island and Great Camanoe. There are reefs lining either side of the channel and you should favor the Great Camanoe side when entering. This anchorage should be negotiated only in good light under power.

Anchoring & Mooring

Several fully maintained moorings are in place, and should be paid for ashore. The holding ground is reasonable for anchoring. Camanoe Island is private and off limits for visitors. Please be considerate with respect to the proximity of the homes on Camanoe. Please keep

Marina Cay, Scrub Island   *Jim Scheiner*

noise levels down and respect the privacy of the residents.

Ashore

Marina Cay has a full service fuel dock offering ice, water, garbage disposal, laundry facilities and showers for yachtsmen. They monitor VHF channel 16. Pusser's Marina Cay provides free ferry service from the main dock in Trellis Bay – check with them for departure times.

Ashore you will find a Pusser's Company Store stocked with their tropical and nautical clothing, unique accessories, gifts and a small mini-mart.

The hilltop Bar at the Robb White House on the highest point of Marina Cay is a great place for a drink with a spectacular view and regular happy hour (and a half) of entertainment. There is an internet café in the house as well as much of the island, including the anchorage, has free wifi access.

The beach restaurant offers casual dining at the grill. The island even boasts four charming rooms and two villas for those wanting some time ashore. There is excellent snorkeling behind Marina Cay.

Dive BVI offers dive trips and instruction daily. An air station is in operation and Ocean Kayaks and Hobie Cat rentals are available. Dive BVI also offer day trips from the island to Anegada.

Scrub Island

Marina Cay   *Simon Scott*

Just to the north of Marina Cay lies Scrub Island which is in the process of becoming a world class resort. Several restaurants are planned, an elegant hotel, spa, shops and the marina. The residences are currently under construction and that section of the island will be private, for residents only.

The Scrub Island Marina will have sixty-five slips for yachts as long as 150 feet and 14 feet deep. The approaching depth to the marina is 25 feet. Slips will be available for lease as well as for short term stays. The marina will have all the amenities, fuel, water, ice, showers and restaurant/bars close by. Several fishing charter boats will be located at the marina for those wishing to experience the thrill of deep sea fishing.

As Scrub Island is a work in progress, you will have to ask when the marina will be completed. Donovan's Restaurant is an easy dinghy ride over from Marina Cay so you can enjoy a meal at Donavan's Restaurant.

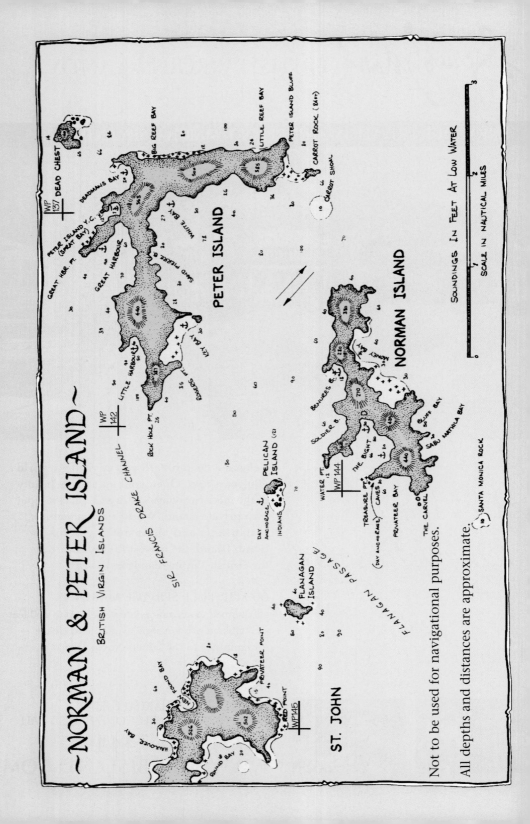

~NORMAN & PETER ISLAND~

BRITISH VIRGIN ISLANDS

PETER ISLAND

NORMAN ISLAND

ST. JOHN

SIR FRANCIS DRAKE CHANNEL

FLANAGAN PASSAGE

SOUNDINGS IN FEET AT LOW WATER

SCALE IN NAUTICAL MILES

Not to be used for navigational purposes.

All depths and distances are approximate.

WP 157 DEAD CHEST

DEADMANS BAY

PETER ISLAND Y.C. (SPRAT BAY)

GREAT HBR. PT.

GREAT HARBOUR

SPRAT BAY

BIG REEF BAY

LITTLE REEF BAY

PETER ISLAND BLUFF

CARROT ROCK (84ft)

GREAT SHOAL

WHITE BAY

SAND PIERCE PT.

LITTLE HARBOUR

RODRIGO PT.

KEY BAY

LITTLE HARBOUR

ROCK HOLE PT.

WP 142

DAY ANCHORAGE

PELICAN ISLAND (72)

INDIANS (72)

WATER PT.

SOLDIER B.

BONAIRES B.

MONEY B.

THE BIGHT

WP 144

TREASURE PT.

CAVES

(DAY ANCHORAGE)

PRIVATEER BAY

THE CARVEL

BLUFF BAY

SABU, MATHLA BAY

SANTA MONICA ROCK

FLANAGAN ISLAND

PRIVATEER POINT

RED POINT

WP 145

HANSEN BAY

ROUND BAY

HANSEN BAY

RAMS HEAD

Norman Island

The Bight

Norman is the first island of any size that, together with the islands of Peter, Salt, Cooper and Ginger, form the southern perimeter of the Sir Francis Drake Channel. Often referred to by the locals as "Treasure Island", legends of Norman Island are resplendent with stories of buried pirate treasure. A letter of 1750 stated, "Recovery of the treasure from Nuestra Senora buried at Norman Island, comprising $450,000 dollars, plate, cochineal, indigo, tobacco, much dug up by Tortolians."

The main anchorage on Norman Island is the Bight, an exceptionally well-sheltered anchorage.

Navigation

On making an approach to the Bight, the only hazard is the Santa Monica Rocks, which lie to the southwest of the Carvel Point. There is in excess of 6 feet of water over them, but watch out for sea swells. If your approach brings you by Pelican Island, remember that you cannot pass between the Indians and Pelican.

The entrance to the Bight is straight onward and without hazard. Enter between the headlands, keeping in mind that there is shoal water just off both points.

Anchoring & Mooring

The best anchorage is well up in the northeast corner of the bay or the southeast section. You will need to get far enough in to anchor on the shelf in 15-30 feet of water. Or there are many mooring buoys in place that you may pick up for the night. Someone will come by dinghy to collect the mooring fee usually in the early evening. If you anchor instead of picking up a mooring be sure that you are well clear of the moorings and have plenty of room to swing without fouling a mooring. Be aware that the wind tends to funnel down through the hills, giving the impression that the weather is much heavier than it is once you are outside of the bay.

Ashore

A dinghy trip to Treasure Point and the caves for snorkeling and exploring is a must. Take your flashlight and tie up your dinghy to the line strung between two small round floats. This avoids dropping an anchor and destroying coral. You may also take your sailboat and pick up a National Parks mooring during

ANCHORAGES OF THE BRITISH VIRGIN ISLANDS

the day (with a permit). Good snorkeling also exists on the reef at the eastern end of the harbor just south of the beach. Please do not feed the fish at the caves, it tends to make them aggressive.

If you are in the mood for a hike, take the track from the beach by the restaurant to the top of the hill. It should be negotiated only with adequate shoes and clothing to protect you from the brush. Caution is also advised when encountering the local population of goats or wild cattle. Stay clear of them.

Located in the Bight of Norman Island is the William Thornton, a floating restaurant named for the architect of the U.S. Capital building. The vessel is a replica of a topsail lumber schooner, measuring 93 feet. Lunch is served from noon to 4pm and dinner from 6:30 to 10 pm daily. Nicknamed the "Willie T," stories abound about many wild nights of partying aboard. The ambiance is casual and often riotously fun! The "Willie T" monitors VHF 16.

Pirates Bight restaurant and bar commands a view of the Bight from the head of the bay. This is a great place to watch the sunset and escape the boat for awhile, or have a couple of rum punches and dance the night away. Happy hour is from 4 - 6pm and again from 10 - 12pm. Lunch and dinner, featuring West Indian cuisine, are served from 11am until the last sailor gets into their dinghy.

At around 5pm daily, the supply vessel Deliverance makes the rounds to the yachts in the Bight, Cooper Island, and Peter Island selling ice, water, fruit, veggies, booze and other goodies you may require. Give them a wave or call them on VHF 16 and they will soon be at your side.

Deliverance   *Simon Scott*

Norman Island / Other Anchorages

Kelly's Cove

A fine alternative anchorage to the Bight is Kelly's Cove, a small, secluded anchorage set against a rugged hillside backdrop. Close enough in proximity to the main anchorage and Treasure Point to allow access by dinghy, Kelly's Cove is a delightful anchorage that provides excellent snorkeling from the boat.

As you approach the Bight, Kelly's Cove is situated under Water Point to the north. The entrance is straight forward, but anchoring needs careful consideration owing to the limited amount of swinging room. There are some overnight moorings in this area leaving limited room for anchoring unless a stern line is taken ashore. If you are dropping the hook, make sure that it is not in coral and the water is shallow enough (20'-25') to control the swinging room due to back winding.

Close by under Water Point, The National Parks Trust has installed several day time moorings for snorkeling and diving.

Treasure Point and Privateer Bay

Providing there is not much sea running, a delightful daytime spot can be had by anchoring approximately 300 – 350 yards south of Treasure Point. You will have to anchor in 30-40 feet of water, avoiding damaging the coral bottom. Make sure the anchor is well set in sand before going ashore. You are likely to be backwinded, so don't be surprised if you end up lying stern to the caves. The National Parks Trust moorings are available with a permit as mentioned above.

The snorkeling is excellent along the mouths of four caves and a dinghy mooring system is in place for those arriving by dinghy to get close enough to the caves without disturbing swimmers and snorkelers

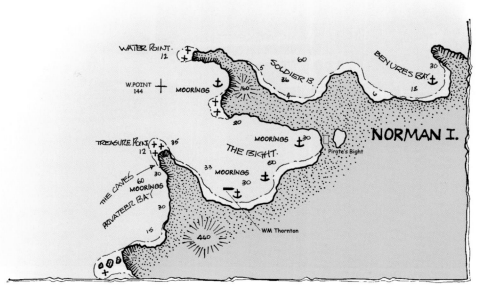

ANCHORAGES OF THE BRITISH VIRGIN ISLANDS

The William Thornton

Simon Scott

in the water. Caution: Do not use your outboard engine between the dinghy mooring line and the shore.

Privateer Bay

Further to the south of Treasure Point is Privateer Bay often used as a day anchorage to access both the caves at Treasure Point and Carvel Rock, which provides excellent snorkeling in the appropriate weather conditions.

Anchoring can prove problematic in this area, since the bottom drops off rapidly and patches of dead coral and rock on the seabed should be identified prior to setting the anchor. Anchor in 15'-20'.

Norman Island / North Coast

Under normal trade wind conditions, there are two delightful anchorages on the north coast that, while limited in available anchoring room, provide a tranquil setting a little out of the mainstream of cruising and charter traffic. Both of these anchorages should be avoided when the wind moves to the north for short periods during the winter months.

Benures Bay (Benares Bay)

The larger and more protected of the two bays, Benures Bay lies to the east on the northern coast of Norman Island. The approach is straightforward as there is no shoal ground to be concerned about until you are in close proximity to the beach.

Anchor up in the northeast corner of the bay and as close to the pebble beach as possible or pick up a mooring. The bottom is sand, so the holding is excellent and the snorkeling is great.

Soldier Bay

A small anchorage capable of accommodating one or two vessels and ideal during the summer months when the wind is light and the trade winds are blowing from the southeast. The entrance to Soldier Bay is free of any foul ground until the shoreline. You will need to identify a sandy stretch to lay down the anchor or pick up a mooring. Holding is good and the snorkeling is excellent.

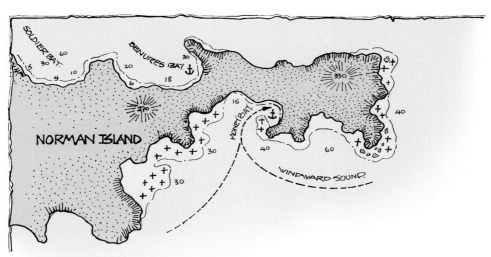

Norman Island/ South Coast

Money Bay

Tucked away on the south coast of Norman is an idyllic anchorage that can be used as a daytime stop or overnight. Under certain conditions the swell can work itself into this little bay and therefore a stern anchor would prove prudent.

Approaching from the east, you will pass the rocky headland forming the southeastern tip of Norman Island, stand well clear since you will be on a lee-shore and the sea conditions will reflect the fact that they have traveled unbroken for 100 miles or so.

Money Bay is located in the eastern end of the second bay to the west of the headland.

Care should be taken to make sure you know exactly where you are. There is plenty of water depth even

Pirates Bight   *Simon Scott*

though the seas are rough in this area. Locate the large rock formation marking the southern end of the bay and proceed into the center of the bay, dropping the anchor in 10' water on a sandy bottom. There is a reef that extends from the rocks at the entrance back toward the beach, so care should be taken to identify its location upon entry.

The most comfortable location is to anchor down toward the reef with a stern line or second anchor run out to the beach. This will keep your bow to the wind and head to the sea. At the time we visited this anchorage in 2008, it appeared that construction of a breakwater was in progress. Be aware that the anchorage could have changed significantly since then.

Pelican Island / The Indians

This would be considered a daytime stop only, but well worth the effort. Do not attempt to sail between Pelican Island and the Indians. Approach them from the north and pick up a Parks Trust mooring. A reef extends between the two and provides excellent snorkeling as does the area immediately around the Indians. As part of the National Parks Trust, this area is protected. You will find National Parks Trust moorings available for use with a permit.

The Indians

Simon Scott

ANCHORAGES OF THE BRITISH VIRGIN ISLANDS

Peter Island

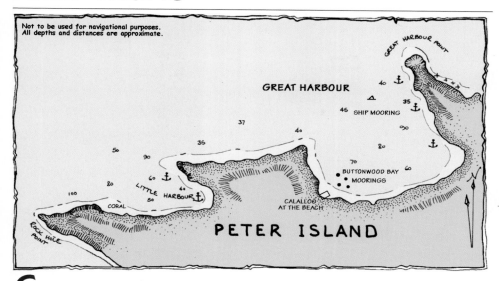

Not to be used for navigational purposes.
All depths and distances are approximate.

GREAT HARBOUR

GREAT HARBOUR POINT

SHIP MOORING

BUTTONWOOD BAY
MOORINGS

LITTLE HARBOUR

CORAL

ROCK HOLE POINT

CALALLOO AT THE BEACH

PETER ISLAND

Sailing to the east, the next island is Peter. Captain Thomas Southey wrote his impressions of the island in his chronological history of the West Indies over 100 years ago:

"In May (1806) the author with a party visited Peter's Island, one of those which form the bay Tortola, a kind of Robinson Crusoe spot, where a man ought to be farmer, carpenter, doctor, fisherman, planter; everything himself."

Little Harbour

There are several good overnight anchorage on Peter Island, the westernmost of which is Little Harbour. Although it doesn't look it on the chart, Little Harbour is a well-protected overnight stop with good holding ground.

When approaching, the first landmark is a dilapidated white house on the north west point which forms the eastern side of the harbor.

Anchoring

The best spot to anchor is well up in the eastern reaches of the bay, in 15-25 feet over a sandy bottom. You will be back-winded, so check your swinging room relative to other vessels and use two anchors if necessary. If the anchorage is crowded, anchor close to shore on the southern coast of the bay in order to stay in 25-35 feet of water. The center drops off rapidly. Be careful not to anchor in the coral reef on the southwestern side of the anchorage. It is 40-50 feet below the surface, and is not easy to see and therefore, easy to damage. Please help protect the coral reefs.

Anchoring in coral is
STRICTLY PROHIBITED
in both the U.S. and B.V.I.

Boats at anchor off of Peter Island   *Julian Putley*

Great Harbour

Most of Great Harbour is considered too deep to make a worthwhile anchorage; however, if you can spend the time, there are two shallow areas and the rewards are those of a quiet anchorage. Buttonwood Bay on the western end of Great Harbour is home to the restaurant Ocean's Seven. You can pick up a mooring and jump in the dinghy, tie up to the dock and pay for the mooring ashore. Ocean's Seven specializes in seafood dishes, but also has chicken and beef dishes. They are open seven days a week serving lunch and dinner. Happy hour is 4-6pm. Check ashore to find out if they are having a pig roast, or other special events. Reservations are requested for dinner only. Ocean's Seven monitors VHF channel 16.

It is important not to get in the way of local fishermen who run their nets out into the bay each afternoon. For this reason, it is recommended that you find the three fathom spot on the northwest shore, about one third of the way in from the point. While the fishing is in progress, the least amount of activity in the bay the better. After the fishermen have gone, you can bring the boat in closer to shore.

Sprat Bay - Peter Island Resort

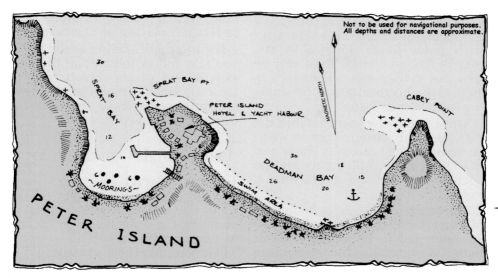

Sprat Bay is easy to spot from the Sir Francis Drake channel by the row of roofs comprising the hotel section of the Peter Island Resort. The entire bay, Deadman's Bay and several beaches on the south coast of Peter Island are part of the resort.

Navigation

Making your entrance to Sprat Bay, it is important to familiarize yourself with the location of the reefs on either side of the channel. The main reef extends north and slightly west of the main bulkhead, so do not get too close to the western shore.

Entering on a heading of 165 degrees magnetic, you can either tie up to the dock, which now sports new finger piers or pick up a mooring. Do not go too far into the southern end of the bay when maneuvering as it is shallow. There are four moorings available for a fee of $65.00 per night (pay the dockmaster ashore). The moorings cannot be reserved in advance. The dinghy dock is located at the western part of

the marina. You may call the dockmaster on VHF channel 16.

The dock has 15 mid-sized slips and three megayacht berths. It is possible to tie up to the dock briefly for a fee of $20.00 per hour (unless you stay for the night). Amenities at the marina include water, fuel (both gasoline and diesel), ice, showers, electricity, and cable TV.

Ashore

Originally built by Norwegians in the late 1960's, the resort has been completely renovated. The 55 unit hotel and restaurant extend along the bulkhead. Reservations for breakfast, lunch and dinner at the Tradewinds Restaurant may be reserved in advance; space available permitting. After 6pm there are no shorts, jeans, tennis shores, flip flops permitted and men must wear a collared shirt, slacks and shoes.

Deadman's Bay

The easternmost anchorage on Peter Island, Deadman's Bay is a spectacular crescent of white sand with palm trees blowing in the trades. The anchorage itself can be rolly due to the surge making its way around the northeastern point, making it a better day stop.

Move your vessel right up into the extreme southeastern corner when anchoring. The bottom is grassy and it is sometimes difficult to get the anchor set, but the snorkeling is excellent.

The beach to the west is for the use of hotel guests only, and yachtsmen are requested to respect the line of buoys designating the swimming beach. However, the Deadman's Bay Beach Bar is open to cruising and chartered yachts as well as the hotel guests. In season the resort often holds beach barbecues here with steel bands playing on the beach.

For those not staying at the resort you may follow the path at the very eastern end of the beach over to Little Deadman's Beach where there are huts available to use and the tradewinds to keep you cool.

The South Coast of Peter Island

There are two anchorages on the south side of Peter that are worthy of mention, but some regard to sea and weather conditions should be noted when planning the anchorage.

Peter Island Spa and beach   *Julian Putley*

White Bay

Named for the white sand beach, White Bay is a reasonable anchorage when the ground swells are not running. Anchor close to shore, but be careful of back-winding.

Key Point

There is an excellent anchorage to the west of Key Point. Make your approach from the south, favoring the key side in order to clear the rock on the west side of the entrance. Anchor between the point and Key Cay in 18 feet of water. This is a small anchorage with room for only a few boats. The snorkeling is excellent and the anchorage is open to the prevailing breeze, keeping it free from bugs.

Anchoring in coral is **STRICTLY PROHIBITED** in both the U.S. and B.V.I.

Dead Chest Island and Deadmans Bay

Julian Putley

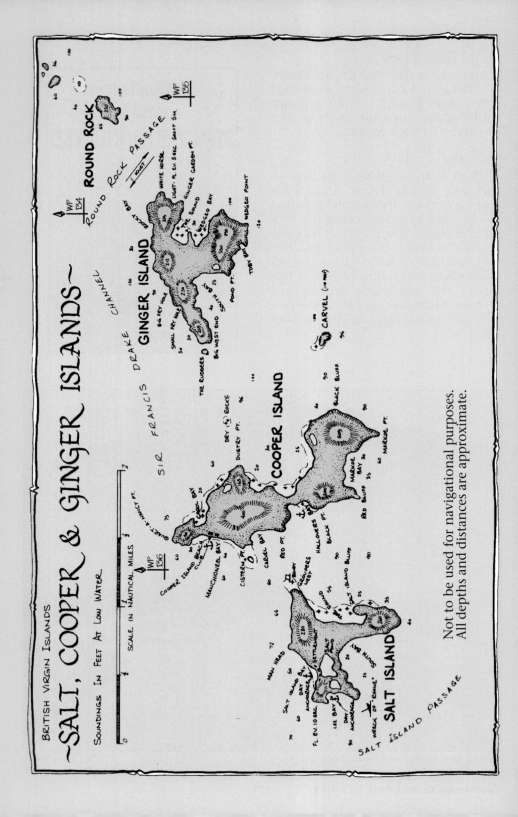

BRITISH VIRGIN ISLANDS

~SALT, COOPER & GINGER ISLANDS~

SOUNDINGS IN FEET AT LOW WATER

SCALE IN NAUTICAL MILES

Not to be used for navigational purposes.
All depths and distances are approximate.

ROUND ROCK

GINGER ISLAND

COOPER ISLAND

SALT ISLAND

ROUND ROCK PASSAGE

DRAKE CHANNEL

SIR FRANCIS

SALT ISLAND PASSAGE

WP 134
WP 135
WP 136

Salt Island

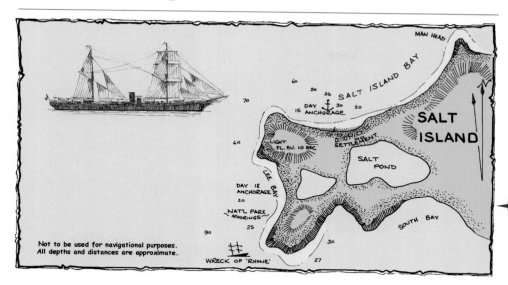

Not to be used for navigational purposes.
All depths and distances are approximate.

Named for the island's three evaporation ponds, Salt Island was once an important source of sale for the ships of Her Majesty, the Queen. The island and its salt ponds, although belonging to the Crown, were operated by the local populace. Each year at the start of the harvest, one bag of salt was accepted by the Governor as annual rent. In 1845, a barrel was quoted at one shilling and, although inflation has taken its toll, salt is still sold to visitors. The residents of the settlement just off Salt Pond Bay have all moved off of Salt Island to the more populated islands with all the modern conveniences.

Anchoring & Mooring

Both of the Salt Island anchorages are affected by a surge and consequently should be considered day anchorages only.

Salt Pond Bay is clear of hazards, but the prudent skipper is advised to ensure that the anchor is well set before going ashore. You may anchor in 10 – 20 feet of water.

Located on the west shore, Lee Bay is an alternative for those wishing to dive or snorkel on the wreck of the Rhone. The National Parks Trust has installed moorings for the use of permit holders only. They are designed for boats under 50 feet to pick up in order to dinghy over to the Rhone. Anchoring over the Rhone is strictly prohibited as it is protected by the National Parks Trust. Constant anchoring by boats has destroyed some of the coral.

It is also recommended that you dinghy to the Rhone from Lee Bay, drop off snorkelers and use the dinghy mooring line available.

Watch out for divers!

Cooper Island   *Jim Scheiner*

Cooper Island

As you sail between Salt and Cooper Islands, you will see a rock off the northeast point, marked by a green buoy with a red stripe. You can go to either side of the marker as there is 20 feet of water.

The principal anchorage on Cooper Island is Manchioneel Bay located on the northwest shore. When approaching the bay from the north, around Quart-O-Nancy Point, you will be on your ear one minute and becalmed the next. The point shelters the wind entirely, and we would recommend lowering sail and powering up to the anchorage.

Anchoring & Mooring

There are many moorings off of Cooper Island you can use for a fee. The white Moor Seacure moorings can be paid for ashore at the Cooper Island Beach Club; the other moorings can be paid to the boat sent to collect the fees.

If you must anchor, be aware that the bottom is covered in patches of sea grass and, consequently, it is often difficult to get the anchor set since the holding is poor. If you are anchoring, make sure to back down on your anchor and check it visually by snorkeling over it.

Julian Putley

Ashore

There is a good, sandy beach fringed with palm trees with views of many of the islands to the west. Between the two main jetties is the Cooper Island Beach Club. Dinghies may tie up at either of the jetties ashore. The menu is varied and the setting unique. Both lunch and dinner are served daily. Reservations are recommended for dinner. Go ashore during the day, or call on VHF 16 or by phone 495-9084. Located near the northernmost jetty, the Seagrape Boutique, open daily from 9am to 7pm, stocks an array of Caribbean resort clothing, souvenirs and sundries.

Sail Caribbean Divers, a PADI Gold Palm, Five Star Resort, offers a full range of scuba diving experiences catering all skill levels. They will meet you at the Cooper Island jetty and within 15 minutes you can be diving on a spectacular reef or enjoying the best wreck diving in the Caribbean including the world renowned wreck of the RMS Rhone. They also have an air-fill station next to the boutique for divers and rent rigid inflatable dinghies, kayaks and snorkel equipment. You may call Sail Caribbean Divers on VHF 16.

The Beach Club operates a supply boat/ferry to and from Road Town, leaving Cooper Island most weekdays at about 7:30am and returning from Road Town in the late morning or early afternoon. Call the Beach Club on VHF Channel 16 for exact timing and availability.

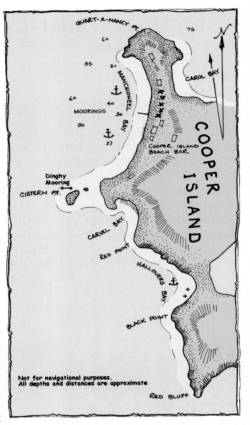

Not for navigational purposes.
All depths and distances are approximate

The Dogs

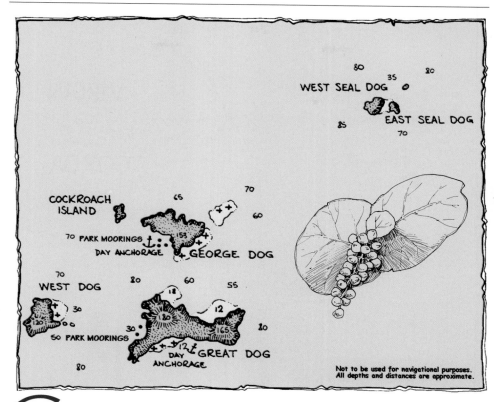

Not to be used for navigational purposes. All depths and distances are approximate.

Great, George, West and Seal Dogs lie to the west of Virgin Gorda, and have good water all around them. They are all in a protected area of the National Parks Trust. It is not possible to sail or power between West and East Seal Dogs. If there is not a sea running there are three good daytime anchorages in the lee of Great Dog and George Dog.

On George Dog, the best anchorage is in the bay to the west of Kitchen Point. Pick up a National Parks Trust mooring off of the beach and stay for lunch and a snorkel trip.

Off of Great Dog there are two possible anchorages depending on the weather. The most common one is on the south side of the island. There are several National Parks Trust moorings you may use with your permit. The depth is between 20 – 30 feet and the bottom is rocky. The second spot is off the beach on the northwest coast and it also has National Parks moorings available.

The snorkeling is excellent in all three locations, but this is not the place to be when there are large swells.

Anchoring in coral is **STRICTLY PROHIBITED** in both the U.S. and B.V.I.

ANCHORAGES OF THE BRITISH VIRGIN ISLANDS

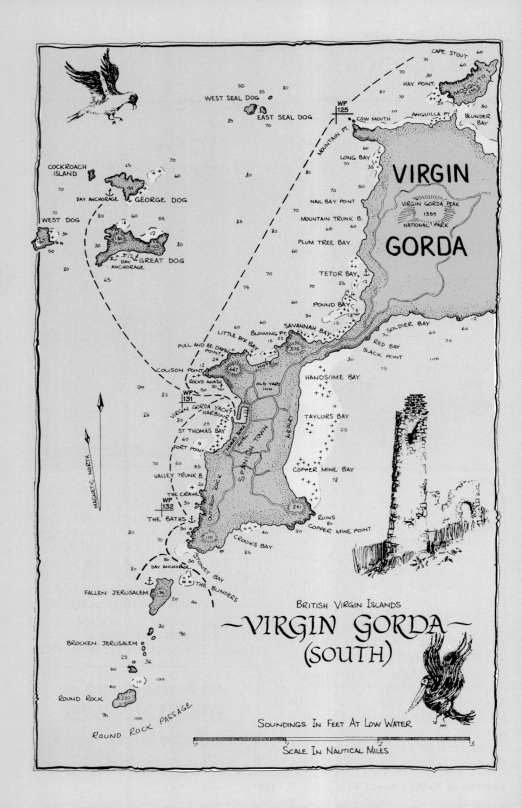

CAPE STOUT 60

80 35 80 HAY POINT 30 30

WEST SEAL DOG 80 MOSQUITO I.

EAST SEAL DOG 70 WP 125 COW MOUTH ANGUILLA PT. BLUNDER BAY

MOUNTAIN PT.

LONG BAY 70 35

VIRGIN

80 80 NAIL BAY POINT 70 50

COCKROACH ISLAND 65 70 MOUNTAIN TRUNK B. VIRGIN GORDA PEAK 1359

70 60 25 80 66 NATIONAL PARK GORDA

DAY ANCHORAGE GEORGE DOG PLUM TREE BAY 60

WEST DOG 70 55 80 10

30 80 60 12 TETOR BAY

50 80 165 GREAT DOG 70 75 70 26 12

DAY ANCHORAGE POUND BAY

65 30 15 18

LITTLE DIX BAY SAVANNAH BAY SOLDIER BAY

60 BLOWING PT. 15 22 RED BAY 60 70 60

PULL AND BE DAMN'D POINT 376 BLACK POINT 100

COLISON POINT 90 24 HOTEL HANDSOME BAY

ROCKS AWASH 447 OLD YARD INN 30

85 30 WP 131 VIRGIN GORDA YACHT HARBOUR TAYLORS BAY 25

ST THOMAS BAY

FORT POINT COPPER MINE BAY 28

70 VALLEY TRUNK B. SPANISH TOWN 20

35 THE CRAWL 30 24

WP 132 OUTCROP ROCK 80

THE BATHS RUINS COPPER MINE POINT

80 110 20

70 CROOKS BAY 40 20

FALLEN JERUSALEM 36 STONEY BAY 25

20 40 DAY ANCHORAGE THE BLINDERS

BRITISH VIRGIN ISLANDS

30 90 ~VIRGIN GORDA~

BROCKEN JERUSALEM (SOUTH)

25 36

10 100

ROUND ROCK 220 100

90 SOUNDINGS IN FEET AT LOW WATER

ROUND ROCK PASSAGE SCALE IN NAUTICAL MILES

MAGNETIC NORTH

THE BLINDERS

COPPERMINE POINT

DEVIL'S BAY

THE BATHS

VIRGIN GORDA

N

SPANISH TOWN

VIRGIN GORDA
YACHT HARBOUR

GORDA SOUND

SAVANNAH BAY

COLISON PT.

VIRGIN GORDA
panorama

Jim Scheiner

Virgin Gorda

The "Fat Virgin", as Columbus irreverently called it because of its resemblance from seaward to a fat woman lying on her back, was once the capital of the British Virgins with a population of 8,000 persons.

The island is approximately 10 miles long with high peaks at the north and central areas. All land over 1000 feet high on Virgin Gorda has been designated National Parks land to preserve its natural beauty.

Laurance Rockefeller built the Little Dix Bay Hotel, as well as the Virgin Gorda Yacht Harbour in St. Thomas Bay.

The Baths

When planning a trip around the island, it is essential to include the Baths. Located on the southwest tip of Virgin Gorda, the Baths are a most unusual formation of large granite boulders. Where the sea washes in between the huge rocks, large pools have been created where shafts of light play upon the water, creating a dramatic effect. The beach adjacent to the Baths is white and sandy and the snorkeling excellent.

The National Parks Trust has initiated a flag system to warn of dangerous seas in the area of the Baths. There is a flag pole at the top of the Baths, and there are plans to install two more on the beach to ensure that they are clearly visible to boaters.

This information will be provided in the marine conservation permit required in order to use National Parks Trust moorings. See page 53 for diagram.

Simon Scott

Navigation

When approaching from the Sir Francis Drake channel, the first landmark will be the large rock formations. There are fine, white sandy beaches of varying sizes and the Baths are located at the second beach from the westernmost tip of Virgin Gorda. If there is a ground sea running, it is advisable to keep sailing into the Yacht Harbour and take a taxi to the Baths.

Anchoring & Mooring

National Park moorings are the only mode of securing the vessel in order to protect the coral as this is in part of the BVI National Park Trust. There is no anchoring at the Baths. If you are powering or sailing further north towards the Yacht Harbour, be mindful of Burrows Rock, which extends 200 feet out from the small headland at the south end of Valley Trunk Bay.

Ashore

If there is any sea at all, landing a dinghy can prove tricky. Dinghies may not be left on the beach, so someone will have to drop everyone off ashore in the dinghy, and pick them up at a designated time, or swim ashore from the boat. Do not leave valuables in your dinghy. Take ashore only those articles that you don't mind getting wet, and wrap cameras and valuables in plastic bags. The entrance to the Baths is unmarked but is at the southern end of the beach under the palm trees. Make your way in between the slot in the rocks and follow the trail. There is excellent snorkeling around the point from the Baths south to Devil's Bay, but the beaches to the north are private. A fabulous trail leads inconspicuously between the Baths and Devil's Bay. Wear reef shoes — it can

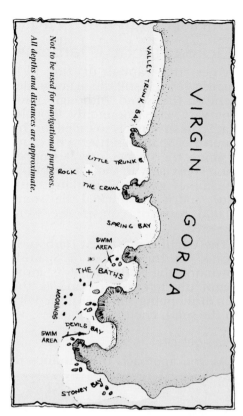

be slippery, but is well worth the challenge.

Colorful stalls on the beach sell souvenirs, crafts and t-shirts. It is also possible to get a cold drink and sandwiches at the Poor Man's Bar or sandwiches and Piña Coladas at Mad Dog's, both right on the beach. At the Top of the Baths you can enjoy breakfast, lunch and dinner while enjoying the view of the Baths and the islands to the west or cool off in their fresh water pool. Meal service starts at 8am and dinner service stops at 10pm. Dinner reservations are recommended by VHF channel 16 or 284-495-5497.

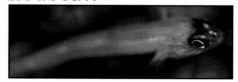

Spanish Town/Virgin Gorda Yacht Harbour

Once the capital of the BVI, Spanish Town is still the major settlement on the island. Although opinions vary, it is commonly thought that Spanish Town is so called for the number of Spanish settlers who came to mine the copper ore at Copper Mine Point early in the 16th century. The mines were still working until 1867, and it is estimated that some 10,000 tons of copper ore were exported.

The Virgin Gorda Yacht Harbour is located in the middle of Spanish Town (or the Valley as it is more commonly referred to) and is the hub of shopping and boating activity on the south end of the island.

Navigation

As you approach the entrance to the Virgin Gorda Yacht Harbour you will be in St. Thomas Bay where there are some moorings for those who prefer not to be in a marina. Pick one up and pay for it ashore at the yacht harbor. To enter the yacht harbor, you should familiarize yourself with the location of the reef that parallels the shoreline. Approach the harbor on a line with the prominent jetty in St. Thomas Bay. The first buoy will be on your port hand and will be green. Immediately to starboard, you will notice a red buoy. Leave it to starboard, as you would with the U.S. system of red right returning.

As you round the red buoy, you will turn approximately 90 degrees to starboard and pass between two more sets of buoys before entering the harbor. Contact the harbormaster via VHF 16 to get your slip assignment before you enter the yacht harbor. A slip reservation the day

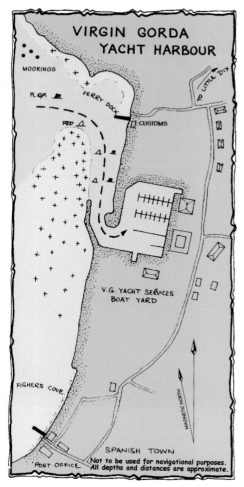

VIRGIN GORDA YACHT HARBOUR

MOORINGS

FL GR

FERRY DOCK

RED

CUSTOMS

TO LITTLE DIX

V.G. YACHT SERVICES BOAT YARD

FISHERS COVE

MAGNETIC NORTH

SPANISH TOWN

POST OFFICE

Not to be used for navigational purposes.
All depths and distances are approximate.

to 4:30pm Monday through Friday and on Saturday from 8am to 12:30pm. Sundays and holidays incur overtime charges.

The marina has dockage for over 100 yachts and can accommodate mega- yachts up to 160 feet in length with a 10 foot draft. Amenities include water, fuel, ice, provisions, showers, wireless internet, and a marine chandlery with computers and internet service available. Garbage can be disposed of in bins at both ends of the marina.

Complementing the marina is a full service boatyard and dry storage facilities adjacent to the harbor. The boatyard is serviced by a 70 ton Travel Lift that can haul vessels over 100 feet in length with beam up to 22 feet. The boatyard offers complete services including shipwrights, marine mechanics, awlgrip and osmosis treatment.

The marina complex offers numerous facilities including a bank, drug store, provisioning, car rentals, taxis, Thee Artistic Gallery and other boutiques. The Bath and Turtle Pub is open daily serving food and drinks from 7am to 11pm or midnight. They frequently have a live band at night with dancing until the wee hours!

before is a good idea to ensure you have a slip when arriving.

There is no anchoring in the yacht harbour.

When leaving Virgin Gorda Yacht Harbour and St. Thomas Bay and heading north to Gorda Sound be sure to give Colison Point a wide berth, as the rocks extend well out from the land into the water.

Ashore

Customs and immigration are located at the town jetty, just a couple of minutes from the V.G. Yacht Harbour. They are open from 8:30am

Julian Putley

ANCHORAGES OF THE BRITISH VIRGIN ISLANDS

Virgin Gorda Yacht Harbour   *Dougal Thornton*

For divers, Dive BVI operates a full service dive shop offering daily tours as well as rendezvous dives from the Virgin Gorda Yacht Harbour.

Little Dix Bay Hotel is a taxi ride away and those wishing to look around the grounds are welcome for drinks and luncheon. Reservations are required for dinner. Although jackets are not required, shorts are not allowed in the dining room after 6pm. Appropriate casual attire is welcome.

The Olde Yard Inn is known for its excellent cuisine and lovely garden. Their Sip and Dip Grill serves burgers and sandwiches for lunch from 11:00am and dinner from 6:30pm daily. For dinner dress should be elegantly casual and reservations are requested. Some nights they have a live band – check with them in advance to confirm.

Other restaurants in the area are the Crab Hole specializing in Creole dishes, The elegant Chez Bamboo creates a specialty bouillabaisse as well as luscious steak and more, Fischers Cove serves breakfast, lunch and dinner from 7:30am to 10pm daily in a casual, friendly atmosphere by the water. The Rock Café is nestled amongst the fabulous Virgin Gorda boulders and is only a seven minute walk from the yacht harbor. They are open daily for dinner from 4pm until close. You can dine in air conditioned comfort, or outside on the terrace where you will also find La Tequila Bar. They often have live music and can be contacted on VHF 16 or by calling 284-495-5482. Check our restaurant section for more listings.

Savannah Bay

During the summer months or when the ground swells are down, there is a very nice daytime anchorage in Savannah Bay, however it can be very tricky to get in. To enter the bay, just north of Blowing Point, you must have good light in order see the reefs. The entrance between the reef is at the southern end of the bay. If you are chartering this bay may be off limits.

Watch for the small reef that extends from the headland on your starboard hand and work your way around the coral heads that comprise the center reef. Once inside, you can anchor in 15-25 feet of water. The snorkeling is excellent.

Giorgio's Table is a charming Italian restaurant located on the point between Pond and Tetor Bays. There is a jetty available for guests having lunch, dinner or drinks at the bar overlooking Sir Francis Drake Channel. They monitor VHF 16.

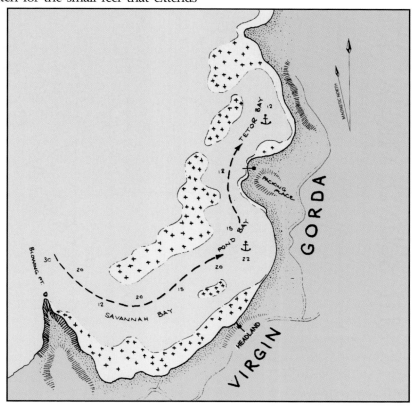

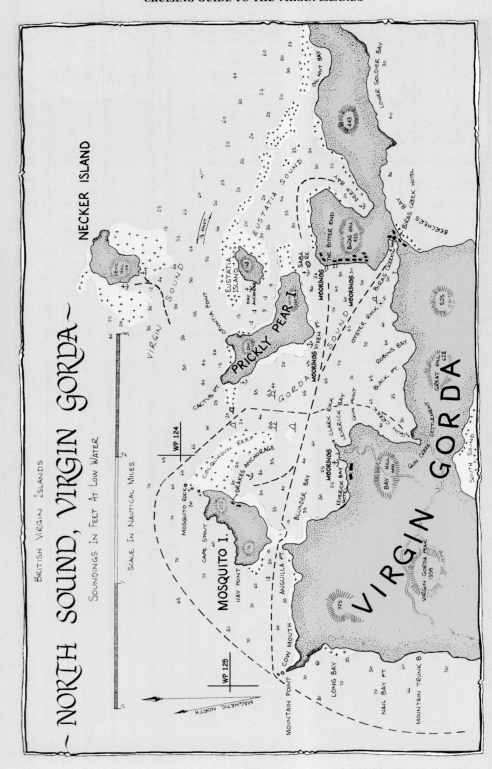

BRITISH VIRGIN ISLANDS

~ NORTH SOUND, VIRGIN GORDA ~

SOUNDINGS IN FEET AT LOW WATER

SCALE IN NAUTICAL MILES

NECKER ISLAND

WP 124

WP 125

MAGNETIC NORTH

VIRGIN GORDA

MOSQUITO I.

PRICKLY PEAR I.

EUSTATIA SOUND

EUSTATIA ISLAND

THE BITTER END

BRAS CREEK HOTEL

OIL NUT BAY

LOWER SOLDIER BAY

DEEP BAY

BRAS BAY

BEECHERS BAY

SABA RK.

MOORINGS

MOORINGS

VIXEN PT.

BURAS HILL
415

525

GORDA SOUND

OYSTER ROCK

BRAS CREEK

ROBINS BAY

BLACK PT.

GREAT HILL
628

SETTLEMENT

GUN CREEK

GUN POINT

GUN CREEK

DEVIL HILL

CACTUS PT.

OPUNTIA POINT

COLQUHOUN REEF

DRAKES ANCHORAGE

MOSQUITO ROCK

CAPE STOUT

HAY POINT

ANGUILLA PT.

BLUNDER BAY

CLARK ROCK

LEVERICK BAY

MOORINGS

LEVERICK BAY HOTEL

BAY HILL

SOUTH SOUND

VIRGIN GORDA PEAK
1359

725

COW MOUTH

MOUNTAIN POINT

LONG BAY

NAIL BAY PT.

MOUNTAIN TRUNK B.

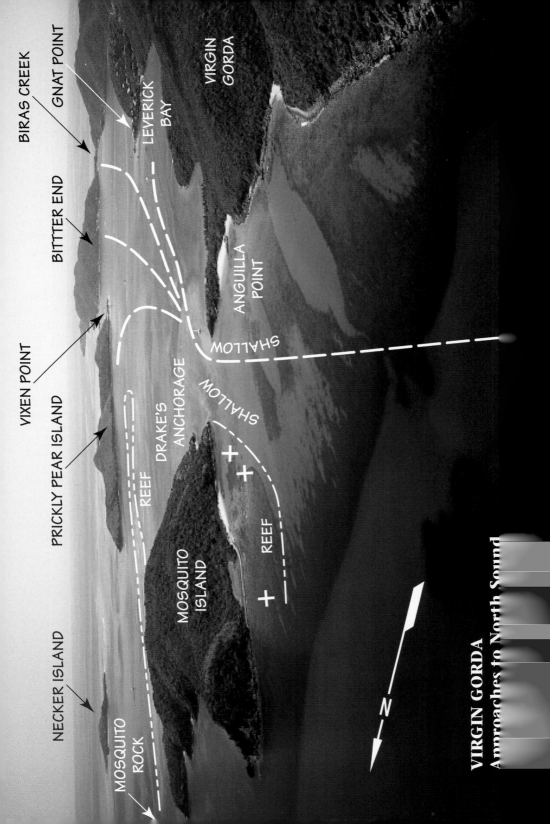

BIRAS CREEK

GNAT POINT

BITTER END

VIXEN POINT

PRICKLY PEAR ISLAND

NECKER ISLAND

LEVERICK BAY

VIRGIN GORDA

ANGUILLA POINT

SHALLOW

SHALLOW

DRAKE'S ANCHORAGE

REEF

REEF

MOSQUITO ISLAND

MOSQUITO ROCK

N

VIRGIN GORDA
Approaches to North Sound

North Sound

Located at the northern end of Virgin Gorda, North Sound or Gorda Sound as it is sometimes called, is a large bay protected all around by islands and reefs. It is an ideal place to spend several days exploring the reefs and relaxing. There are numerous restaurants and marina complexes here to suit everyone.

Navigation
Northern Entrance
Via Colquhoun Reef

When making your approach to the Sound you will easily recognize Mosquito Rock just to the north of the tip or Mosquito Island. There are reefs on both sides of the channel so proceed with caution.

Leaving the rock well to starboard, head for the flashing green can buoy (flashing green 4 seconds) that marks the port side of the channel when entering. This will keep you clear of both reefs. Leaving the green can to port, you will proceed past a red cone or nun (flashing red 4 seconds) to starboard. Continue through the red and green buoys keeping well in the middle of the channel.

If you are proceeding to Drakes Anchorage, there is another red buoy (flashing red) marking the lower end of the reef. It is imperative that you leave it to starboard in order to avoid going aground. Once past the buoy, you can proceed directly to the anchorage with clear water.

Mosquito Island has been purchased and plans are being made to build an eco-friendly "green" resort. At this time, we have no details as it is early in the planning stage.

If you are heading for Saba Rock, Bitter End, or Biras Creek, continue into the Sound past the sand-spit on

Caribbean Yacht Chart C12, C12a, C13

Simon Scott

Vixen Point (leaving good clearance from the end of the spit) and then head for the cottages on the hill that comprise the accommodations at the Bitter End Yacht Club.

There is one other navigational hazard in the Sound and that is Oyster Rock, which is to the west of the Biras Creek anchorage. The rock is marked with a red cone buoy.

Anguilla Point Entrance

This entrance is tricky, but can, in fact carry 6 feet; however, it is recommended that bareboat charters not use this entrance at all and vessels of over 5 foot draft should use the northern approach.

Leverick Bay

Anchoring & Mooring

Leverick Bay Resort and Marina is one of those destinations that make North Sound a water sports haven. Heading for the marina from North Sound the water is fairly deep with a minimum 16 feet at the marina. Leverick Bay monitors VHF 16 or you may call 284-495-7275. Pull in to the T dock for water, fuel and ice. There are approximately 36 moorings in the bay available to pick up and pay the $25.00 per night fee at the marina. On the southern side of the marina you will find the dinghy dock. The marina has 25 slips with electricity, fuel, ice, showers, trash disposal and laundry facilities. Both moorings and dock customers are entitled to 200 gallons of fresh water and a free bag of ice along with use of the resort's swimming pool. The marina can also accommodate up to three mega-yachts for overnight stays. The deepest part of the marina is 24 feet and has room for a 300 foot mega-yacht.

Ashore

Located on the northern shore of Virgin Gorda, Leverick Bay is an entertaining water sports recreation center. You will find all the amenities you need including a pool, grocery

Caribbean Yacht Chart C12, C12a, C13

store, spa, laundry, wifi, and air conditioned rooms and villas. For the shoppers, the Pussers Company Store carries a unique line of nautical and tropical clothing, watches and luggage. Palm Tree Gallery has an extensive collection of Caribbean art, jewelry and ceramics. The Chef's Pantry has a wide selection of mouth watering gourmet foods. All the resort facilities are available to both villa and visiting boat guests.

The Restaurant at Leverick Bay had open air dining and bar on the second story. It offers a breezy view of North Sound. Breakfast, lunch and dinner are served, with reservations for dinner recommended. Mooring fees will be refunded if a party of four or more purchase full dinners every night (with the exception of Friday)! Friday nights feature a beach barbeque with the lively mocko jumbies show (Caribbean stilt dancers). Live music starts at 7pm until.

Leverick Bay is a good base for exploring by land or by sea. Dive BVI

is a full service dive shop servicing divers in Virgin Gorda since 1975. They provide a good opportunity for diving on some of the unique dive sites around North Sound. Leverick Bay Water Sports have power boats, dinghies, Sunfish and kayak rentals for exploring North Sound.

If fishing is your passion, Charter Virgin Gorda will arrange to take you to the Sea Mount or the North Drop. Both are renowned fishing areas by anyone's standards.

North Sound is a microcosm of the BVI chartering area in itself. Leverick Bay is the closest water sports resort as you enter the Sound. Following are more North Sound destinations.

Gun Creek

To the east Leverick Bay around Gnat Point, Gun Creek provides a protected anchorage. Ashore there is the local settlement of Creek Village. Should you need provisions check out the Gun Creek Convenience Center and Eatery. You may tie your

Simon Scott

dinghy up to the ferry dock and find the store about two hundred yards up the main road.

Vixen Point

Anchoring & Mooring

Several moorings are available off of the sandy beach at Vixen Point on Prickly Pear Island. You may register and pay for them ashore at the restaurant. This anchorage has fairly good holding on a sandy bottom, but be sure to avoid anchoring too close to the moorings.

Ashore

The Sand Box serves lunch from 11:00am to 5pm daily and dinner from 6:30 to 11pm in a casual beach bar atmosphere. They also serve a mean margarita! The beach is good for swimming and you have a clear view of the activity in the Sound while you relax. The Sand Box monitors VHF 16 or call 284-495-9122.

Bitter End

Anchoring & Mooring

Located on John O'Point, the Bitter End is a resort hotel that features water sports and recreational activities. The resort includes restaurants and a marina with overnight dockage, guestrooms and moorings.

There are two sets of lighted buoys marking the approach for the North Sound Express ferryboat. Avoid anchoring near this channel to keep it clear for ferry traffic. The Bitter End channel and mooring field is a no wake zone.

Bitter End has two dinghy docks – both marked with signs saying "Dinghy Dock".

One is directly in front of the main lobby at the end of the channel. The

Caribbean Yacht Chart C12, C12a, C13

Bitter End and Saba Rock North Sound   *Jim Scheiner*

other dinghy dock is inside the Quarterdeck Marina to the right of the main lobby building.

The Quarterdeck Marina sells fuel and water at the separate fuel dock open from 8am to 4:30pm with a depth at the fuel dock of 12 feet. Vessels taking a berth will also have electricity hookups. Depth in the marina is approximately 10-12 feet and the marina can accommodate yachts with a length of 120 feet and 12 feet of draft. Megayachts 200 feet long and up to 18 foot draft are docked at the concrete L dock. Please make arrangements in advance. The Bitter End monitors VHF 16 or can be called by phone at 284-494-2745 ext 315.

The Bitter End has 70 moorings available for boats up to 60 feet at $30.00 per night that can be paid for at the Quarterdeck Office with cash or credit cards (8am – 3pm) or paid to the launch driver every evening from 5pm to 10pm (cash only).

Ashore

The Bitter End is a unique nautical village catering to yachtsmen. Ashore you will find the Provisions Emporium which stocks a wide array of meat, fish, breads and pastries baked fresh every day, dairy products, fresh fruits and vegetables as well as beverages including beer, wine, and liquor.

The Clubhouse Steak and Seafood Grille serves breakfast (8 – 10am), lunch (12:15 – 2pm) and dinner (6:30 – 9:30 pm) daily. The English Pub serves drinks as well as lunch and dinner daily from 11am until closing. Free wireless Internet is available in the Clubhouse and the Pub. Both fax and telephone services are available from the front desk in the main

Caribbean Yacht Chart C12, C12a, C13

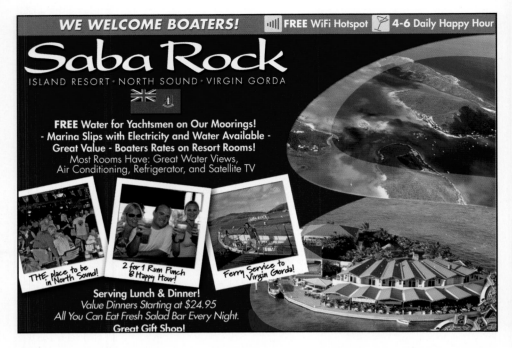
lobby. Bitter End often has entertainment at night. Check ashore to find out what is going on!

For shopping try the Reeftique with clothing, jewelry, sunglasses and Bitter End logo-wear. The Bitter End Outfitters stocks sundries, gifts, local art, books, games and dive gear. For those needing to relax and unwind from a long day on Sir Francis Drake Channel, The Spa at Bitter End is the place to do it, with massages, aromatherapy manicures, facials, and private yoga sessions.

Bitter End is known as a water sports center with over 100 boats to rent, plus windsurfers, kiteboarding, fishing, Sunday regattas, and US Sailing-certified lessons. Kilbride's Dive Centre has their base at Bitter End for the divers in your crew. To document it all is Yacht Shots who will photograph you and your crew on board your boat with all sails up heeling over and gliding through North Sound.

Boat supplies can be purchased at

the Chandlery. Mechanical services are available through the Quarterdeck Marina.

One could stay here for a whole charter and experience something new and exciting every day.

Saba Rock

Saba Rock is a tiny island sitting between the Bitter End on Virgin Gorda and Prickly Pear Island. The island boasts an amazing resort for such a tiny rock island. It includes gardens, a hotel, restaurant, gift shop, and a beach with hammocks to get rid of that last stubborn bit of stress.

Anchoring & Mooring

Several moorings are available at $25.00 per night (payable in the gift shop) with free 250 gallons of water and a bag of ice. Pull up to the T dock to take on water from 7am until it gets dark. A deep water marina along the shoreline has slips up to 24 feet wide, water, electricity, ice and a

Simon Scott

Caribbean Yacht Chart C12, C12a, C13

place to dispose of garbage. Check your email as Saba Rock provides a free wifi hotspot.

Ashore

Amazingly spacious, air-conditioned rooms with satellite TV are available with special boater's rates. The restaurant is open daily and has a pub or a dinner menu to select from. Check ashore to see when they have live music scheduled.

The Moorings Charter company has a sub-base here to assist their charterers with anything they need.

If you want to visit any other docks in North Sound, try the free ferry service, available from 7am to approximately 11pm.

Biras Creek

A well protected anchorage fringed by mangroves, Biras Creek Resort, at the head of the harbor, straddles a hill with stunning views of the beach on one side and the harbor on the other. The harbor is accessible directly from North Sound where twenty-two moorings are available for a fee of $30.00 per night. The mooring field is set up with a 60 foot swinging radius, therefore vessels using a mooring must be under 60 feet in length. An attendant will come to the boat to collect the fee. During a storm these moorings are designated as a hurricane shelter area.

The marina can accommodate vessels not exceeding 50 feet long. To make reservations for dock space, contact them at 284-494-3555 or hail them on VHF channel 16. When slips are available you can pay by the hour, daily or by the month. The dinghy dock is located at the base of the marina dock to your right when facing the resort. Trash is accepted at the fuel dock only, for a fee of $3.00 per bag.

Ashore

Guests from visiting yachts are welcome at the resort's panoramic hilltop restaurant. Breakfast is served from 8 – 10am, lunch is served from 1 – 2pm at the beach five days during the week and the other two days a light lunch is served in the restaurant, dinner is served from 6:30pm to 8:45pm. A private dining room is also available for special occasions. Reservations for dinner are required and must be guaranteed with a credit card. In order to maintain a calm, stress-less holiday environment, children under eight years old are not allowed at the resort.

The Biras Creek Restaurant is well-known for its superb meals served in a romantic atmosphere. The resort requests that after 5:30pm men wear trousers and a collared shirt and ladies wear suitable resort attire and please no shorts, jeans or tennis shoes. The grounds, beach and swimming pool are reserved for resort guests only.

On your starboard side as you enter Biras Creek are the service buildings for the resort and also the location of the Fat Virgin Café and Boutique. This is a casual, fun establishment serving from 10am for sandwiches, burgers, chicken and roti.

Bitter End Resort, Saba Rock, and Leverick Bay Resort are all within dinghy range of Biras Creek and they all have gift shops, restaurants and bars.

Jim Scheiner

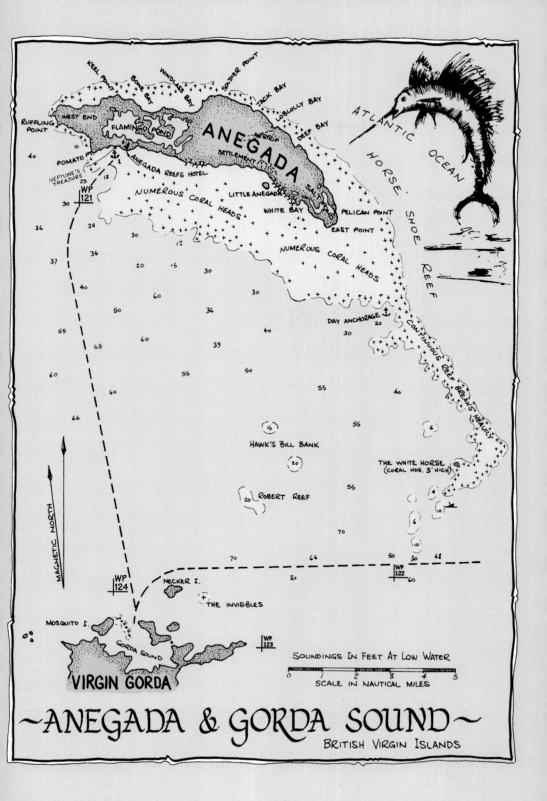

~ANEGADA & GORDA SOUND~

BRITISH VIRGIN ISLANDS

SOUNDINGS IN FEET AT LOW WATER

SCALE IN NAUTICAL MILES
0   1   2   3   4   5

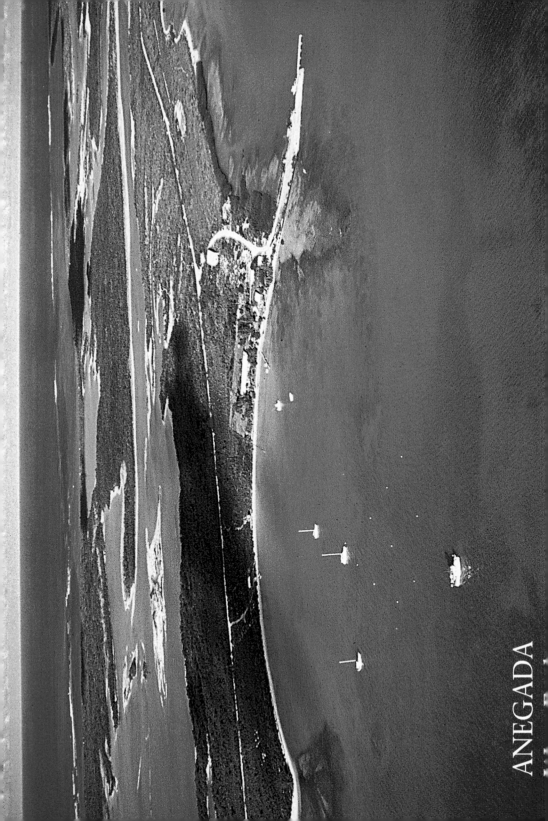

ANEGADA

Anegada, The Drowned Island

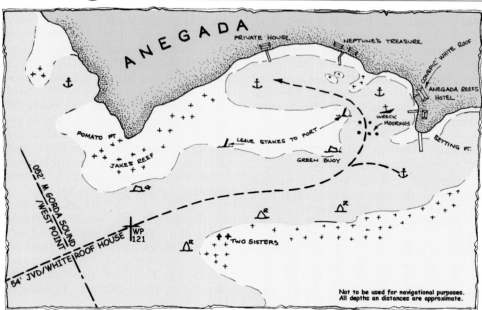

Not to be used for navigational purposes.
All depths an distances are approximate.

In contrast to the mountainous volcanic formation of the remainder of the Virgin Islands, Anegada is comprised of coral and limestone, and at its highest point is 28 feet above sea level. Created by the movement between the Atlantic and Caribbean plates, which meet to the northeast of the island, Anegada is 11 miles long and fringed with mile after mile of sandy beaches.

Horseshoe Reef, which extends 10 miles to the southeast, has claimed over 300 known wrecks, which provide excitement and adventure for scuba diving enthusiasts who descend on them to discover their secrets. The reef also provides a home for some of the largest fish in the area, as well as lobster and conch. The numerous coral heads and tricky currents that surround the island, along with the difficulty in identifying landmarks and subsequent reef areas, make it off limits for many charter companies.

Day excursions from Marina Cay, Leverick Bay and Virgin Gorda Yacht Harbour are operated by Dive BVI's high-speed catamaran several times a week. Double "D" Charters also operate day trips from Virgin Gorda Yacht Harbour.

Navigation

Because of its profile and surrounding coral heads, Anegada should be approached only in good weather conditions and with the sun overhead in order to see the bottom. Leave North Sound between 8 and 9:30am to arrive at the west end of Anegada with good light to see the reefs.

Steer a course of 005 degrees magnetic, which will take you from Mosquito Rock to Pomato Point. The

1-2 knot current will set you down to the west. Approaching the island, you will see coral patches, but if you are on course, they will have 10-20 feet of water over them. Owing to the low elevation of the island, the palm trees and pines will be sighted first. Do not turn off course until you have identified Pomato and Setting Points and located the red buoy marking the entry into Setting Point. When in line with the eastern tip of Jost Van Dyke, head in towards Anegada steering 050 degrees magnetic (no need to go further west).

There are four markers, 2 reds and 2 greens. As you approach the first red and green, go between them keeping the red to starboard and the green to port maintaining 070 degrees. Follow the next red, keeping it to starboard. The last buoy is a green and this must be kept to port. Steer around this buoy and come into the anchorage on 015 degrees magnetic. If in doubt, call Anegada Reef Hotel, or Neptune's Treasure on VHF channel 16 for assistance.

Anchoring

Yachts drawing over 7 feet should anchor off the commercial dock, which is in line with the green buoy in 10-15 feet of water. All others can make their way into the inner harbor, watching out for the coral heads that extend out from the small headland between the hotel and Neptune's Treasure and the coral off the dock (see chart). Drop the hook in 8-10 feet of water on a good sandy bottom. Moor Seacure have ten mooring buoys in the anchorage (white/blue and marked Moor Seacure). After picking up one of these buoys, please go ashore and pay the $25.00 fee to the Anegada Reef Hotel. There are ten more buoys painted orange in front of Potters by the Sea. A dinghy will come around to pick up mooring fees from the boats using these buoys. Again, the fee is $25.00.

Continue west of the Setting Point anchorage towards Neptune's Treasure. There are ten moorings in front of Neptune's Treasure.

Anegada

Dougal Thornton

Approach these moorings from the east going between the red and green channel markers. Draft is around 6-7 ft. Fees for these moorings are $25.00. Please go ashore and pay at Neptune's Treasure.

Ashore

Anegada has both interesting and fun activities to offer the visiting yachtsman. For exploring this unique island on your own, there are several car rental companies to select from: DW Jeep Rentals, Anegada Reef Hotel (Garfield's Rentals), Egbert Wheatley Car Rentals. Additionally, there are bicycles and motor bikes available from Lil Bit Cash & Carry at Setting Point.

For those preferring to use a bus shuttle service or taxi, there are services at Potters by the Sea, Anegada Reef Hotel and Neptune's Treasure. It is advisable in all cases to ask what the rates are before accepting a ride. There is always transport available here, just come ashore or call ahead on VHF Channel 16. Also the other establishments with dinghy docks will assist you with obtaining a taxi.

There are dinghy docks at Potters, Anegada Reef, Lobster House, Lobster Trap, Whistling Pine, and Neptune's Treasure. Anegada Reef Hotel and Neptune's cater to the larger boats also, with approximately 4 ft. 6 in. draft and in length, 46ft.

You can obtain fuel from Kenneth's Gas Station at Setting Point just a few steps from Potters and Anegada Reef docks. Note: This is the only place to buy gas on the island. If you wish you can bring your boat, or dinghy around to his dockside and there you are close to Lil Bit Cash & Carry, Sue's Boutique at the Purple Turtle, Potter's by the Sea, VnJ's and Anegada Reef Hotel.

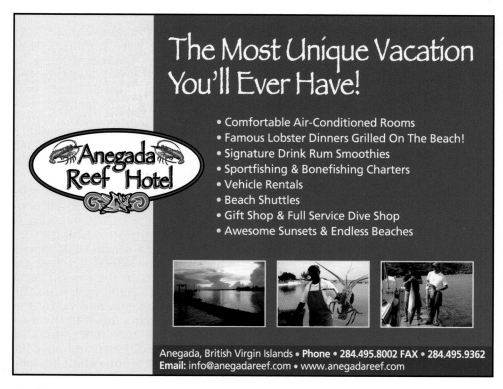

Dougal Thornton

Bags of ice are available at Lil Bit, Potter's, Anegada Reef Hotel and also at Neptune's Treasure (a short dinghy ride from Setting Point).

Lil Bit Cash & Carry at Setting Point offer groceries, and also a laundry. Sue's Boutique at the Purple Turtle is also on the dockside and offers some groceries, including cheeses, paté and wines together with a wide selection of gift items, tee shirts, etc. Here you can also use the internet for checking and sending emails, and a mailing service is offered. Visitors can also purchase phone cards and use the phone situated outside the Purple Turtle building. There are two grocery shops in the village (called the Settlement), Faulkner's Country Store and Vanterpool's Grocery Store. Dotsy's Bakery and Cafys Restaurant offer freshly baked bread and pastries and both serve local foods.

Gifts and boutique items: visit Sue's Boutique at the Purple Turtle at Setting Point, Anegada Reef Shop, or VnJ's. Heading east towards the Settlement, at Nutmeg Point, visit VnJ's and next door, Henny's Gift shop/DW Car Rentals. Pat's Pottery is also situated here on the ocean side of the road. Several restaurants will also sell t-shirts and gift items at their various locations.

Visitors must experience the wonderful north shore beaches, particularly Loblolly where the snorkeling is spectacular. For those wishing to 'lagoon swim' and beach walk, Bones Bight and Cow Wreck beaches are some of the best in the world. For a very long, beach walk, walk from the anchorage westwards and enjoy the spectacular beaches down to the west end. However, remember, most of the beaches are deserted and have little shade, so it is important to take some cold drinks with you, sunscreen, a hat and a t-shirt for sun protection.

For the avid fishermen, the island has fabulous bonefishing flats from Setting Point eastwards towards the end of the island. There are several guides who will take you by boat to the flats. They also rent fishing gear and will assist fishing novices. The boat ride in itself is stunning and some guides will take you to their special little snorkeling areas within the Horseshoe Reef.

The salt ponds in the center of the island are the habitat for many migrating birds and also the home of a flock of Caribbean flamingoes, reintroduced to Anegada. Eighteen birds were brought from Bermuda Zoo fourteen years ago and have successfully bred. These birds are thriving and now the flock far exceeds 100 birds. The habitat is perfect for them.

Heading west, look for the fields of wild orchids and also the endangered Anegada Rock Iguana, sometimes seen around the Bones Bight area. There is now an iguana "head-start" facility in the Settlement where visitors can view young iguanas being raised safely in captivity, so they may grow to a suitable size before being released into the wild.

Accommodation ashore includes rooms and/or guest houses at Anegada Reef Hotel, Neptune's Treasure (at Setting Point anchorage), Ocean Range Guest House (in the Settlement), and the Sands at Bones Bight. There are various beach cottages for rent, but generally this is for periods of longer term accommodation.

Beach restaurants that offer perfect day facilities are Cow Wreck Beach Bar & Restaurant, Big Bamboo and Flash of Beauty. Just order lunch and go for a swim and your lunch will be ready when you come back. They also offer dinners and will arrange transportation from the anchorage.

For dinner at Setting Point, if you prefer not to drive so far, Potters,

Julian Putley

Jim Scheiner

Caribbean Yacht Chart C12

Anegada Reef, Lobster House, Lobster Trap, Whistling Pine and Neptune's Treasure are all very pleasant places to eat, offering lobster and seafood as their specialties. A little further west at Pomato Point is the Pomato Point Restaurant. This is a lovely tranquil setting for dinner. Although they do not have a dinghy dock, they will arrange for transportation to and from Pomato Point.

Most restaurants need to have your dinner reservations by 4 p.m. at the latest. Dinners are by order only, so don't just show up and expect dinner without a reservation. The majority of restaurants monitor channel 16.

In the Settlement, there is a medical clinic, school, police & fire station and post office. As mentioned earlier, there are two grocery shops and a couple of bakeries/restaurants for local food. There are also several churches situated in the village.

Only some establishments accept credit cards, so it is advisable to check ahead. Most businesses do accept travelers checks in U.S. dollars and of course, U.S. currency. Euros are not accepted in the Virgin Islands. There is no ATM or bank in Anegada at present.

ANCHORAGES OF THE BRITISH VIRGIN ISLANDS

the anchorages of the

United States
Virgin Islands

National Park Service Headquarters

Dougal Thorton

THE UNITED STATES VIRGIN ISLANDS

OFFICE OF THE GOVERNOR
GOVERNMENT HOUSE
Charlotte Amalie, V.I. 00802
340-774-0001

MESSAGE FROM THE GOVERNOR

Welcome to my home, the beautiful United States Virgin Islands! Our islands are blessed with an abundance of beauty – wide, white beaches; translucent turquoise water; year-round warm weather and sunny days, punctuated with cool tropical breezes; and lush, colorful vegetation on our hills and mountains. Our islands offer so much to visitors as you will quickly learn

The United States Virgin Islands is a premiere destination for travelers from around the globe. Surrounded by some of the finest cruising waters, it's no wonder that the Virgin Islands is recognized as the Yacht Charter Capital of the World. The dozens of islands and cays that make up the Territory have an unspoiled beauty and accessibility unmatched anywhere else.

Since Christopher Columbus first arrived on St. Croix more than 500 years ago, our islands have been a haven for free-spirited seafarers. That spirit still lives today and can easily be found by cruising our waters and mooring in isolated harbors and bays; fishing for the elusive Blue Marlin, snorkeling and diving through living coral reefs and world-famous shipwrecks; and relaxing on the beaches that hug our tropical shoreline. Your options for a perfect visit are many - from enjoying the solitude of an isolated cove, to fine harbor side dining, to legendary waterside parties. The choices are yours.

And when you step on shore, you'll find more new experiences waiting to be discovered. Our history and culture are rich and varied, and our architecture reflects the influence of the seven nations which at one time or another claimed these islands as their own. Because our favorable customs regulations were originally established under Danish rule, our retail shops offer quality items that are less expensive than found elsewhere.

As a proud Territory of the United States of America, U.S. passports are not required to visit our islands.

On behalf of the residents of the United States Virgin Islands, I welcome you to our islands, our home, and a place where families and friends can truly experience paradise! Enjoy your stay and come back again!

John P. de Jongh, Jr.

Governor

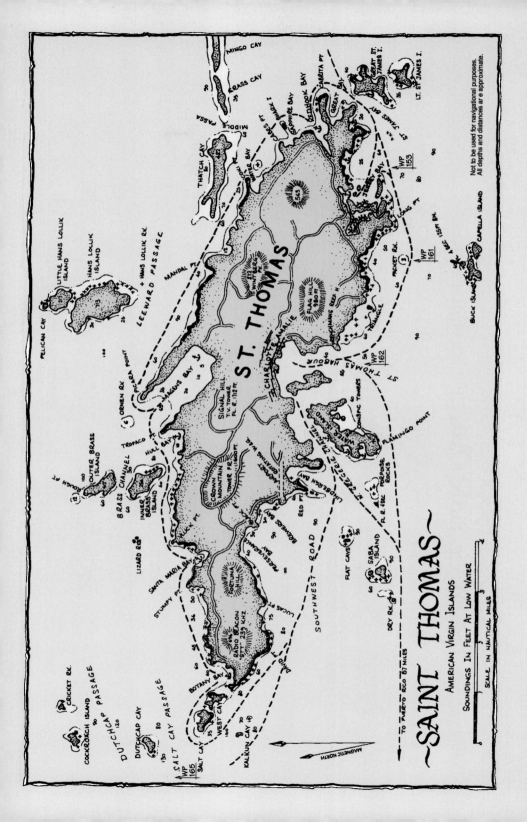

~SAINT THOMAS~

AMERICAN VIRGIN ISLANDS

Soundings In Feet At Low Water

SCALE IN NAUTICAL MILES

Not to be used for navigational purposes.
All depths and distances are approximate.

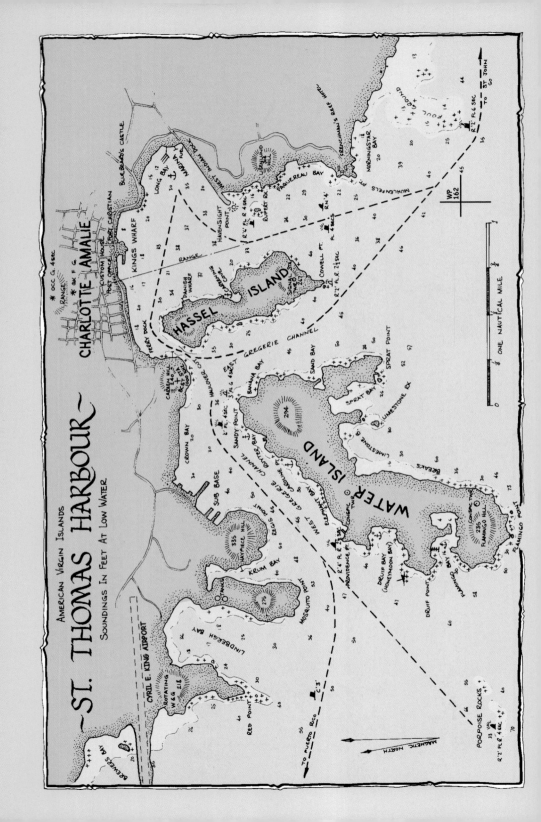

AMERICAN VIRGIN ISLANDS

ST. THOMAS HARBOUR

CHARLOTTE AMALIE

Soundings In Feet At Low Water

ONE NAUTICAL MILE

MAGNETIC NORTH

ST. THOMAS HARBOUR
U.S. Virgin Islands

Charlotte Amalie/ St. Thomas Harbor

Named after a Danish Queen, Charlotte Amalie is the capital city of the U.S. Virgin Islands and a major seaport. Used extensively over the centuries as a haunt of pirates and privateers, St. Thomas was declared a free port by the Danes thus enabling the sale of goods, livestock and ships acquired in honest trade or under the flag of piracy.

The town still has many of the original Danish buildings and mansions on the hillside overlooking the harbor. Picturesque alleys and stairways will lead you from large mansions to traditional West Indian houses surrounded by gardens.

Sheltered in all weather, St. Thomas Harbor tends to have a surge, especially when the wind moves around to the south, making it uncomfortable for small boats. Since it is a commercial harbor, swimming is not recommended.

A.J. Blake

Navigation

If you are making your approach from the east, you will pass the red nun buoy marking Packet Rock, which lies due north of Buck Island. It is best to stay well off the coast.

Another red nun "R2" marks the shoal ground that lies to the south east of the harbor entrance. You will also be able to see the Frenchman's Reef Hotel that sits atop Muhlenfels Point.

As you continue in, you will pick up two more red buoys marking Rupert Rocks. Leaving them to starboard, you can head directly for the anchorage.

Once inside the harbor, you will note several buoys off the West Indian dock. These designate the turning area for the many cruise ships that come and go on a daily basis and the anchorage lies to northeast of them.

Anchoring

The traditional anchorage for yachts is off the Yacht Haven Grande Marina complex. Take care not to foul any of the private moorings that have placed by the charter yachts operating out of the harbor. It is not recommended to tie up to the quay in Charlotte Amalie as the surge is both dangerous and uncomfortable.

Ashore

Customs clearance can be carried out wharf-side at the ferry dock at the west end of the harbor; the hours are from 8am to 4:30pm daily including weekends. This is the only customs and immigration facility on St. Thomas for yacht clearance. Cruisers planning to stay on the east end of St. Thomas may find it easier to clear in at Cruz Bay, St. John. They do not monitor the VHF radio.

When clearing at customs, bear in mind the dress code ashore calls for shirts and shoes, as wearing just bathing suits is deemed generally inappropriate.

Virgin Island Customs and immigration law requires that all people aboard must accompany the skipper while clearing. Non U.S. citizens or residents arriving by private or chartered boat must have a visa and passport in order to clear U.S. Immigration. U.S. citizens must have a passport to check in to the U.S. Virgin Islands from other countries, including the British Virgin Islands. U.S. resident aliens must have a green-card. For questions call immigration at 340-774-4279.

Yacht Haven Grande is situated in Long Bay, near the cruise ship docks. This state of the art marina has 5200 linear feet of dock designed for luxury yachts and can accommodate megayachts over 400 feet in length. High speed fueling is from a pedestal right at your slip – no need to move to a fuel dock. They will also dispose of oil, black water etc. The marina complex has everything you need and want including fine dining in several restaurants, catering, laundry, a florist, provisioning, and ships chandlery. Adding to the experience is an elegant upscale group of shops on the premises.

If you need some time off the boat, relax in the pool, use the tennis courts, or hone your skills on the putting green. Yacht Haven Grande has included some fantastic condominiums in their complex. In the center of the marina is an exclusive, private yacht club.

Security is a priority in the marina complex. Your personal safety and the security of your vessel will be assured. The marina can be reached on VHF channel 16.

Nearby, within walking distance are a number of helpful shops such as a grocery store, bank, car rentals and more. You will also come across various restaurants, bars and fast food for those craving a burger and fries.

Near Yacht Haven Grande is a cable car that will carry you to the top of Flag Hill to Paradise Point presenting incredible vistas of Charlotte Amalie and the harbor. You can get a variety of tropical drinks and food as you gaze out on this spectacular view, as well as finding some fun things to buy to remind you of your trip.

A short walk from the marina brings you to Havensight Shopping Mall full of gift shops like A.H. Riise, Royal Caribbean and Little Switzerland, and a collection of glamorous jewelry shops like Colombian Emeralds, Cardow, and Amsterdam Sauer. Many other shops of all descriptions provide for more than a few hours of shopping gluttony.

Charlotte Amalie

Main Street, or Dronningens Gade (which means Queen Street) with its Danish buildings and stone alleys is laced with shops and restaurants. Known as a free port, St. Thomas bustles with shoppers from the cruise ships, and visitors from all parts of the Caribbean and many other parts of the world.

Frenchtown Marina
A.J. Blake

U.S. citizens are allowed a $1600 duty-free exemption on imports purchased in the U.S.V.I. Excellent values can be found on such luxury items as perfumes, camera gear, liquor, jewelry and other treasures.

Many attractive gift shops offering attractive prices line Main Street. Be sure to stop in at the Leather Shop, A.H. Riise's, Cardow Jewelers, Royal Caribbean, Little Switzerland, and Colombian Emeralds, all in the Main Street area as well as Havensight.

Charlotte Amalie has many historical buildings steeped in a myriad of cultures. A tour of the town will take you through many fascinating labyrinths of old stone buildings and wooden houses.

Across Tolbod Gade from the brightly colored Vendors Plaza is the office of the V.I. Government Visitors Bureau and the Native Arts and Crafts Co-op. This was once the old customs building and is a good place to get your bearings before shopping. Emancipation Park, named for the freed slaves, borders the vendors market on the seaside of the park. You can easily find it by looking for the rainbow of umbrellas with vendors selling local handicrafts and assorted other mementos. Next to the park is Fort Christian, now a museum, it is the oldest building in St. Thomas having been built in the 1600's.

Market Square, just west of the busy shopping district of Main Street, was a slave market in earlier days, and later became a market for local farmers. Note the wrought iron roof, which came from a European railway station at the turn of the century.

The second oldest synagogue in the United States is located on Crystal Gade. The sand floors in the synagogue are characteristic of Sephardic Carib Synagogues.

On Norre Gade stands the Frederick Lutheran Church, the official church of the Danish Virgin islands. It was rebuilt in 1826 after a fire. You may visit the church Monday through Saturday from 8am to 5pm and on Sunday from 8am to noon.

Above Main Street, the Governor's House and other government buildings, are painted with traditional bright red roofs to be easily spotted from sea. This lovely building has housed both the governor's residence as well as his offices. The spacious second floor reception room can be viewed by appointment.

Bluebeard's Castle tower guarded the harbor and the Danish settlers, with the help of Fort Christian and Blackbeard's. The hotel and grounds command an excellent view of the entire harbor.

Beaches

Charlotte Amalie offers a central location to either rent a car, join a tour, or hire a taxi to tour the island. Remember if you will be renting a car

Charlotte Amalie, Waterfront

A.J. Blake

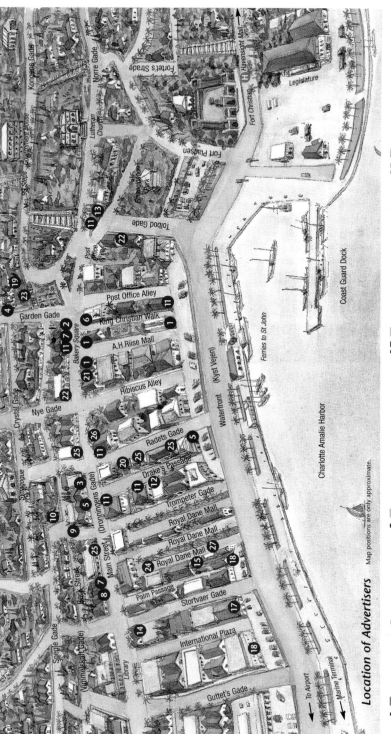

Location of Advertisers

Map positions are only approximate.

1	A.H. Riise Stores 🅗	9	Coconuts
2	Amsterdam Sauer 🅗	10	Cuzzin's Caribbean Restaurant
3	Beverley's Jewelers	11	Diamonds International 🅗
4	Blue Turtle Gallery	12	English Shop
5	Captain's Corner 🅗	13	Fujiama
6	Cardow Jewelers	14	Gemstone House
7	Crystal Shoppe	15	Glady's Cafe
8	Club Cigar	16	Going Seanile

17	Green House	25	Omni Jewelers 🅗
18	Hard Rock Cafe	26	Royal Caribbean 🅗
19	Hervé Restaurant & Wine Bar	27	Scandinavian Center 🅗
20	House of Rajah Jewelers 🅗		Tropical Memories
21	Jewels Boutique 🅗		
22	Little Switzerland 🅗		
23	Marisol Restaurant		
24	Okidanokh		

■ Shopping   ■ Wining & Dining   🅗 = Havensight Mall

Map Courtesy of Ralston Publications, Ltd.

to drive on the left hand side of the road.

There are many beautiful beaches that should be visited, some with restaurants and dressing rooms. Magen's Bay Beach is located on the north side of the island in the curve of a sparkling bay. Small sailboats and snorkeling gear can be rented, changing rooms and showers are available. There is a nominal charge for admission. Hull Bay Beach, also on the north shore, offers some wave action for surfing, a snack bar and a restaurant.

Bordeaux and Stumpy beaches are on the western end of the north shore, but are accessible only by a rough road, and then a long walk.

Brewers Beach is near the University of the Virgin Islands. Lindbergh Bay is near the airport and three hotels.

Morningstar Beach, next to Frenchman's Reef Hotel is close to Charlotte Amalie, and offers dressing rooms and a restaurant.

Secret Harbour is a great beach for windsurfing, as is Sapphire Beach Resort on the eastern end of the island. Sapphire Beach Resort provides rentals of beach chairs, rafts, snorkel gear, sunfish, and jet skis. A restaurant is convenient and there is live music on Sunday afternoons.

Coki Beach on the northeastern part of the island has rentals of snorkel gear, floats and chairs and a small snack bar. You can also take time to visit Coral World at Coki Point.

These are just some of the highlights of the sights to see in St. Thomas. Pick up one of the tourist publications such as St. Thomas this Week or pay a visit to the Tourist Board of the Virgin Islands for more details of what to see and where to go.

Crown Bay

Navigation

Located immediately west of the historic Charlotte Amalie Harbor and Hassel Island, and north of Water Island Crown Bay lies within the area known as Sub Base. Yachts may approach via either West Gregerie Channel or East Gregerie Channel; both of which are well marked, as is the reef extending northward from Water Island. While in Gregerie Channel, yachtsmen may approach Crown Bay Marina by leaving the cruise ship dolphin piling to port. The signed entrance to the marina is immediately north of the northernmost cruise ship dock. The tall Texaco sign on the fuel dock marks the entrance to the marina.

Upon entering, the marina's 315 foot fuel dock with high volume pumps lies hard to starboard and is open from 8am to 5pm daily. Water, diesel, gasoline and a pump-out station are available. There is ample maneuvering room inside the turning basis with a controlled depth of 20 feet. The wet slips have a depth of 15 feet. The marina monitors VHF channel 16.

Ashore

Situated on four acres of landscaped grounds, the facilities at Crown Bay Marina are exceptional. There are 99 slips available ranging from 25 to 200 feet, including 16 alongside and stern-to-berths catering to megayachts up to 200ft in length.

The slips have metered power, water, telephone hook ups, satellite TV service and wifi high speed broadband internet service. The marina office is open from 8am to 5pm and provides on-site security, specialized ship's agent service for port clearance and wire

Julian Putley

transfer banking assistance. Crown Bay Marina is in close proximity of the airport.

Dockside retail shops include Island Marine Outfitters, a chandlery, and Gourmet Gallery for provisioning with an extensive selection of wine, specialty cheeses, choice meats, fresh seafood, fruits and vegetables. Tickles Dockside Pub, with a casual atmosphere is open daily serving dinner until 10pm with the bar staying open for late night drinks.

Blue Island Divers and Water Sports are a full service scuba diving facility that cater to an international clientele from beginners to more challenging dive experiences. The Drop-or-Doo Laundromat offers self-service washers and dryers or the convenience of drop-off services. BodyWorks Delivered

offers professional therapeutic massage by appointment. Le Face by Zina is a day spa that provides the full spectrum of face and body pampering services. Monica's Hair Studio can help tame that wind-blown hair look offering a full range of services.

Messages, Mail and More can assist with mail, courier service, mail boxes, notary services, photocopying and more. Yacht captains and owners without Caribbean bank accounts are able to wire transfer money via the marina account to facilitate with emergency funds.

The Water Island Ferry Service provides several round-trip runs daily between the marina and Water Island. Check with the operators for schedules and fares. A private inter-island shuttle for guests of the Westin Resort & Villas

ST. THOMAS AND ST. JOHN
PUBLIC MOORINGS INFORMATION

The Reef Ecology Foundation in an effort to further protect the coral reefs in St. Thomas and St. John have installed 80 public moorings for public use. The following are the guidelines and locations of these moorings:

- Moorings are colored white or orange and have Reef Ecology Stickers on them.
- Moorings are for public use on a first come basis.
- Moorings are for day use only, with a three hour time limit.
- Use of the moorings is limited to vessels 60 feet or less.
- No fees will be charged for use of the moorings.
- Mooring use is at your own risk and therefore you must inspect the mooring to see that it is securely fastened to the mooring buoy and is holding the vessel as intended. It is your responsibility for the safety of your own vessel.

- After picking up the mooring line, please run your bow line through the loop on the mooring line to tie off.
- Not to be used overnight or in storm situations.
- Moorings are maintained by the Reef Ecology Foundation for the preservation of the coral reefs.

Locations of Moorings:

Thatch Cay, Grass Cay, Congo Cay, Carvel Rock, Great St. James, Little St. James, Cow and Calf, Capella Island, Flat Cay, Buck Island, Mingo Cay, Lovango Cay, Water Island, Dog Island, French Cap and Saba Island. For more details call the Reef Ecology Foundation at 340-775-0097.

PROTECT
OUR
CORAL

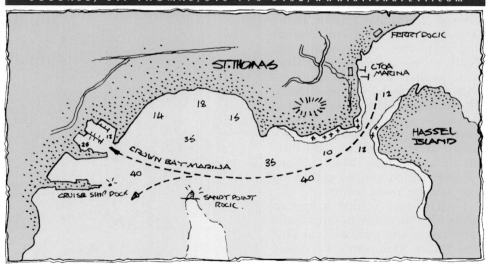

in St. John makes daily trips between its D-Dock Annex terminal at the marina and their private dock on Great Cruz Bay.

More and more luxury yachts today are utilizing the services of United Yacht Transport to facilitate the movement of yachts to and from the Caribbean region. Crown Bay Marina's close proximity to the United Yacht Transport staging area is advantageous for yachtsmen utilizing UYT which ferries dozens of luxury yachts across the Atlantic in dry-dock cradles secured to the deck.

Caribbean Yacht Chart C16, C16a   227

Sub Base Dry Docks

On the western side of Crown Bay is the Sub Base Dry Docks and Shipyard, providing a complete repair facility including yacht repairs, machining, welding, painting, fiberglass work electrical and carpentry shops, as well as a sail loft and rigging facility. Sub Base Dry Docks has a 100 ton crane and a 100 foot long drydock.

Quantum Sails, Island Rigging and Offshore Marine are all located at the marine center. They are open from 8am to 5pm Monday through Friday and on Saturday as needed. Sub Base Dry Docks monitors VHF 16.

Frenchtown

Frenchtown Marina, near the ferry dock in the far western section of St. Thomas Harbor, is the base for the CYOA Yacht Charters and their fleet of power and sail boats. The marina is open from 8am to 5pm daily and monitors VHF 16. The water is from 6 feet to 18 feet deep and they can accommodate vessels from 30 to 150 feet long, stern to the dock. Water, electricity, showers and garbage drop off are all available. Moorings just off the marina can be picked up and paid for at the marina.

Frenchtown is quaint, steeped in history and is home to some really great restaurants such as Hook Line and Sinker, Alexander's, Craig and Sally's, and the Frenchtown Deli. It is worth the stop for that alone! Frenchtown is also a convenient spot to get to the ferry terminal if you are planning to go to St. John or the British Virgin Islands, or it is only a very short walk to the Main Street shops and restaurants.

A pelican relaxing in the mangroves   Simon Scott

Water Island

This island was once a military base, and then was owned by the U.S. Department of the Interior, but now the land is owned by individuals.

Water Island is two and one half miles long and one half mile wide. It can be reached via the ferry that leaves from Crown Bay Marina on St. Thomas. Water Island divides the east and west Gregerie channels. On the southern most part of the island is an old lookout tower on the top of Flamingo Hill.

Flamingo Bay

Flamingo Bay is a daytime anchorage in Water Island. The bay can develop a surge and therefore is not recommended for overnight anchorage. Honeymoon Bay, or Druif Bay, slightly to the north of Flamingo Bay, is a favorite anchorage in normal weather. A beautiful white sand beach attracts swimmers.

The designated swimming area is well marked so you can avoid motoring through. Dinghies may be beached on either side. The anchorage has a sandy bottom in 15 to 20 feet of water. Good snorkeling can be found along the southern shore.

Hassel Island

Hassel Island, just minutes from the Charlotte Amalie waterfront, is under the domain of the National Park Service. You can still see some 18th and 19th century fortifications, as well as some private homes and a shipyard.

The park has a limited trail system at this time, amongst the cactus and orchids. Green iguanas can be spotted from time to time. There is a small anchorage in the Careening Cove on the eastern side of the island, often full of local boats.

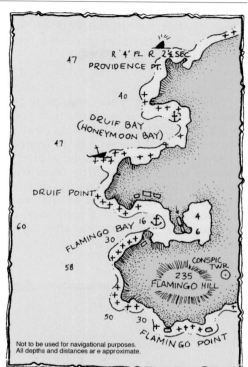

Not to be used for navigational purposes.
All depths and distances are approximate.

Dougal Thornton

The Lagoon, St. Thomas

Yachts drawing up to 6 feet have access to the Lagoon, the best hurricane shelter on the island of St. Thomas. Yachts drawing over 5 feet should enter on a high tide.

Navigation

When making your approach to the Lagoon, it is imperative that you not confuse it with the tricky "False Entrance" to the west. As its name implies, there appears to be a direct passage when approaching from the south or west, and boats at anchor can be seen at the head of the bay, but beware — there is a reef extending all the way across the false entrance.

A good rule of thumb would be to say: if you can't see a green can buoy on the port side of the channel, don't go in! The channel into the Lagoon is well marked and provides no problems once you have identified Rotto Cay and its relationship to other landmarks. Leaving the green buoy on the tip of Cas Cay to port, and Coculus Rocks to starboard, proceed to Grassy Cay. You will pick up a green buoy on your port hand and red nun marking the southern tip of Grassy Cay. Leave it to starboard. Take Grassy Cay to starboard by 25 feet, and round the red buoy on the northwest side. Leave the anchored boats to port and follow the channel. The channel is marked with red and green buoys and is easily followed leaving the red nuns to starboard when entering from the sea.

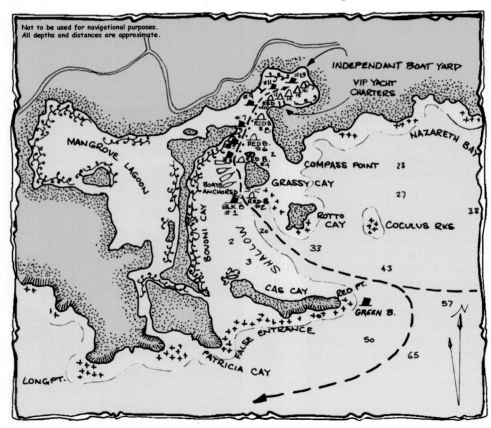

Not to be used for navigational purposes. All depths and distances are approximate.

THE LAGOON
BENNER BAY

GPS COORDINATES
WAYPOINT 153-A CLEAR ENTRY POINT   N 18° 18.5   W 064° 51.5
WAYPOINT 153-B GREEN MARKER   N 18° 18.4   W 064° 51.6
WAYPOINT 153-C CENTER CHANNEL ENTRANCE   N 18° 18.86   W 064° 52.06

Jim Scheiner

Simon Scott

Ashore

Independent Boatyard and Marina provide a full-service boat yard, complete with a 50 ton Travel Lift and a 10 ton crane. The boat yard maintains a group of private contractors to accommodate boats requiring services, including: Bruce Merced's Marine Repair, Benner Bay Marine (outboard repairs), Carpentry Plus, Dave Gott Refrigeration, Mike Sheen's Fiberglass Shop, Island Marine Outboards, Tim Peck Enterprises (Awlgrip work), and Mace of Arts who do boat lettering.

Adjacent to Independent Boatyard is Caribbean Inflatables. They can service life rafts and sell and repair inflatable boats, along with selling emergency gear. They are open from 8:30 to 5pm.

The marina includes 85 slips, with full services for both transients and live-aboards. The depth is 7 feet. Daily hours are from 8am to 5pm.

Compass Point Marina, across the Lagoon, over 100 slips and will accommodate boats up to 60 feet in length, with a 19 foot beam and 5 foot draft. They monitor VHF channel 16. The marina provides electricity, water, showers, storage, marine services, and a public dinghy dock on the southeast side of the marina.

Skippers must contact the marina by telephone (340-775-6144) to make a reservation before coming to the marina. Most slips are rented on a yearly basis, but occasionally there is a slip available for a night or two. Compass Point Marina is the head-

Jim Scheiner

quarters for VIP Yacht Charters with their fleet of late model power and sailing yachts.

Located at the marina are two restaurants, with three other restaurants within dinghy distance. St. Thomas Yacht Sales along with a dive shop and several marine repair businesses are based at Compass Point.

Pirate's Cove Marina has 24 slips with depths from 3 to 7 feet. The marina primarily rents slips on a yearly basis. They sell gas and diesel, provide water, ice and electricity and have internet access. You can purchase provisions from the General Store and items from the Pirate's Cove Gift Shop and Boutique. The Pirate's Cove Bar and Grill is a casual, breezy spot for breakfast, lunch and dinner daily. The marina monitors VHF 16.

Nazareth Bay (Secret Harbor)

From Christmas Cove, head towards the entrance to the Lagoon. Look for the white buildings of Secret Harbor Beach Hotel on the right.

The east side of the bay is full of coral heads, so head to the west side and anchor in about 20 feet of water. Do not use the moorings as they are private.

Do not attempt to bring your boat in to the dock as it is extremely shallow. You may tie your dinghy up to the hotel dock. The dock to the right of the hotel dock is private.

Ashore

The Blue Moon Café and Aqua Action Dive Center are located on the property of the Secret Harbor Beach hotel. The restaurant, with a stunning view of the sea, is open daily and serves breakfast, lunch and dinner with reservations.

Christmas Cove / Great St. James

Current Rock sits astride the channel and is marked with a light. The easternmost channel is recommended, although the other can carry 8 feet.

As the name implies, there can be

Simon Scott

a strong current of up to 4 knots running in either direction depending upon the tide. If approaching from the west, start your engine in advance, as the island of Great St. James tends to blanket the wind. The Cow and Calf, a group of rocks awash to the southwest of Current Cut, are easy to see.

Navigation

Making your approach to Christmas Cove, you will notice it is divided by Fish Cay. There is a reef extending from the Cay northeast to the shoreline of St. James.

Current Cut

Approaching Christmas Cove and the south shore of St. James from the north you will have to negotiate Current Cut. Current Rock sits astride the channel and is marked with a light. The eastern most channel is recommended, although the other can carry 8 feet.

Anchoring

Anchor on either side of Fish Cay in 15 feet of water. Do not anchor too far out as the wind tends to become erratic. Do not pass between Fish Cay and the shore. If anchoring to the north of Current Cut, ensure that you are anchored close enough to the shore in order to be out of the current flow.

Ashore

There is good snorkeling toward the southern tip of the island. When the weather is calm, take the dinghy and explore the waters and reefs around the south end of St. James Island.

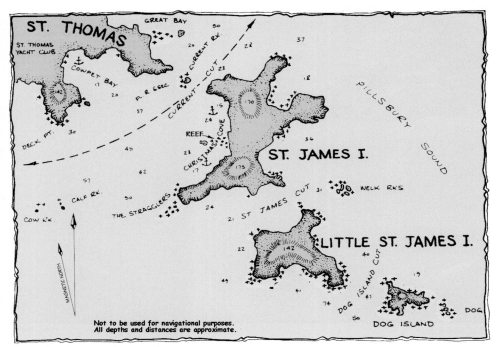

Not to be used for navigational purposes.
All depths and distances are approximate.

Red Hook

Just to the north of Cabrita Point on the eastern end of St. Thomas, Red Hook is a busy harbor with ferries departing for Cruz Bay, St. John on the hour. American Yacht Harbor, on the north side of the bay provides yachtsmen with all services. Because of its exposure to the east, Red Hook is often a choppy anchorage.

Navigation

Once around Cabrita Point, favor the northern side of the bay where the water is deepest. Keep an eye out for ferry traffic and stay out of its way. There is a marked channel into Vessup Bay.

Anchoring

As there are numerous private moorings and a considerable amount of ferry, and other traffic, it is recommended Muller Bay on the southern side of Red Hook be used for anchoring. Stay clear of the channel and ferry dock and don't go too deep into the bay, as it shoals off rapidly past the last set of docks.

Care should be taken when laying an anchor not to foul a vacant mooring.

Ashore

American Yacht Harbor has more than just the basic marina amenities. This includes dockage, ice, water, showers, fuel, electricity, satellite TV, telephone hook ups and free wifi! The marina can accommodate vessels up to 110 feet in length with a 10 foot draft and a 30 foot beam. Mail,

Red Hook Bay

Jim Scheiner

≡ARRIVE

AMERICAN
YACHT HARBOR
ST. THOMAS, USVI

As host of many IGFA qualifying events and with direct access to the famous North Drop, American Yacht Harbor is a world-class sportfishing destination not to be missed!

- World-class sportfishing with access to North Drop
- Host of ABMT Boy Scout Tournament & other IGFA events
- Full-service marina with 128 fixed slips
- Vessels up to 110' LOA, 10' draft, 40' beam
- Dockside electric & water
- In-slip fueling & pumpout
- Restrooms, showers, laundry, 24-hour security
- Mail, phone, fax, internet
- Duty-free shopping, fine dining & exciting nightlife

18°19.36'N / 64°51.06'W

T +1 340 775 6454
F +1 340 776 5970
6100 Red Hook Quarters #2
St. Thomas, USVI 00802
ayh@igymarinas.com
igy-americanyachtharbor.com

For information or reservations
WWW.IGY-AMERICANYACHTHARBOR.COM   1.888.IGY.MARINAS

ISLAND GLOBAL YACHTING

AMERICAS I CARIBBEAN I EUROPE I MIDDLE EAST

American Yacht Harbor and Ferry Dock

Dougal Thorton

telephone, fax and internet services are also provided at the marina office. A mobile pump-out service is also available in the marina. The marina monitors VHF channel 16.

Several sport fishing charters, power boat rentals and sailing charters are based here. American Yacht Harbor hosts some very well known billfish tournaments and is located across from the Virgin Islands Game Fishing Club.

The marina complex includes a shopping village, with convenient stores and businesses for provisioning, marine supplies, a bank, laundry service, movie rentals and a host of gift shops and boutiques. Several restaurants are in the marina complex as well as many in the Red Hook vicinity.

Just to the east of the marina is the ferry dock, convenient for a trip to St.

John or the British Virgin Islands. Across the street is Red Hook Plaza with a grocery store, mail services, restaurants (including the popular Duffy's Love Shack), and a chiropractor. The Marina Market is less than a block away and is a very well stocked market with an excellent selection of wines and champagne, meats, seafood and more. These are among many other shops and businesses in the Red Hook area.

Red Hook is a busy center for bareboat charters, crewed boat charters, fishing charters and many other marine oriented businesses. For more information and directions, check ashore at the marina office. The ferry to St. John leaves from Red Hook every hour and the ferries to and from the British Virgin Islands stop here as well. Rental cars and taxis are readily available.

Coki Point around the corner from Red Hook is the home of Coral World Marine Park. Situated on four beautifully landscaped acres, this marine park offers incredible views of the ocean coral reef life twenty feet below the sea through a unique underwater observatory. Feedings for the fish and the sharks are scheduled during the day. The park is complete with gift shop, dive shop, and restaurant. It is well worth a visit.

Sapphire Bay Marina

To the north of Red Hook Bay and the American Yacht Harbor is the Sapphire Bay Marina, a part of the Sapphire Bay Resort complex. The marina has 67 slips, fuel, water, electricity and fresh water showers. The depth is 10 feet. The resort has several beachfront restaurants, a fresh water pool, ATM and car rentals are available.

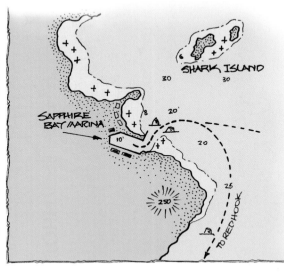

Sapphire Resort   Jim Scheiner

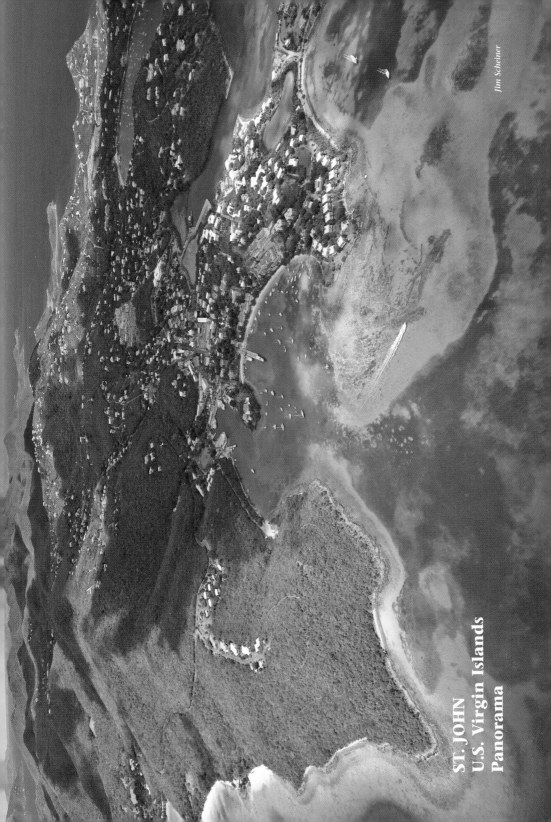

ST. JOHN
U.S. Virgin Islands
Panorama

Jim Scheiner

~ST. JOHN~
AMERICAN VIRGIN ISLANDS

TORTOLA

WEST END

FORT RECOVERY
780

FRENCHMAN'S BAY

FRENCHMAN'S CAY
400

580

SOPERS HOLE

THATCH CUT

LITTLE THATCH I.

GREAT THATCH ISLAND

13

MARY PT.

LEINSTER BAY

FRANCIS BAY

CINNAMON BAY

WHISTLING CAY

FL. G. 4 SEC. JR.

JOHNSON REEF

TRUNK BAY
962

HAWKSNEST BAY

HAWKSNEST

CANEEL BAY

DURLOE CAYS

CONGO CAY

LOVANGO CAY
24

MINGO CAY

GRASS CAY
253

MAGNETIC NORTH

TWO BROTHERS
FL. 6 SEC. 23 FT. 6 M.

LIND PT.

CRUZ BAY

FL. 4 SEC. 14 FT. 5 M.

STEVEN CAY
4

CABRITA PT.

GREAT ST. JAMES I.

LITTLE ST. JAMES I.

DOG ISLAND

DOG ROCKS

ROUND BAY

MOOR PT.

RED POINT

PRIVATEER PT.

FLANAGAN ISLAND

HURRICANE HOLE

BATTERY PT.

CORAL HARBOUR

LAGOON PT.

SABBAT PT.

LEDUCK ISLAND

CORAL BAY

EAGLE SHOAL

SCALE IN NAUTICAL MILES

RAM HEAD

SALT POND

CABRITHORN PT.

LAMESHUR BAY

WHITE PT.

REEF BAY

RENDEZVOUS BAY

DITTLIF POINT

FISH BAY

CHOCOLATE HOLE

CONTANT PT.

GREAT CRUZ BAY

BOVOCOAP PT.

334

250

1272 BORDEAUX MT.

995 MINNA HILL

ST. JOHN

CAMELBERG PEAK
192

GREAT HILL
227

1000

921

873

NOT TO BE USED FOR NAVIGATIONAL PURPOSES.
ALL DEPTHS AND DISTANCES ARE APPROXIMATE.

VIRGIN ISLANDS CORAL REEF NATIONAL MONUMENT

242

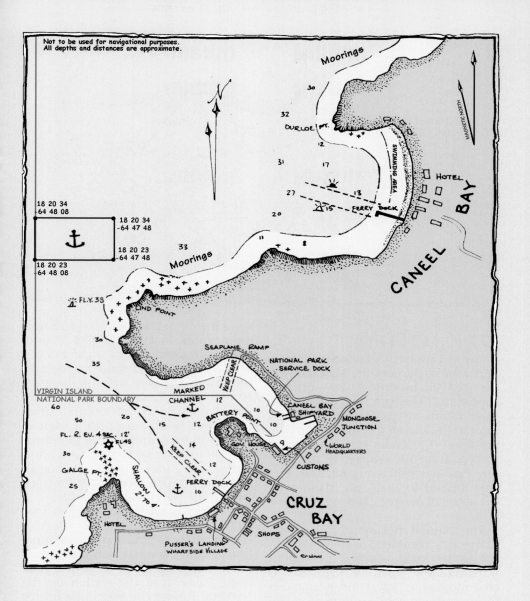

The Virgin Islands National Park

Anchoring is permitted within this zone designated by the following GPS coordinates:

18 20 34 -64 48 08	18 20 34 -64 47 48
18 20 23 -64 48 08	18 20 23 -64 47 48

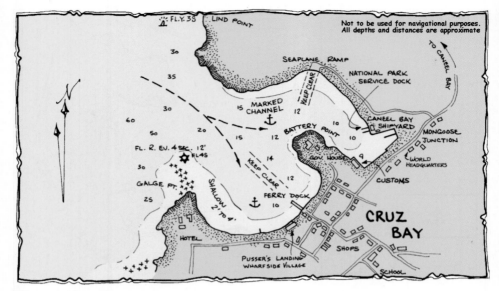

St. John

Two thirds of this fabulous island is under the auspices of the National Park Service, maintaining its pristine appearance. The Park Service has taken great efforts to provide moorings in most of the anchorages in order to help preserve the underwater reefs and seabeds from the damage of anchors. The Park has stringent guidelines that have helped to keep this island from the abuse of overuse. It is well worth a visit.

The natural beauty of the island mountains combined with the exquisite white sand beaches are mouth watering. The town of Cruz Bay is charming with excellent restaurants tucked away or commanding spectacular views. You don't compete with the cruise ships for bargains, but the same duty free status applies here. With the thriving artist community in St. John there are some original and interesting treasures to see and buy. You may even wish to check into villa rentals for your next trip.

Virgin Islands National Park was established by Congress in 1956 to pre-serve the natural and cultural resources on St. John. In 1962 the park boundaries were expanded to include 5,650 acres of submerged land adjacent to the island. The park was also designated a Biosphere Reserve, part of an international network of natural areas established to demonstrate the value of conservation. A presidential proclamation created Virgin Islands Coral Reef National Monument in 2001 adding an additional 12,708 acres of submerged land to the National Park Service.

It is highly recommended you stop at the National Park Service Headquarters in Cruz Bay for information on the park as a national monument, tours, things to see and regulations. Please read the section on the National Park at the beginning of this guide before visiting St. John for essential information.

Cruz Bay

Cruz Bay, a port of entry, is the main town on St. John and, without doubt, the best place to clear customs. Serviced by ferries to St. Thomas on an hourly basis, many charters elect to leave their vessels in Cruz Bay and take the ferry to Red Hook. Cruz Bay offers the yachtsman all of the basic services, including banks, post office, grocery markets, etc. Often crowded, the anchorage, though protected, is not necessarily a good overnight stop, as the movement of the ferries tends to make it uncomfortable. Vessels under sixty feet may anchor in the Cruz Bay Creek area near the boat ramp for a maximum of three hours for the purpose clearing customs and immigration or other business in Cruz Bay.

Navigation

Approaching Cruz Bay from the southwest or Great St. James, it is not recommended to go between Stephen Cay and St. John, as there are numerous coral heads. Leave Stephen Cay to starboard.

Two Brothers Rocks are always visible in the middle of Pillsbury Sound, and have good water all around.

Entering Cruz Bay, there is a reef extending out from Gallows Point, marked with a red flashing marker. Stay well to the north of it, as it is in very shallow water. A flashing yellow buoy to the west of Lind Point marks the port side of the channel. There are two marked channels within the harbor, one servicing the ferry dock to starboard, and one servicing the National Park dock and customs to port.

Anchoring

Shoal water extends from the marker on the end of the reef about 50 to 60 feet toward the ferry dock, so be careful when anchoring. Be sure to avoid obstructing both channels or you will incur the wrath of the ferry boat captains. Do not tie up to the dock as it is reserved for commercial traffic. A public dinghy dock has been built on both sides at the base of the pier. Tie up on the west side of the dock using a short scope so that the dinghy doesn't get caught under the dock. Dinghies are not permitted on the beach.

All moorings in Cruz Bay, Great Cruz Bay and Coral Bay are private and subject to stiff fines for unauthorized use.

"Iron Ranger" drop box for mooring fees   *Courtesy of Virgin Islands National Park*

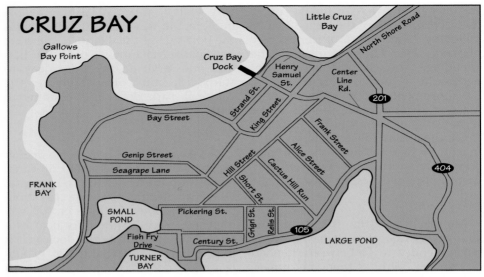

Ashore

The customs house is on your right in the northern section of the bay known as the Creek. Vessels clearing into the U.S.V.I. may tie up to the dock or they may clear in by dinghy as the dock is often full. The depth at the dock is 9 feet. There is a dinghy dock pier off the ferry dock for those anchored out in the bay who are coming ashore to clear customs. If coming ashore this way, turn left along the waterfront to the customs building.

Caneel Bay Shipyards, across from customs, is a full service facility offer-

Jim Scheiner

ing repair services for fiberglass, sails, refrigeration, woodwork and storage, as well as ice, fuel and water.

Several shops and offices are located within the waterfront area. Jeep rentals are available and a tour of the islands is highly recommended to visit some of the beautiful beaches St. John has to offer. Caribbean Connections offers mail, internet access and telephone answering services both in Cruz Bay and in Coral Bay. Islandia Real Estate can make your dream come true if you are ready to trade it all in and move to the islands. They are located on Centerline Road. Or check out Holiday Homes of St. John, a complete real estate firm including commercial property.

For medical emergencies dial 911. There are doctors and clinics in St. John.

To replenish the galley Starfish Market is open daily from 7:30am to 9:00pm and they do provide provisioning. Check out their wine room and the walk-in humidor. Marina Market is open from 7:00am to 8:45pm Monday through Saturday and 8am to 8pm on Sunday.

St. John is an artistic community boasting painters, musicians, song writers and writers. For information on art galleries, restaurants, accommodation and happenings contact the Tourist Office near the post office, which is open on week days only. The last Saturday of every month is St. John Saturday with music, crafts, special food in the park, and other activities.

Scheduled taxi buses leave from Cruz Bay to many of St. John,s exquisite beaches. You can also ride the bus all the way to Coral Bay or round trip to any-where on the island for a very inexpen-sive fare - a real bargain.

The National Park Service

One of the first stops you should make is to visit the National Park Service Visitor,s Center next to Caneel Bay Shipyard. There are many new rules and regulations that you should be familiar with before spending time sail-ing and boating in the park. Besides the boating you should also familiarize yourself with the fishing and diving regulations. See our section on National Parks at the front of this book for many of these important regulations.

Almost two thirds of the island of St. John is protected as a National Park. Park rangers schedule hikes and tours throughout the park on both land and sea trails, identifying flora and fauna. Annaberg Sugar Mill can be toured on your own with the assistance of a pam-phlet.

A.J. Blake

Courtesy of Virgin Islands National Park

Any beach in the U.S.V.I. can be used by anyone according to U.S.V.I. law. However, you cannot gain access to that beach by crossing private property, or go beyond the beach onto private property. Some beaches therefore, are accessible only by sea.

At the base of the ferry dock you will find many wonderful shops and restaurants all within easy walking distance. There is tourist information available to guide you to all of the wonderful activities St. John has to offer. You can easily walk to the Fish Trap Restaurant for lunch and dinner located at the Raintree Court. Try Morgan's Mango for a Caribbean culinary experience, just across from the National Park Dock.

Mongoose Junction

Just past the Park Service Center is a charming shopping arcade built of natural stone, known as Mongoose Junction. Visitors should stop by and browse in the quaint, interesting shops. You will find it hard not to part with some money here!

The Ocean Grill restaurant is now open and serves a fresh gourmet lunch and dinner in a romantic tropical setting. Sun Dog Café/Gecko Gazebo bar overlooks the courtyard and has an eclectic menu and can cool you with tropical drinks. The Deli Grotto will serve you hot breakfasts and lunches and provide you with beach/picnic and snack items.

Island Fancy Gallery and Gifts features tropical gifts and St. John specialties. Bamboula features a collection of primitive art, clothing, beads, baskets and textiles. Rent or buy your snorkel gear and beach chairs at Hurricane Alley; it is the perfect place for casual wear, sandals and T-shirts for the entire family. Bougainvillea Tropical Sportswear has clothing and accessories just right for the islands. Big Planet Adventure Outfitters specializes in beachwear clothing, footwear and accessories.

R & I Patton Goldsmithing design and craft stunning gold and silver jewelry. Caravan Gallery, voted best jewelry on St. John, has an awesome selection of silver and gold jewelry, authentic artifacts and affordable gifts. The Best of Both Worlds has fine jewelry and crafts including home accents representing a diversity of talented craft artists. Bajo El Sol Gallery, voted best art gallery in the U.S.V.I., represents works by local artists Aimee Trayser, Kimberly Boulon, Deborah St. Clair, Avelino Samuel and Livy Hitchcock. The Fabric Mill offers the colors of the Caribbean in everything, from designer clothing, to rugs, and fabrics for your home or boat. Wicker, Wood & Shells features gifts inspired by nature.

If you are thinking of making the Virgin Islands your home, the following call either Islandia Real Estate or Town & Country Real Estate.

Wharfside Village

Adjacent to the ferry dock is a wonderful collection of shops and restaurants overlooking the action in Cruz Bay. From clothing to fine jewelry it is a great place to poke around if you've got some time and a bit of pocket money or credit cards!

To find your St. John dream home stop by American Paradise Real Estate. Lowkey Watersports will help with dive and snorkel adventures and gear; Ocean Runner Power Boat Rentals give you the freedom to go on your own expedition on power boats from 19 – 28 feet. Noah's Little Ark offers smaller dinghies with outboards for smaller expeditions.

There are many choices for dining at Wharfside Village like Panini Beach Trattoria who offer authentic Italian dinners, Rumbalaya Caribbean Bar & Grill who open for breakfast, lunch and dinner offering open air dining with a view. Dizzy D's has pizza and tacos. The Beach Bar is as casual as it gets with sandy feet and wet bathing suits welcome. Café Wahoo is upstairs and serves a Euro- Caribe fusion style of dining with flair. The Paradise Café will entice you with their frozen drinks, smoothies and tropical juices.

Cruz Bay Clothing sell casual clothes

Jim Scheiner

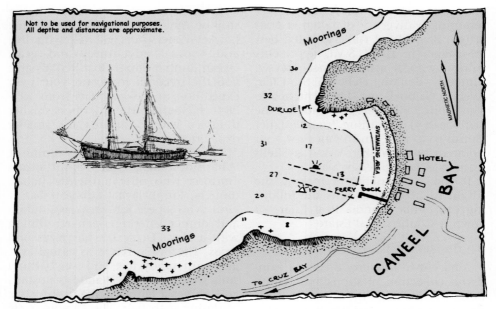

Not to be used for navigational purposes.
All depths and distances are approximate.

Moorings

30

32

DURLOE PT.

12

31

17

27

13

20

15 — FERRY DOCK

SWIMMING AREA

HOTEL

CANEEL BAY

MAGNETIC NORTH

33

Moorings

11

8

TO CRUZ BAY

and swimwear. Cruz Bay Photo Center can help with film processing or digital camera accessories. Pussers is known for their tropical and nautical travel clothing and accessories. Have a look at their excellent storm proof hand luggage. Karmah offer a line of casually elegant clothing for women. Dreams & Dragonflies have gifts, jewelry, clothing and collectibles. A good gift to bring home for yourself or others can be purchased at St. John Spice. They offer exotic spices, tea, coffee, lotions and other gift items.

For those wanting to go home with some glitter visit Blue Caribe Gems. They carry fine jewelry from a diverse group of talented designers. Freebird sells costume jewelry, watches, unique silver and gifts. Galeria del Mar have fine arts and crafts. Verace Designer Jewelry features the work of many fine, well known jewelry designers. All are located at the charming Wharfside Village!

Stone Terrace Restaurant and Bar on the waterfront offer a sophisticated cuisine for dinner. Chloe and Bernard's at the Westin on Gallows Point, offer European cuisine in an open air setting

with superb views of Pillsbury Sound. Cruz Bay and surrounding area has some wonderful restaurants and bars. Most of the details are in the restaurant section of the directory in the back of our book.

Caneel Bay

Traveling north from Cruz Bay, you will pass several beautiful white beaches, but they represent marginal anchorages because of the surge.

Caneel Bay is the home of the resort of the same name, which is built on the site of an 18th century sugar plantation. The property extends to the east side of the bay, to Turtle Bay, including the Durloe Cays.

Visiting yachtsmen are welcome in the bay, but are requested to keep noise to an acceptable level and to refrain from hanging laundry on the lifelines.

Mooring

There is a ferry channel marked that services the small jetty in the middle of the bay. Stay outside of the line of buoys off the beach that designates the swimming area. There are several NPS moorings to pick up. If the moorings are taken, anchoring is only permitted 200 feet seaward of the mooring field.

Ashore

During the day visitors may go ashore, and are welcome to visit the gift shop and the Beach Terrace. Outside guests may make reservations for lunch and dinner at the charming Equator Restaurant. There may be times when the hotel must request that outside guests return at another time if the hotel management feels their visitor capacity has been reached. Uniformed hosts and hostesses are stationed throughout the complex to give directions and answer questions.

Eastbound

If you are sailing east, care should be taken negotiating the channel between the Durloe Cays and St. John. The wind can change around the headland and strong currents can create a choppy sea. On occasion, it is prudent to start the motor while negotiating this passage.

Hawksnest Bay

This lovely, peaceful bay is great for swimming and snorkeling. Hawksnest has 13 NPS moorings installed for overnight use. If the moorings are taken, or if your vessel is over 60 feet, anchor 200 feet seaward of the mooring field.

Trunk Bay   *Mauricio Handler*

ANCHORAGES OF THE UNITED STATES VIRGIN ISLANDS

Trunk Bay / Johnson's Reef

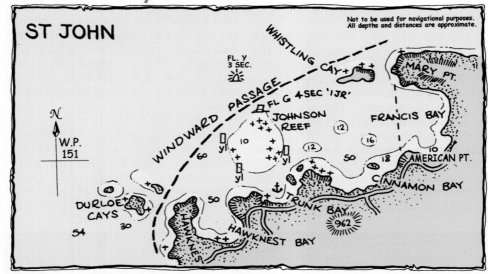

One of the more spectacular beaches in the Virgin Islands, Trunk Bay is the site of an underwater snorkel trail for beginners. During the winter months or when a ground sea is running, it is not recommended as an overnight mooring area because of the bad swell.

Johnson's Reef

A large reef a half mile to the north of Trunk Bay, Johnson's Reef, although well marked, continues to claim its share of wrecks due to negligence. The reef is marked at the northern end by a flashing yellow buoy (National Park boundary buoy) every three seconds and a lighted green buoy. The reef is surrounded by several yellow buoys, three of which are flashing. Do not go between them. The safest way is to stay to the north of the flashing green buoy. Care should be taken to give the reef a wide berth.

Navigation

The approach to Trunk Bay is straight forward with the exception of Johnson's Reef, as previously noted. If approaching from the west, there is a small cay off the headland to watch for. When leaving for the east, you can proceed between Trunk Cay and the yellow markers marking the southern tip of Johnson's Reef, taking care to stay at least 200 yards off the shoreline. When a ground swell is running, there will be considerable surface action and it is recommended to go around the outside, once again giving the reef a good offing.

Mooring

There will be a line of marker buoys off the beach, which indicates the swimming area. Dinghies going ashore must use the channel marked with red and green buoys toward the western end of the beach.

During ground seas, the surf on the beach can make the landing of dinghies a difficult, if not a dangerous, task.

Ashore

The National Park Service maintains an underwater snorkel trail at Trunk Bay. Picnic grounds and facilities are also maintained by the Park Service and snacks and cold drinks are available.

ST. JOHN N.W. COAST
Johnson's Reef, Trunk Bay
& Francis Bay

Jim Scheiner

Cinnamon Bay

The site of the National Park Campground, Cinnamon Bay provides a good daytime spot to pick up a mooring. Being exposed, it can be uncomfortable during ground seas. The NPS has provided 8 mooring buoys for day or overnight use. Accommodations at the campground include cottages, tents, and bare sites. The watersports center offers snorkel gear and beach chairs for rent, as well as diving, sailing and windsurfing.

Maho Bay

Like Cinnamon Bay, Maho Bay is another pleasant place to pick up a mooring in calm weather. There are 28 moorings provided for day or night use at Maho Bay. Maho Bay Camps welcomes boaters and has a well stocked store, as well as showers. Camping accommodations include canvas covered cottages hidden on a hillside in the National Park. A restaurant is open for breakfast and dinner. Dinghy in from Maho Bay or Francis Bay.

Francis Bay

Located on the northern shore of St. John, Francis Bay is the large bay extending to the very southeast of Whistling Cay.

Navigation

If you are making your approach from the west, you will be rounding Johnson's Reef. Favor the northern end leaving the large green buoy to starboard. There is also a channel between Trunk Cay, and the yellow buoy (leave to port or north). If you are approaching from the north, there is plenty of water through the Fungi Passage that lies between Mary Point on St. John and Whistling Cay. A small shoal area extends south from Whistling Cay, where the decaying ruins of an old customs house can still be seen.

Mooring

This bay is the only bay in the National Park that allows yachts from 125 - 210 feet to anchor following the NPS guidelines.

All vessels over 125 feet and less than 210 feet in length must anchor in sand at depths of 50 feet or greater, in Francis Bay, at least 200 feet shoreward of a line from Mary Point to America Point according to NPS regulations. Yachts 60 feet or under in length may pick up a NPS mooring. Twenty-nine moorings are provided in Francis Bay.

When the wind is light, it may get buggy if you are close to shore. A small sandbar lies in the northeastern corner. Stay outside the buoys designating the swimming area.

Ashore

For those who feel like taking a healthy walk, the National Park Service maintains a trail that extends from the picnic site to an abandoned plantation house. From there you can follow the road to the Annaberg Ruins. The National Park Service maintains garbage facilities ashore.

Departing

If you are heading east, you will find yourself in the Narrows with the wind and current against you. Many of the local skippers prefer to lay a tack toward Jost Van Dyke, and then tack back through the cut between Great Thatch and Tortola, rather than fighting the Narrows with its strong adverse currents.

Leinster Bay

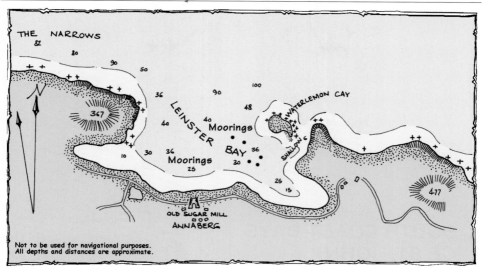

THE NARROWS

82

20

90

50

36

90

100

WATERLEMON CAY

367

LEINSTER

48

40

Moorings

40

40

SHALLOW

BAY

10

30

36

36

Moorings

30

25

25

15

00

4.77

OLD SUGAR MILL
ANNABERG

Not to be used for navigational purposes.
All depths and distances are approximate.

Located on the north coast of St. John, Leinster Bay lies directly to the south of the western most tip of Little Thatch. The bay is well protected and quite comfortable.

Navigation

Leaving Waterlemon Cay to port, work yourself up into the eastern end of the bay, known as Waterlemon Bay. It is not recommended to go between Waterlemon Cay and St. John.

Anchoring

Leinster Bay has 20 overnight moorings provided by the National Park Service. Only anchor in sand 200 feet from the mooring field if there are no moorings available.

Ashore

Aside from snorkeling around the cay, there are one or two interesting walks ashore. In the southwest corner of the bay, there is a trail that leads to the Annaberg Sugar Mill, the ruins of which have been restored by the Park Service.

If leaving your dinghy, please make sure that it is well secured. If the nature of the sea is such as to make it difficult, land it on the sandy beach back up in the bay and walk along the beach to the foot of the trail.

ANCHORAGES OF THE UNITED STATES VIRGIN ISLANDS

Courtesy of Virgin Islands National Park

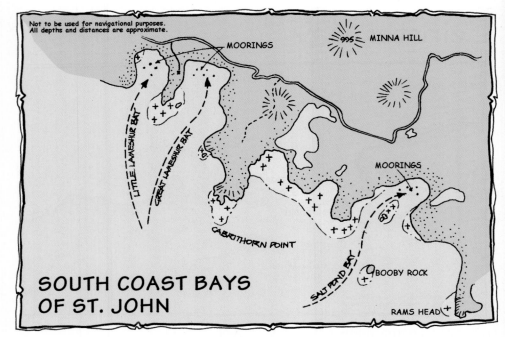

Not to be used for navigational purposes.
All depths and distances are approximate.

MOORINGS

MINNA HILL
995

LITTLE LAMESHUR BAY

GREAT LAMESHUR BAY

MOORINGS

CABRITHORN POINT

SALT POND BAY

BOOBY ROCK

RAMS HEAD

SOUTH COAST BAYS OF ST. JOHN

South Coast Bays of St. John

Beyond the point of Ram's Head, there are a number of bays, less frequently visited by the cruising yachtsman. We have listed below several of these anchorages, along with any pertinent information. In the south bays no anchoring is permitted by the National Park Service, however, there are some moorings available to pick up that are maintained by the park service.

Salt Pond Bay

Salt Pond Bay is an excellent spot to pick up a NPS mooring. It is easy to enter, although there are rocks awash at the entrance. You can pass on either side of them; however, there is more room if you leave them to starboard.

When approaching and leaving, Booby Rock is easy to see (35 feet) with good water all around. Anchoring is forbidden, but the Park Service has provid-

ed moorings. The snorkeling around this anchorage is excellent.

A word of caution is that this bay has been subject to some petty thievery. Sun-bathers, rental cars and boats all seem to be fair game.

Great Lameshur Bay

Another well-protected bay, Great Lameshur Bay is easy to gain access to. Once inside, pick up a Park Service mooring. Anchoring is forbidden.

Little Lameshur Bay

To the west of Great Lameshur, Little Lameshur offers good protection except when the wind is in the south. This is another bay with restricted anchoring. Pick up a mooring and head for the water. Snorkeling here is excellent.

Coral Bay and Hurricane Hole

Comprised of a series of bays, coves, and fingers of land, Coral Bay and Hurricane Hole are located on the southeast corner of St. John. Hurricane Hole is now part of the Coral Reef National Monument and anchoring is strictly prohibited. However the park service maintains 11 moorings for day use only – overnight use is prohibited. Hurricane Hole/ Coral Reef National Monument is a no-take zone, so fishing, and collecting are not permitted. At the time of the slave days, when the sugar mills were at their peak, Coral Harbor was the main anchorage on St. John. There are some interesting ruins still in existence.

Navigation

If you are approaching from the east, the route is straight forward. Leave Flanagan's Island to port. Make your entry midway between Red Point on St. John and Leduck Island. It is wise to give all headlands in this area a wide berth as most have rocks extending out from them.

If you are approaching from the south or west, then care must be exercised to avoid Eagle Shoal, which is very difficult to see. When rounding Ram's Head, it is possible to hug the shoreline, passing midway between Sabbat Point and Leduck Island, but the safer route is to stay south of a line drawn between Ram's Head and Water Point on the northern tip of Norman Island until Leduck Island bears northwest. Then enter midway between Leduck Island and Red Point.

Coral Harbor

The entrance is straightforward. Stay mid-channel until the stone house on the eastern side of the bay bears northeast. The channel is marked by 3 sets of red and green buoys that are privately maintained. You should then be able to anchor in 15-20 feet of water. Keep the channel clear for fishing boats, and do not pick up the private moorings you will see here.

Hurricane Hole   *Jim Scheiner*
Caribbean Yacht Chart C14, C14a   257

Ashore

There is no customs service at Coral Bay. There are a number of buildings left over from slavery days, including the Moravian Mission and the ruins of an old sugar mill and a fort. Coral Bay has become the place to eat in St. John. Try the Shipwreck Landing, Island Blues Seaside Bar and Grill, and Skinny Legs Bar and Grill. Sputnik's is open for breakfast and pizza on Wednesdays and a couple of other days - best to check with them first. The Jolly Dog Island Outpost at Shipwreck Landing has "stuff you want". Coral Bay Marine monitor VHF 16 from 9am to 5pm Monday through Friday and 9am to 1pm on Saturday. Sunday they are closed. They provide engine repairs, sail repairs, ice and miscellaneous items. The Coccoloba Center is the home of Lily's Gourmet Market with full deli items, liquor and beer along with meats and seafood. Or, if you prefer to eat out, try the Aqua Bistro with its circular bar or the Big Belly Deli. For a bit of fun shopping (for women anyway) is the Sugar Apple Boutique with gems and jewelry, accessories and sarongs. Coral Harbor is home to some

wonderfully eccentric and dedicated cruising sorts. It is considered more of a haven from the tourists, rather than a tourist destination.

A.J. Blake

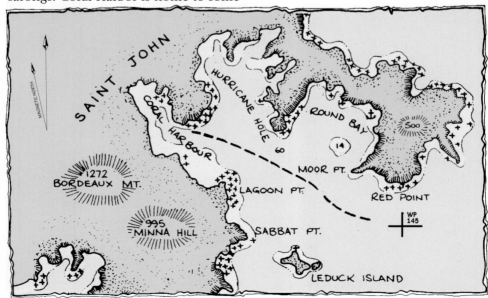

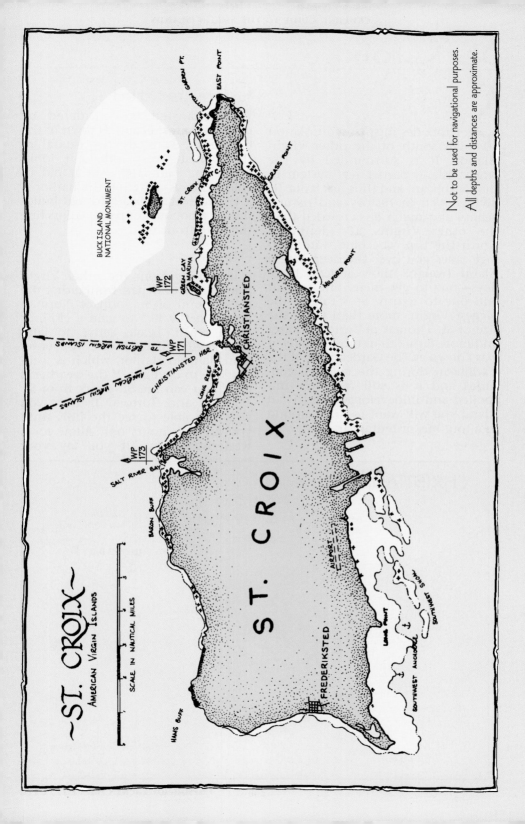

~ST. CROIX~
AMERICAN VIRGIN ISLANDS

SCALE IN NAUTICAL MILES

BUCK ISLAND
NATIONAL MONUMENT

ST. CROIX

FREDERIKSTED

CHRISTIANSTED

HAMS BLUFF

BARON BLUFF

SALT RIVER BAY

WP 173

WP 171

WP 172

GREEN CAY MARINA

CHRISTIANSTED HBR.

LONG REEF

ST. CROIX YACHT C.

GARDEN PT.

EAST POINT

GRASS POINT

MILFORD POINT

AIRPORT

LONG POINT

SOUTHWEST ANCHORAGE

SOUTHWEST SHOAL

To BRITISH VIRGIN ISLANDS

To AMERICAN VIRGIN ISLANDS

Not to be used for navigational purposes.
All depths and distances are approximate.

St. Croix

St. Croix lies in splendid isolation 40 miles south of the other Virgin Islands. It is surrounded by the largest island barrier reef system in the Caribbean, and thus has fantastic diving. Rich in history and natural beauty and much less crowded than the other Virgins, it's definitely worth the trip. The blue water passage takes you over the deep Virgin Island Trough. Allow at least three days—one to get there, one to tour and one to return. St. Croix is the biggest Virgin, more than twice the size of St. Thomas or Tortola. Flatter and more fertile than most islands, it was known as The Garden Spot of the Caribbean during the colonial centuries and it is still relatively unspoiled and undeveloped. This is an island you will want to drive around in a tour bus or rental car.

Christiansted

Christiansted is considered by many the most beautiful town in the Caribbean. Formerly the capital of the Danish West Indies, it looks much the same today as it did in colonial days. Entering the harbor is a visual treat, as beautiful old buildings in a bouquet of pastel colors line the waterfront.

Navigation

If coming from the other Virgin Islands, try to depart from either the eastern end of St. John or Norman Island in the BVI to gain a close or beam reach. Leave early, no later than 8:00 am, to ensure you enter Christiansted Harbor, which is well-marked, in daylight. If the weather is clear you can see St. Croix from St. Thomas and Tortola. If not, you won't be able to see the hills until you are two hours out. Allow for a westerly current. If you lay your

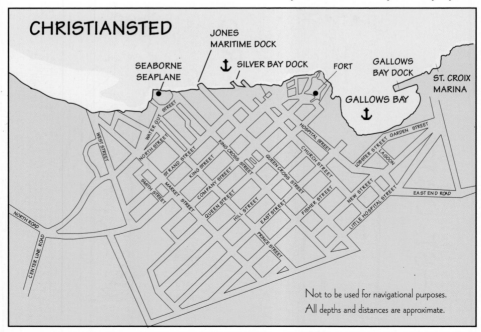

Not to be used for navigational purposes.
All depths and distances are approximate.

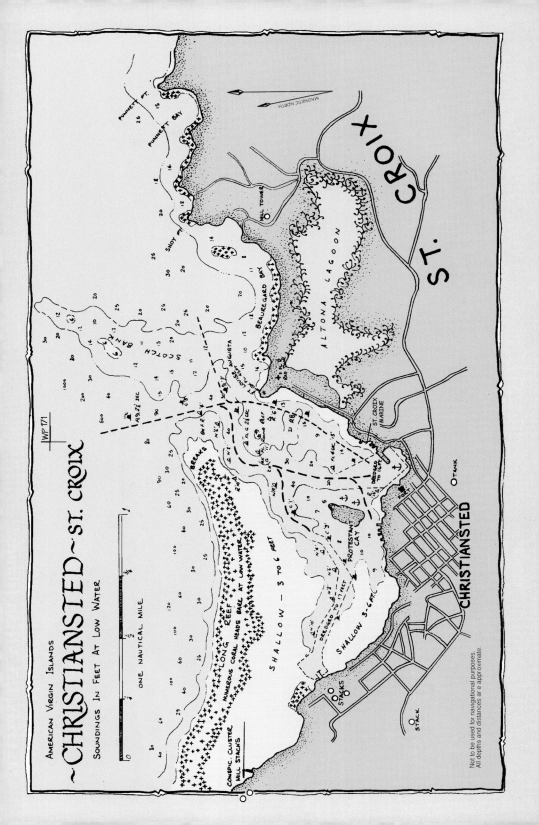

AMERICAN VIRGIN ISLANDS

~CHRISTIANSTED~ ST. CROIX

Soundings In Feet At Low Water

WP 171

ONE NAUTICAL MILE

ST. CROIX

CHRISTIANSTED

MAGNETIC NORTH

PUNNETT PT.

PUNNETT BAY

SHOY

MILL TOWER

BEAUREGARD BAY

ALTONA LAGOON

SCOTCH BANK

AUGUSTA

ST. CROIX MARINE

FORT

TANK

BREAKS

NUMEROUS CORAL HEADS BARE AT LOW WATER

LONG REEF

CONSPIC. CLUSTER MILL STACK'S

SHALLOW — 3 TO 6 FEET

PROTESTANT CAY

DREDGED TO 16 FT.

DREDGED TO 17 FEET

SHALLOW 3-6 FT.

STACKS

STACK

Not to be used for navigational purposes.
All depths and distances are approximate.

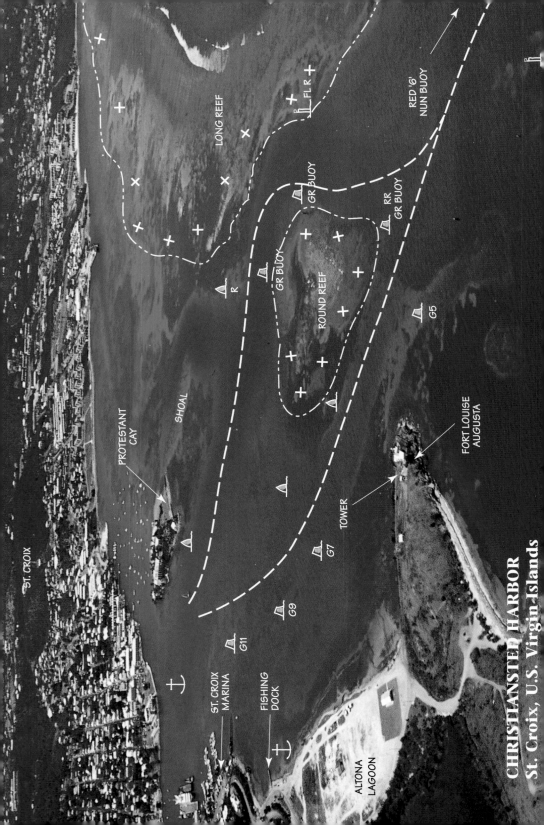

CHRISTIANSTED HARBOR
St. Croix, U.S. Virgin Islands

ST. CROIX

PROTESTANT CAY

SHOAL

LONG REEF

FL R

RED '6'
NUN BUOY

GR BUOY

GR BUOY

RR
GR BUOY

GR BUOY

R

ROUND REEF

G5

TOWER

G7

FORT LOUISE
AUGUSTA

G9

G11

ST. CROIX MARINA

FISHING
DOCK

ALTONA
LAGOON

course for the eastern end of the island you can alter as you near the island. The saddle formed by Lang Peak and Recovery Hill makes an easy landmark. Head for a point midway between them until you pick up the radio tower on Fort Louise Augusta. Pass the first green buoy to port, then line up the radio tower between the channel markers. This should be approximately 170 degrees magnetic.

Long Reef, which extends across the harbor (and offers good diving), will be seen breaking to starboard. On your port hand is Scotch Bank and, although the charts indicate that parts of it are covered with adequate water, it is wise to stay clear as it breaks in a ground swell.

Although the harbor entrance to Christiansted Harbor is well buoyed, note that Round Reef, which lies to the west of Fort Louise Augusta, is a major navigational hazard. You can go to either side of it if you draw under 10 feet.

Anchoring

The anchorage in the lee of Protestant Cay is quite crowded with the permanent moorings of boaters who call this home and seaplanes coming and going to St. Thomas and San Juan from the Seaborne base at the west end of town. Visiting yachts are asked to anchor to the east of the Cay or in Gallows Bay on the east side of the harbor, east of the fishing dock at Altona Lagoon. (Don't tie your dinghy up to the fishing dock. Go to St. Croix Marine, where there is a dinghy dock at the end of Dock C.) Vessels over 50 feet should use Gallows Bay. Holding is good in both locations.

Ashore

Vessels sailing from the B.V.I. or other foreign ports must clear customs and immigration at the Gallows Bay Harbor Dock. If your boat is registered in the U.S. and you have no

date boats up to 375 feet.

Gallows Bay is a convenient location with most services nearby: bank, post office, laundry, hardware store, supermarket, travel agency, internet café, bookstore, boutiques and restaurants. It's also in walking distance of Christiansted town.

In Christiansted Harbor there are two small marinas. Jones Maritime Company has a 15-slip dock, sailing school, yacht management service and charter opera-

foreigners aboard, you can clear by phone 340-773-0216. Foreigners must visit in person, with passport and visa. Hours are 8-4:30 Monday through Friday. If you arrive after 5, on a holiday or on a weekend, phone in to 340-778-0216. St. Croix Marine, a full service marina and boatyard, is just east of the customs dock. It can dock vessels up to 200 feet and 10-foot draft, and it offers discount fuel, showers and ice. There is a popular restaurant/bar, the Golden Rail, open all day every day. The boatyard offers long and short term storage, a marine railway, 60-ton Travelift, fiberglass repair, USCG and ABS certified welding, custom painting, mechanical and electrical repairs, refrigeration and air conditioning service. Also on the premises is Island Marine Outfitters, a comprehensive chandlery open Monday through Saturday from 7:30am to 5:00pm. The marina is operated by Larry and Ginny Angus and can be reached by phone at (340) 773-0289. They and their staff can help you arrange for car rentals or tours or for delivery from purveyors of food and drink.

A mega-yacht marina is proposed for the Gallows Bay Harbor Dock location. When operational, the Gallows Bay Marina will accommo-

tion. The marina offers all services but fuel. There are bathrooms with full size showers, laundry service, ice, water, power, courtesy car, 5-dog security and management that lives on the premises.

Close by is Silver Bay Dock, with slips, electricity and water available for boats up to 40 feet long. Cars can park nearby. Dockage can be obtained by calling 778-9650.

A boardwalk lined with small hotels, restaurant/ bars and shops runs along the entire waterfront, from the seaplane terminal to the town wharf and fort area. (Plans call for continuing the boardwalk all the way to Gallows Bay.) You can tie your dinghy up anywhere along the boardwalk and hit the watering holes or walk to town. Stixx on the Waterfront is a boater's hangout and the unofficial dinghy dock. The Fort Christian Brew Pub has crab races Monday during happy hour. On Protestant Cay in the middle of the harbor you'll find Hotel on the Cay. Its Harbormaster Beach Club has a beach barbecue and Caribbean show on Tuesday nights, with limbo and broken bottle dancing, fire eating and Mocko Jumbie stilt dancing. In town there are several remarkably good restaurants. This is the place to splurge on a gourmet dinner at Kendrick's, Bacchus or Savant.

The Town of Christiansted

This gem of a town was built early in the Danish era (1733-1917). Basically neoclassic, the stately architecture was gracefully adapted to the tropics, with arched arcades to protect pedestrians from the sun and rain. The outskirts of town have deteriorated, but restorations are underway.

The Christiansted National Historic Site preserves the wharf area and surrounding buildings much as they were in Danish times. Five yellow buildings are administered by the National Park Service: the imposing Fort Christiansvaern, complete with cannons and dungeons; the Steeple Building, the first church on the island; the Scale House, where merchants weighed their produce before shipping it abroad and where you can find a visitors' center with tourist information; the old Customs House, currently undergoing renovation; and the Danish West India & Guinea Company Warehouse, where slaves were auctioned in the courtyard. A museum dedicated to the slave trade is planned for this building, currently used for NPS offices. A short way up King Street are two other historic landmarks, imposing Government House, which once was the seat of government and boasts a lovely ballroom upstairs, and the pretty Lutheran Church.

The heart of town is a triangle bound by the waterfront, Queen Street and King Cross Street. Here you can do your duty free shopping in a pleasant, laid back ambiance of charming and uncrowded stores. There are a few really interesting gift shops featuring tropical items and one that carries only locally made arts and crafts: Many Hands. Jewelry stores are abundant but most of them are small and personal, with the designer on the premises. This island is famous for

Julian Putley

its bracelets, most notably "the St. Croix Hook" originated by Sonya and copied by everyone else and "the Crucian Bracelet" by Crucian Gold. IB Designs has found a niche with jewelry that incorporates chaney, bits of broken old china found on the ground. There are also a number of attractive boutiques selling island fashions. The V.I. Tourism Bureau is in Goverment House. You have to go through security to get there but it is open to the public.

The island is home to many artists, and Christiansted has numerous galleries. You can visit them all in one evening during Art Thursdays, the third Thursday of each month except in summer.

Three nights a year you can join a terrific town party called Jump Up, when the streets are full of bands, vendors and mocko jumbies, and the shops and restaurants offer special sales.

If you happen to be here the first Sunday in May you'll luck into a half-ironman triathlon that draws hundreds of international athletes every year. If you're here on the Saturday closest to St. Patrick's Day, you'll catch a parade.

Island Tour

St. Croix has been under seven flags, most notably Denmark, which ruled for almost 200 years and divided the island into 375 plantations of about 150 acres each. Sugar cane was the dominant crop. The Danes left a stunning architectural legacy, and the countryside is full of restorations and ruins of the plantation era: greathouses,

slave quarters, rum factories and many hurricane-proof windmills, where the sugar cane was ground. They are known locally as sugar mills. The Heritage Trail is a self-guided driving tour that covers many of these historic sites. Follow the brown signs featuring windmills. For information about it see www.stcroixheritagetrail.com.

The island is 28 miles long by 7 miles at its widest point. Topographically diverse, it is close to desert on the east end and almost rainforest in the west. In between are mountains and valleys and, on the south shore, miles of grasslands grazed by Senepols, a breed of cattle developed by St. Croix ranchers.

A good way to see most of the island and its highlights within a day is to make a circle tour. If you're driving yourself, remember to keep left! If you start in Christiansted and head east on Route 82, you will pass the lovely old Buccaneer Hotel; Green Cay Marina; Southgate Coastal Reserve, a bird haven owned by the St. Croix Environmental Association; the St. Croix Yacht Club; Cramer Park, a public beach with picnic facilities; and an 82-foot dish antenna, part of the Very Long Baseline Array of the National Radio Astronomy Observatory. The island to the north is Buck Island Reef National Monument, a popular sailing and snorkeling destination. Stop at Point Udall, the easternmost point of the U.S., where there is a monument to the millennium. It overlooks beautiful bays on both sides. To the south are Jacks and Isaacs Bays, recently acquired by The Nature Conservancy as a preserve.

Continuing along the south shore on Route 60, you will see the Divi

Carina Bay Resort and across the road its casino. Turn left on 624 and left again on 62 and pass miles of cattle ranches. Go left on 68 to see HOVEN-SA, the largest oil refinery in the western hemisphere; and St. Croix Renaissance Park, a huge environmentally-oriented industrial and business park on the site of an old alumina refinery (the red mountain is the waste from that process). This road will deliver you to Route 66, the Melvin Evans Highway, the only four-lane road on the island. You'll pass the airport off to your left. Route 64 is a U-shaped road that skirts the airport, first as East Airport Road and later as West Airport Road). Go right at the latter and you're soon at the Cruzan Rum Distillery, where you can tour the factory in half an hour and sample one of their famous flavors. Make a slight departure from your circle tour by turning right on 70 (Queen Mary Highway, also known as Centerline Road), to see St. George Village Botanical Garden, where an excellent collection of native plants and ornamentals is displayed among relics of the pre-Columbian and colonial periods. Back on 70, head west to Whim Museum, a restored sugar plantation. Both the Botanical Garden and Whim Museum are worth touring, and both have attractive gift shops. Also on this road is a K Mart, the island's only department store.

Follow 70 into the quaint town of Frederiksted. This is a good stop for lunch and a swim at Sunset Grill north of town or Beach Side Café on the Beach south of town. In town check out Strand Street on the beautiful waterfront, site of the new Caribbean Museum Center for the Arts, and the cruise ship pier. At the north end is Fort Frederik where, on July 3, 1848, thanks to a progressive governor, Peter von Sholten, and a non-violent slave leader named Buddhoe, the slaves of the Danish West Indies were emancipated peacefully. Frederiksted is thus known as Freedom City.

When you leave the town head north on 63 and take the second turn to the right, Mahogany Road (Route 76). This takes you through the tropical moist forest (there is not enough rainfall to qualify as a rainforest) where you will pass the Lawaetz Museum, a charming old farmhouse built by Danish settlers whose descendants still live on the island; St. Croix LEAP, a woodworking shop using fallen trees; the turnoff to Mount Victory, an eco-camp, and Creque Dam Farm, a sustainable farm institution, two bright stars in the island's growing eco-tourism field; the Domino Club, a thatch-roofed bar featuring beer-drinking pigs; and the Bottle Museum, a yard full of decorative vignettes made from recycled trash. Turn left on 69, which takes you past the beautiful Carambola Golf Course designed by Robert Trent Jones (one of three golf courses on the island), then down The Beast, a monstrous hill triathletes ride their bikes up in the half ironman competition every May.

You are now back on the north shore. Carambola Hotel is to the left and Route 80 to the right, which takes you past Cane Bay with its famous dive site, the Wall; and Salt River Bay National Historical Park and Ecological Preserve, the only place on U.S. soil where a Columbus party landed and the site of his first hostile encounter with indigenous people. When you reach the end of 80, turn left on 75 and follow it back into Christiansted. You will enter town at Sunday Market Square, a newly restored block that looks as it did when the slaves gathered there on their day off to visit and buy and sell their own produce and handiwork.

ANCHORAGES OF THE UNITED STATES VIRGIN ISLANDS

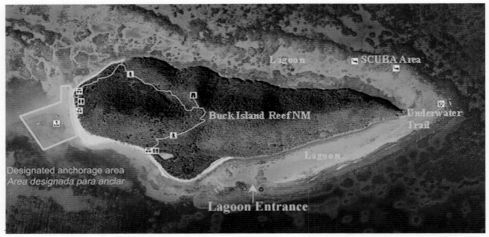

Courtesy of Virgin Islands National Park

Buck Island Reef National Monument

This is the only offshore sailing destination from St. Croix, but it's so good the locals go back time after time. Several charter boats are National Park Service concessionaires and make day and half-day runs. A small, uninhabited island about a mile off the northeast shore, Buck Island has a gorgeous beach on one end and a snorkeling trail on the other. You're likely to see sea turtles and sting rays here, as well as plentiful reef fish. Schools of Blue Tang abound, swimming through the underwater coral garden and its grottos. The trail has underwater signs guiding snorkelers through the reef and identifying the fish and coral, and there are a couple of buoys to rest on so that you won't be tempted to set down on the coral. The boundary of the National Monument was expanded in 2001, adding over 18,000 acres of submerged lands to the park. Fishing is prohibited.

Navigation

If going from Christiansted Harbor, leave the same way you came in until you reach the sea buoy. Proceed northeast for 2 miles along Scotch Bank, then head for the prominent point on the south end of the island. An alternate route is to proceed out of the harbor to buoy C7 off Fort Louise Augusta. Do not go further inshore, as there are two shoal areas. Leave Green Cay to starboard and head for the white beach on the western end of Buck Island. There are two white buoys that mark the extremities of the park's western patch reef area. If you want to go to the snorkeling trail, proceed eastward along the south shore of the island, keeping the white buoy to port, until you see green and red buoys marking the entrance through the reef into the lagoon. Follow the lagoon passage to the eastern end of the island and pick up one of the Park Service moorings. Depth inside the lagoon varies, averaging only 6 feet. Stay in the middle to avoid shoal areas.

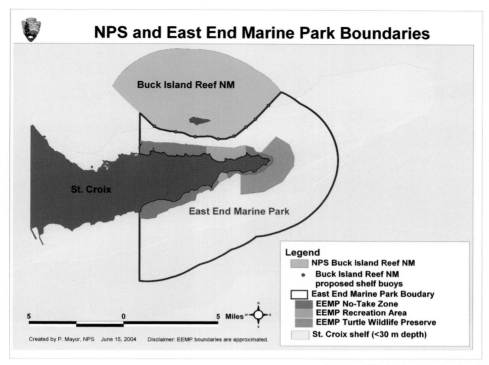

NPS and East End Marine Park Boundaries

Buck Island Reef NM

St. Croix

East End Marine Park

Legend
- NPS Buck Island Reef NM
- • Buck Island Reef NM proposed shelf buoys
- ☐ East End Marine Park Boudary
- EEMP No-Take Zone
- EEMP Recreation Area
- EEMP Turtle Wildlife Preserve
- ☐ St. Croix shelf (<30 m depth)

5   0   5 Miles

Created by P. Mayor, NPS   June 15, 2004   Disclaimer: EEMP boundaries are approximated.

Courtesy of Virgin Islands National Park

Anchoring & Mooring

There is no anchoring inside the reef. At the underwater trail you're welcome to pick up one of the Park Service moorings for day use only. For the time being anchoring is allowed at the designated area off West Beach. Boaters are requested to obtain a permit (good for one year) from the National Park Service office near the wharf in Christiansted. You can anchor anywhere off the beach in about 15 feet of water in deep sand. Please avoid sea grass areas!

Buck Island is a nesting site for four species of endangered or threatened sea turtles. If you anchor overnight between June and December, you are not allowed ashore between sunset and sunrise, and bright lights and loud noise are not permitted. You may see monitors and researchers at work ashore.

Ashore

There are two picnic areas on Buck Island with pit toilets, picnic tables and barbecue grills, a pavilion east of the small pier on the south shore and one without shelter on the western end. Visit the information kiosk located at each picnic area for park guidelines and information.

An overland hiking trail provides a 45-minute walk from beach to beach with a stop at the north side reef overlook. Avoid contact with any plants on the island as many will burn or cause an allergic reaction. There is no collecting in the park.

Jim Scheiner

ANCHORAGES OF THE UNITED STATES VIRGIN ISLANDS

Jim Scheiner

East End Marine Park

The entire eastern tip of St. Croix has been designated a marine park to protect and replenish corals and fish by regulating boating, diving and fishing within its boundaries, from Chenay Bay on the north to Great Pond on the south. The local government is placing single-point moorings (16" yellow balls) at Chenay Bay, Teague Bay and Cotton Garden for daytime use only. Similar moorings will also be found in Christiansted Harbor, Frederiksted Harbor, Salt River (outside the reef) and along the west end from Sandy Point to Sprat Hall.

Green Cay Marina

Green Cay Marina is a full service, well protected marina on St. Croix's northern coast east of Christiansted and just south of Green Cay, a small nature preserve. It should be approached from the western side of

Buck Island. Look for the yellow buildings with white roofs of Tamarind Reef Hotel close by the marina.

Leave Green Cay to port and head for the rock jetties to either side of the entrance. The marina monitors VHF16 and 340-773-1453. If you call ahead, the dockmaster will meet you at the fuel dock and lead you to a slip. Depths are 8 to 9 feet.

Marina hours are 8-4 weekdays and 8-3 weekends and holidays. Wireless hookup is available in the office.

Ashore

The marina is well kept and has all the amenities including showers, laundry, water, electricity, fuel and ice. In addition to the 46-room luxury, beachfront hotel, beach, tennis courts, and state of the art gymnasium, there are two restaurants, a casual open air spot on the waterfront and an air-conditioned fine dining establishment with piano bar overlooking the marina.

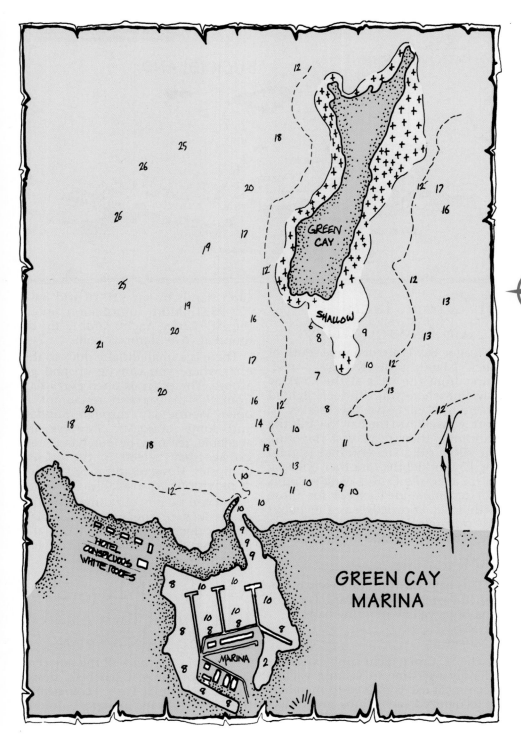

GREEN CAY
MARINA

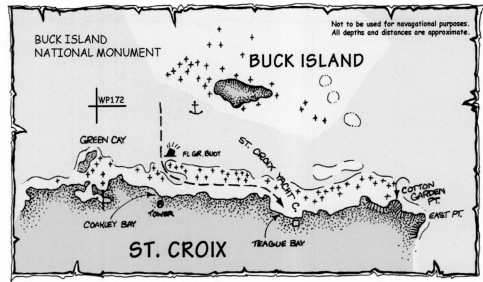

Not to be used for navagational purposes.
All depths and distances are approximate.

BUCK ISLAND
NATIONAL MONUMENT

BUCK ISLAND

WP172

GREEN CAY

ST. CROIX YACHT C.

FL GR. BUOY

COTTON
GARDEN
PT.

TOWER

COAKLEY BAY

EAST PT.

ST. CROIX

TEAGUE BAY

St. Croix Yacht Club/Teague Bay

Teague Bay is about a mile south of Buck Island, protected by a reef. Enter from the west at the Coakley Bay Cut where you will see a lighted green marker. Leave the marker to port, go well into the bay towards the windmill, then head east, favoring the shore side. The entrance is good for 12 foot depths. Another opening in the reef, the Cotton Valley Cut, is not recommended except for those with local knowledge as the buoys are privately maintained and there are patch reefs inside the cut.

Mooring

This bay is within the newly established East End Marine Park. Look for one of its yellow mooring balls.

Ashore

The St. Croix Yacht Club extends a friendly welcome to visiting yachts. Reciprocal use is offered to members of recognized yacht clubs, and others may request a guest pass. The yacht

Club stands by on VHF16 and 340-773-9531. More information about the St. Croix Yacht Club can be found at www.stcroixyc.com.

There is a small dinghy dock to the east, where you can tie up and go ashore. The office is open every day from 9-5. A bar and restaurant is open Wednesday through Sunday and some holidays. Showers are available, ice may be purchased and garbage may be left in the on-site dumpster. However, no fuel, laundry or provisions are available.

You can tie up your dinghy on the main dock to the west or a small dinghy dock to the east. Across the road from the restaurant is a convenience store and deli.

Salt River National Historical Park and Ecological Preserve

Salt River Bay and all the adjacent land surrounding it has been designated a National Park. Ecologically, the bay, with its mangrove forests and sea grass beds, is the heart of a

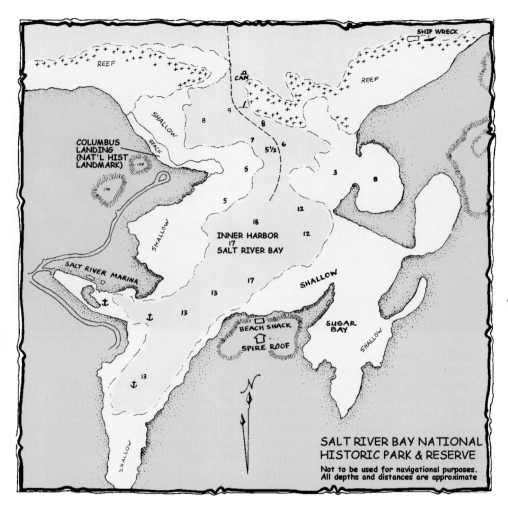

Not to be used for navigational purposes.
All depths and distances are approximate

SALT RIVER BAY NATIONAL
HISTORIC PARK & RESERVE

ANCHORAGES OF THE UNITED STATES VIRGIN ISLANDS

still healthy chain of ecosystems. Historically, this is the only documented Columbus landing site on U.S. soil, and it wasn't a pleasant experience. His armed men went ashore looking for water and were confronted by a canoe full of Indians with bows and arrows. In the altercation that followed, each side had one fatality and all the remaining Indians were taken as slaves.

In 2004, the Park acquired the large white house on the western point, which is now a visitors' center and will eventually include a museum of pre-Columbian artifacts found within the park. The Park is managed jointly by the National Park Service and the V.I. Government.

Navigation

Salt River Bay is in the middle of the island on the north shore. It is a very safe anchorage and a popular hurricane hole but is suitable for shallow draft only, a maximum of 6 feet. Local knowledge is advised to enter, as the channel through the reef is narrow, its marker is privately maintained, and sandbanks extend from both sides of the bay. Use of your engine and your depth sounder

Courtesy of seahawkpaints.com

is advised. Some distance west of the bay you will see a tall marker. This is a scientific device monitoring various physical attributes of the reef. It is part of a NOAA project called CREWS (Coral Reef Early Warning System).

If approaching from the east, avoid White Horse Reef off the eastern point of the bay. This is a small patch reef that doesn't always break. Another reef spans the entrance to the bay, with a narrow channel about midway. There is a green marker at the opening, which you leave to port. Approaching the cut you will see two red mooring buoys about 100 and 150 yards out. Line those up with a spire roof on the south shore of the bay and follow this course through the cut. Once inside the reef, after three or four boat lengths make a dog-leg turn to port.

Turn to starboard as soon as you can align the spire roof with a beach shack in front of it and continue toward that range into the anchorage.

Anchoring

You many anchor anywhere you find sufficient water except in the marina channel. You can leave your dinghy at the marina. There is a dinghy dock near the restaurant and dive shop.

Ashore

Salt River Marina is a small and homey facility tucked into a very protected basin on the west side of the bay. This is a perfect hurricane hole, but as such can be hot and buggy. Space is limited and advance notice is recommended. The marina is open 7 days a week and monitors VHF 16 during daylight hours. All services are available to dockside customers, with fuel requiring 24-hour notice. An open-air restaurant/bar, Columbus Cove, is open every day but Monday. Anchor Dive is also on the premises, offering a very short boat ride to the Salt River Canyon, one of the best dive sites in the

Caribbean. Kayaks can be rented for touring the mangrove-fringed fingers of the bay. Gold Coast Yachts custom designs and builds 40 to 80-foot catamarans on the property. Otherwise, Salt River is not convenient to shore-based services, but taxis can be called and rides to town can be arranged.

Frederiksted

Frederiksted is an open roadstead protected from the prevailing tradewinds, but it can be dangerous in westerlies, which are rare. It's a quaint and charming laid-back town with a mixture of Danish Colonial and Victorian architecture and beautiful parks along the waterfront. Many buildings are in ruins, but a number of restorations are underway.

Navigation

Frederiksted makes a good landfall when sailing from the Spanish Virgin Islands to the west or the Dutch ABCs to the south. Approaching from the south or west, give Sandy Point (the SW extremity of St. Croix) a wide berth. A new red buoy (R2) at 17:39:40Nx64:54:37W is in 60 feet of water outside a shifting sandbar. Approaching from the north you can hug the shore closely at Hams Bluff on the NW corner of the island, but once around stay about 100 yards offshore of the west coast to avoid shoals. At the red destroyer mooring ball you can head east to the beach (Sunset Grill beach bar) and run close to the beach on into Frederiksted.

Simon Scott

Anchoring

South of the cruise ship pier the holding is poor with a thin layer of sand over rock. Holding is better on the north side of the pier and improves as you head north along the beach. The anchorage along the beach away from town is usually quiet but can be rolly if northerly swells are running. Dinghies can be landed on any stretch of the beach or at low docks on either side of the cruise ship pier.

Ashore

This small town has all the basics: a post office, banks, drug store, laundromat, small grocery stores and clothing shops, a barber shop, dive shop and coffee shop. It also has some very special attractions, notably the Caribbean Museum Center for the Arts; the Crucian Chistmas Festival, the local version of carnival, a loud, colorful and boozy event; and, every third Friday, Sunset Jazz, a free concert featuring excellent musicians that brings out a diverse family crowd.. There are quite a few good restaurants in this quiet town—Blue Moon, St. Tropez, Turtles Deli, Motown (for local food), Aqua West and Lost Dog. Good food (and beautiful beaches) can also be found south of town at Beachside Café and north of town at Sunset Grill. Across the road is Sprat Hall Plantation, a small hotel in an historic house. From there you can go horseback riding through the tropical forest. The Department of Tourism has an office near the cruise ship pier in the Courtyard of Pier 69 Restaurant.

Rum Distilleries of the BVI By Julian Putley

Rum is synonymous with the Caribbean. It is as popular today as it ever was and is enjoyed in increasing quantities in cocktails like rum punch, piña coladas, painkillers and Cuba libres. But in many cases rum distilleries have fallen victim to progress where sugar cane fields have become more valuable as real estate and manufacturing costs have made rum production prohibitive except by large modern plants. In the BVI, though, there is a rich heritage of the sugar industry, and its by product rum, and the territory boasts the oldest operational rum distillery in the West Indies.

In the 18th and 19th Centuries the sugar plantation was one of the most dramatic sights in the BVI and the core of the islands' economy. The north shore hillsides were covered in sugar cane, where seedlings were planted in steppes or terraces. During the spring months the cane was harvested, stripped of their leaves and sent to the mill for crushing. Mills were powered either by wind, oxen or mules. Tortola's only surviving windmill is at Mount Healthy and today it is a National Park.

Once the cane was crushed the juice was sent to the factory where it was boiled in a series of iron kettles called "coppers," the fire being fed by bagasse, the cane refuse. The many stages of boiling down the juice were overseen by a Chief Boiler whose expertise on timing and tempering was invaluable. The liquid in the last kettle was cooled and stirred until sugar crystals called muscovado developed. Residue from this process was called molasses, the base for rum.

The molasses was taken to the stillhouse where it was mixed with water, finely chopped bagasse, sugar skimmings from the sugar boiling, lime for tempering, and flavoring like tamarind or citrus fruit. This mixture was known as mash and each plantation had its own recipe, often secretly guarded; a plantation was held in high esteem if the quality of its rum was mellow and flavorful. The mash was allowed to ferment for about a week before it was fed into the still.

The copper potstill was an enclosed cylindrical tank with a gooseneck pipe coming out of the top, which led down to a coil of pipes or "worms," submerged in a bath of cold water. The still was heated and the hot vapors ran down through the cold worms and out came rum. Aging the product in oak casks and blending to taste finished off the process.

When the last of the cane was pushed through the grinders, sounds from a conch shell horn summoned everyone for a bacchanal known as "Cropover." This festival still exists in Barbados but in Tortola has been replaced by the August Emancipation Festival. All the workers got together on the factory grounds and cooked, ate, drank and sometimes danced to the music of a scratch band.

In Tortola today there are reminders of this thriving industry everywhere. The name Cane Garden Bay is self-explanatory. The hillsides rising up from this spectacular beach were alive with waving cane fields while schooners and square riggers were loaded with hogsheads of sugar and demi-johns of rum directly from local "moses" boats. At one time there were seven sugar factories in or near Cane Garden Bay. Just to the east is Brewers Bay, and the ruins of the distillery here are probably the most intact and easily accessible of any on the island. The building with the fireplaces and stoking holes are adjacent to the road and the four coppers, all in a row can be viewed by an easy

Julian Putley

climb into the building. Through the undergrowth the huge copper still is clearly visible. Then there is Cooper Island. Could this have been home to barrel and cask makers?

The Callwood distillery in Cane Garden Bay still produces rum in much the same way as it did 200 years ago. The distillery is at the eastern end of the bay partly sheltered by huge breadfruit trees. Approaching the distillery across a rickety bridge is like walking into a time warp. The old stone building with the potstill resting atop a crumbling fireplace, its tapering gooseneck disappearing into a wall, the smell of smoke and liquor, cane trash lying in a pile and a donkey tethered to a post, are all reminiscent of a bygone era.

The Callwood distillery has been handed down from generation to generation and is now run by Michael Callwood. His family bought the estate in 1899 when it was known as the Arundel estate, and the rum pro-duced today is still called Arundel rum. The distillery began life in the early 18th Century and soon became renowned for producing an excellent quality of liquor, cane being brought from all over Tortola and even Virgin Gorda. Today the rum is made directly from sugar cane juice and the standard of excellence has been maintained. You can buy a dark aged rum which has matured in oak casks for four years or a white rum from demijohns. There is an extravagant claim that Callwood's Arundel rum does not produce hangovers because it is free of chemicals.

Close to Tortola's summit, near Chalwell lies the ruin of another distillery, Joe's Hill Distillery. The old engine that ran the mill, the still itself and the coppers are being removed to the H. Lavity Stoutt College where plans are in progress to build a replica of a 19th Century mill, sugar factory and distillery as part of a "Heritage Village." Directly opposite the Brewers Bay turn-off on Joe's Hill

Julian Putley

themselves, together with the smacks of their thongs and the mules kicking, while their heavy burdens creaked over the tortuous descent..." It is not surprising that most distilleries were built close to the water's edge.

On the north shore at the island's eastern end lies Josiah's Bay and the grounds behind the beach were once home to a thriving plantation. During the prohibition era when it was illegal to export rum to the U.S. the estate was converted into a distillery that used an oil-powered engine to crush the cane. The rum was smuggled to the U.S. Virgin Islands in the hulls of boats covered with charcoal and it proved to be a very lucrative business. The distillery ceased operation sometime during the forties.

Josiah's Bay Plantation has today been partially restored and the outbuildings have been converted into an art gallery and gift shop. There is also an excellent restaurant and bar, The Secret Garden, and around the grounds can be seen the coppers, old still and a cistern that was once used for cooling the "worm."

Road begins an interesting walk through thick undergrowth, past banana fields and wild citrus trees that takes you to the site of the distillery. It is now quite dilapidated as a result of the tenacious roots of tropical trees and vines but one interesting feature here is that the "worm" is still intact in the ruined cistern and large coppers are strewn over the site.

Distilleries that were situated in the hills had the problem of transporting the rum to a transshipment point and the following excerpt from a letter written in 1843 describes loads being brought down from Windy Hill "with mules bringing tierces (casks) down the mountain for shipment. To effect this, they harness the animals by couples into shafts that bear the casks as its poles do a sedan... the drivers' incessant bawling with the beasts and

Baugher's Bay near Road Town is the site of another distillery that is now in a state of such ruin that only the foundations are still visible along with the cistern. But the almost indestructible engine is there for all to see. Rowan Roy who interviewed the late Captain Ernest Pickering, principal owner of the distillery, around 1970 when the factory was still in operation, wrote that, "A mill sits outside the factory and is positioned so that the crushed cane juice runs by gravity into coppers in the factory, while a rum still also outside the factory building is so placed that the fermented mash can also be run by gravity to the still." This was obviously an operation that considered laborsaving important and the accessibility to Road Town harbor was also convenient.

Julian Putley

For about 200 years the production of sugar and rum was the mainstay of the islands' economy and it is only in the last 40 years that tourism and later in the mid 80s offshore financial services have supplanted this once invaluable industry. Road Town is unrecognizable from the way it looked in 1965 with modern office blocks and tourist oriented marinas, retail shops and restaurants. So next time you lift that irresistible rum concoction to your lips think back on its origins – after all in terms of generations it was only yesterday.

Addendum:

Today the popularity of rum and rum drinks has spawned many blended rums. The most famous blended rum in Tortola is Pusser's, a blend of five rums and the recommended ingredient of many cocktails, the most famous being the "Painkiller."

The term Pusser is derived from Purser, the man on board ship responsible for ship's stores, and for over 200 years the Royal Navy distributed a rum ration to the sailors: this ceased in 1970. In 1979, Charles Tobias, founder of Pusser's West Indies Ltd., obtained license from the Admiralty to blend the famous rum and soon it was being bottled in Tortola, where it is widely available today.

Other blended rums in Tortola are Foxy's Firewater available from the famous beach bar on Jost Van Dyke; Saba Rock Rum from North Sound, Virgin Gorda and the "Rum Stoned Captain's Choice" from the Last Resort in Trellis Bay. The Sandcastle also has its own rum as does the Bitter End, which also makes a spiced rum. Probably the best loved spiced rum in the islands is Tortola's Spiced Rum, Pirates' Blend. It is made from Tortola's own Arundel rum and blended with cane syrup, fresh cloves, cinnamon and ginger.

Regional rums are available in the islands' liquor stores and perhaps the most popular is Barbados' Mount Gay. Bacardi of Puerto Rico and Cruzan of St. Croix are also popular. Anyone wishing to learn more about rum should pick up a copy of Ed Hamilton's book, *"Rums of the Eastern Caribbean."*

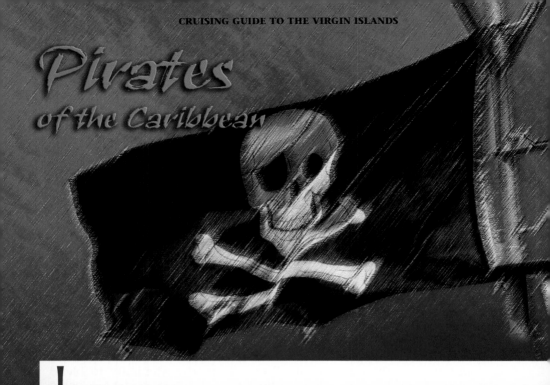

Pirates
of the Caribbean

I t is just as well that there are no longer any pirates in the Virgin Islands. Imagine yourself reclining in the cockpit of the yacht after a difficult hour trying to make the anchor stay put. The piña colada is nice and cold. The kids' yelling has receded into the distance as they explore the shoreline, collecting sea urchin spines in their feet. Your wife is perfecting her suntan on the foredeck and the other couple, who used to be your oldest friends until you decided to charter a yacht together, are arguing through clenched teeth in the galley. A perfect vacation in the Caribbean.

Then, as the sun begins to sink towards the horizon, a small sloop veers into the cove you thought you had to yourselves. An anchor splashes overboard and, before you have finished spraying your ankles with insect repellent, a horde of noisy, unshaven thugs row across to your boat and, without so much as a by-your-leave, swarm on deck, empty your wallet, your liquor cabinet and your fridge, and steal your camera and your wife.

It wouldn't do much for the charter business.

Although piracy is no longer a popular pastime in the V.I., it is really not that long since it was all the rage throughout the Caribbean. In the early 1700s, a sympathetic governor in St. Thomas was still fencing goods for pirates like Charles Vane and Edward Teach (the legendary Blackbeard), and as late as 1869 the steamship Telegrafo was detained in Tortola and charged with piracy.

Nor is there anything new about sailors dabbling in "the sweet trade".

As long as men have transported anything of value across the ocean, there have been others willing to relieve them of it. Even the Bible speaks of "princes of the sea". Julius Caesar had first-hand experience of these — he was kidnapped and held for ransom by them, and his invasion of Britain was partly in order to subdue the Veneti pirata and their British crews.

For several hundred years the Vikings made annual raids along the coasts of Western Europe, and in the Middle Ages, as trade and travel by sea expanded, piracy got underway with a vengeance.

"Privateering" also came into vogue at this time. A pirate called Eustace The Monk, who was believed to have black magic powers, did well plundering French ships on behalf of England's King John. Privateering was basically government-sponsored piracy — tacit approval given to raids on the ships of potential enemies. Privately owned vessels manned by civilians were commissioned with "letters of marque" as auxiliaries to the Royal Navy. They were used mainly against merchant shipping and were actively encouraged by monarchs in times of war or hostility. (As the 16th and early 17th centuries saw Europe in a fairly constant state of turmoil, this meant that they were encouraged most of the time.) Since a healthy percentage of the "purchase" went to the Crown, there was an added incentive for Royalty to turn a blind eye to the often extreme actions of the privateers and a deaf ear to the whining and complaining of the Ambassadors from semi-hostile nations.

A prime example of this sanctioning of successful piracy was, of course, the way in which Queen Elizabeth I dealt with Sir Francis Drake. His famous round-the-world voyage actually evolved from a plan to raid the Spanish-American towns along the Pacific coast during an interval when England was theoretically at peace with Spain.

However, when he returned with a treasure worth at least $5 million, the Virgin Queen boarded his ship, the Golden Hind, ignoring the Spanish demands that "El Draque" be hanged, and knighted him instead. This led Sir Walter Raleigh to make the (still pertinent) comment, "Did you ever know of any that were pirates for millions? They only that work for small things are pirates."

Having laid claim to all of the Americas and the West Indies, Spain was the most powerful nation in the world at this time. Other nations, though afraid to challenge the monopoly directly, were happy to see pirates siphoning off funds intended for the Spanish Reformation by intercepting the treasure ships loaded with Aztec gold. The increasing number of privateers also provided a handy pool of trained sailors who could be called upon in times of outright conflict.

Numerous ex-pirates played an important role in the eventual defeat of the Spanish Armada. In times of covert hostility they could go back to being privateers (the "legality" made visiting ports for supplies easier), and in the infrequent and uneasy intervals of peace they resorted to plain piracy — their status was largely dependent upon the diplomatic label given to it at the time.

In reality their lives changed very little. If pressganged into the Navy they could expect long voyages, harsh discipline, vile food and a good chance of an early demise — all for a pathetic pittance which would be cut off abruptly in peacetime. As pirates, their conditions at sea were little better but were offset by a freer democratic lifestyle, a similar chance of survival and the possibility of vast financial reward. As Bartholomew Roberts, one of the most successful pirates of the early 18th century, commented, "In an honest service there is thin rations, low wages and hard labor; in this, plenty and satiety, pleasure and ease, liberty and power; and who would not balance creditor on this side, when all the hazard that is run for it, at worst, is only a sour look or two at choking. No, 'a merry life and a short one' shall be my motto."

The defeat of the Armada intensified the harassment of Spanish merchant ships and allowed English, French and Dutch colonies to germinate in the now undefended West Indies.

Some of the first colonists were the inerrant French boucaniers who settled on Hispaniola.

They made a meager living barbecuing beef in smokehouses called boucans and selling it to passing vessels. Foolishly the Spaniards drove them off the island; in revenge they took to the sea where, instead of hunting wild cattle, they went after Spanish ships instead.

"Buccaneer" became a new and fearful term for "pirate", and their ranks swelled as out-of-work naval crews drifted to the new world. New colonies struggling desperately to gain a

Jost Van Dyke from Smuggler's Cove   Simon Scott

foothold were a willing market for plundered goods. The governors of these new settlements gained a 10% commission for issuing letters of marque to privateers and, as a result, Jamaica's Port Royal became one of the richest towns in the hemisphere because of pirate gold. It also became known as "the wickedest city in the world," but it was largely due to the transient population of fighting sailors that the British were able to keep Jamaica. As late as 1774, historian Edward Long wrote, "It is to the buccaneers that we owe possession of Jamaica to this hour."

So the pirates were a vital part of the colonization of the West Indies. Henry Morgan, for example, dealt terrible blows to Spanish dominance when he attacked Spanish shipping, ransomed Puerto de Principe in Cuba, assaulted Porto Bello and burned Panama City to the ground. Despite a new treaty with Spain, neither Morgan nor the governor who issued the commission was ever punished, possibly because of the shares received by the King and his brother, the Duke of York.

The Spanish meted out their own punishment if they caught pirates or privateers. They made no distinction between the two except that privateers were sent to the gallows with their commissions tied around their necks. Hanging was the usual end for captured pirates, although, if they were unlucky enough to fall into the hands of the Inquisition, they might receive a more drawn-out demise on the rack.

Some of the evil vermin who gravitated to a life of piracy were very capable of perpetrating their own unique atrocities. Most pirates had a weakness for "rumbul-lion" and

in their cups would often torment their prisoners for entertainment. Blackbeard was said to have made one victim eat his own nose and lips; another Englishman named Thomas Cobham sewed 20 Spaniards up in a mainsail and threw the whole squirming package overboard.

"Going on the account" was the term used when a man signed up for a career in piracy; this basically meant "no prey, no pay," but all the crew were shareholders in the "company" and part owners of the ship. The company typically began with a very modest vessel — some of the early buccaneers used dug-out canoes —but after a few killings on the market, they would generally acquire more suitable headquarters.

The ideal pirate vessel was small and fast. Bermudan sloops were felt to be ideal because of their speed (over 11 knots) and maneuverability, and could carry up to 75 men. A bigger company might go for a brigantine, a two-masted vessel that could carry either a square or fore-and-aft rig or a versatile combination of the two.

This was often how pirates made their assaults, sneaking out from the coast in poor light to spring upon a sluggish merchantman. The Virgin Islands made an excellent hunting ground with their myriad coves and passages. Situated right on the treasure route from South America to Europe, the area was visited by many notorious Caribbean pirates such as Edward England, whose kind treatment of prisoners so disgusted his crew that he was deposed; Charles Vane, who Defoe reported, "died in Agonies equal to his Villainies but showed not the least Remorse for the Crimes of his past life"; Calico Jack, well known for his romance with lady pirate Anne Bonny; Bartholomew Roberts, who became one of the greatest pirates of all "for the love of novelty and change alone"; and the formidable Blackbeard, who would go into battle with slow-burning matches alight in his beard and behind his ears to enhance his devilish resemblance.

By the early 18th century, competition for prizes in the Caribbean was strong. A treaty in 1713 allowed the Navy time to begin protecting merchant shipping (for a price that was almost robbery in itself).

As the colonies in the island began to stabilize, law and order made the pirates less welcome as members of the community. Many of them set off for the North American mainland, where the newer colonists, already muttering about Independence, were quite pleased to help the newcomers harass British shipping magnates. Others headed for the Orient, the Red Sea, the Indian Ocean and Madagascar.

Since then piracy has continued to flourish in the Far East, but has been quelled fairly effectively in the West.

Smuggling, however, is another matter —

recent years have seen a resurgence in the "sweet trade".

The traditions haven't changed much; seaport bars still abound with tales of sailors sneaking around dark shores in small, fast boats, dodging the authorities, sending coded messages at dead of night and risking life and liberty for high stakes.

Ivan's Local Flavor Stress Free Bar **Simon Scott**

The Real Dead Chest

By Julian Putley

The second of the hugely popular Pirates of the Caribbean movie series, Dead Man's Chest opened in 2006 to record breaking attendance and rave reviews.

However, though there are few that haven't at least heard of the film, most are unaware of the identity of the real Dead Chest Cay, Dead Man's Bay, and the actual hidden treasure chest full of "Pieces of Eight". The story unfolds in the British Virgin Islands, our very own veritable paradise.

On the south side of the Sir Francis Drake Channel and just to the east of Peter Island is the cay named Dead Chest. In the days of yore a "dead man's chest" was the name for a coffin, the outline of which you can make out when viewing the island from the northwest. Look even longer and the coffin appears to contain a shrouded body with a raised head. As long ago as the late 1700s the cay's moniker was Dead Chest, clearly marked on Jeffrey's 18th century chart of the Virgin Islands. Folklore has it that the infamous pirate Blackbeard marooned fifteen men on the cay with nothing but a bottle of rum. Some apparently tried to swim the half mile to Peter Island's eastern cove but didn't make it, giving this beautiful palm lined bay the ominous name, "Dead Man's Bay".

At a much later date author Robert Louis Stevenson researched events in the area, studying nautical charts (his passion), as well as historical events and Caribbean lore. The well documented piracy of a huge treasure, much of which had been buried on Norman Island, most likely provided him with valuable information the culmination of which resulted in the much loved Treasure Island. Thus, Dead Chest Cay came to be immortalized in the famous refrain:

Fifteen Men on the Dead Man's Chest,
Yo-ho-ho and a bottle of rum!
Drink and the devil had done for the rest.
Yo-ho-ho and a bottle of rum!

Perhaps the most captivating aspect of the many similar themes of the film and the true story of the piracy in the Virgin Islands is that both involve treasure chests. In the BVI a daring act of piracy led to the burying of a cache of treasure on Norman Island in the year 1750. Some 160 years after the event a treasure chest of "Pieces of Eight" was discovered in the southernmost cave on the leeward side of the peninsula that crests at Treasure Point. Mention of the discovery is made in no less than three publications. We won't tell you what happens in the film... you have to go and see it!

It is interesting to note that the 2006 film Pirates of the Caribbean, Dead Man's Chest and Robert Louis Stevenson's book of 1883, Treasure Island   (and over 50 films based on the book) were both phenomenal successes of their time. It is also remarkable that our tiny cay in the British Virgin Islands, Dead Chest Cay, should be such a major player.

"Yo-ho-ho and a bottle of rum!!"

Julian Putley is the author of "The Virgins' Treasure Isle," the story of the daring piracy and subsequent burying of it on Norman Island in the BVI.

The BVI Music Fest: Sun, Sand and Music
By Claudia Colli

For the past seven years, Cane Garden Bay has been the site of the Virgin Islands most ambitious music festival, the BVI Music Fest by the Sea, a three-day extravaganza that features some of the worlds top musical performers. Concert-goers stand at the edge of the sea on beautiful Cane Garden Bay, water lapping at their feet and sand between their toes as music legends like Jimmy Cliff, Percy Sledge, Roberta Flack and Maxi Priest play from the big stage.

This is not your ordinary concert, but then again Tortola is a magical place where extraordinary things can happen and an international music fest on a palm fringed beach is just one of them. For three nights and two days, Cane Garden Bay turns into a musical Mecca where people from around the globe come to share music and the beauty of Cane Garden Bay with hundreds of music-loving islanders.

Many of the festival-goers are yachtsmen, who cruise into Cane Garden Bay, one of the B.V.I.s most popular anchorages, for one or more days. There are no better seats in the house than sitting on the deck of a boat with the sounds of reggae, soca and jazz being carried off-shore by the trade winds. But of course, the main action is on shore, and as the night cools down, and the music heats up, sailors dinghy to shore and join the throngs on the beach as the artists take to the stage.

Held the last weekend of May, the event is hosted by the BVI Tourist Board and is organized by BVI entrepreneur Frank Mahoney, a music lover who saw the festival as a way of attracting visitors to the Territory in the off-season. There are also a plethora of local sponsors from cell phone companies to banks.

The 2008 Music Festival was once again jam packed with stars from the

Caribbean and the US. As always, Friday, the Festivals opening night, was primarily devoted to Calypso. David Rudder is from Trinidad, the birthplace of Calypso, and his fresh and original songs have helped usher in a new era for Calypso music. Arrow, a Soca superstar from Montserrat, also performed on Friday night. His best selling number, Hot, Hot, Hot has taken Calypso to a brash new level.

Saturday night, or Reggae Night, traditionally attracts the greatest crowds, and the beach was packed with lovers of the cool sounds of Jamaica. Damien Junior Gong Marley, the son of reggae icon, Bob Marley, had the crowds rocking until the early hours. He was followed by popular Jamaican Dance Hall artist, Beenie Man, who closed out the night at 4am.

On Sunday, the Bay became more mellow as R&B star, Jerry Butler, took to the stage. Known as the Ice Man Butlers career has spanned four decades, and his iconic song, Your Precious Love, had the crowd slow dancing on the sand. He was followed by En Vogue, the popular 90s girl group and another R & B legend, Jeffrey Osborne, who wowed the audience with hit songs that included his emblematic ballad, On the Wings of Love.

You dont necessarily have to be a late night person to enjoy the Festival. There is plenty to do in the daytime as well. For families, the days activities include all the normal beach fare swimming, sunning and liming on the beach. There are fashion shows and beach games, and the many restaurants on the Bay open special beachside booths serving local food and drink. Music, though, is always present, whether it is local fungi band music, steel pan or a DJ spinning his platters.

Each year, the music gets better, but the setting always remains the same as one of the worlds most beautiful bays becomes one of its most vibrant musical stages. For more information on the BVI Music Festival and its artists go to www.bvimusicfest.net

West Indian

Grub & Grog

Few recipes have actually survived from the days of the Arawaks, although we know they hunted agouti and iguana, made cassava bread and seasoned their foods with salt and pepper. Arawak hunters reputedly caught wild duck and fowl by covering their heads with gourds (cutting tiny eye slits) and standing neck-deep in the swamps or lagoons until an unwary bird passed near enough to grab it by the legs and drown it!

The Caribs' favourite recipes are unlikely to prove popular today, but the pirates provided us with a still-popular cooking technique: The word boucan means to cure meat by smoking strips over a slow fire, which is what the early brethren did with the wild pigs and cattle which escaped or were "liberated" from the farms of Spanish settlers. Hence these men came to be called boucaniers. Eventually they returned to the sea as buccaneers, where, of course, they drank rum, still the basis for many West Indian drinks. Made by the fermentation of molasses or cane juice, rum was defined in 1909 as "the spirit of sugar" and was originally called kill-devil or rumbullion.

Generally, West Indian foods represent the cosmopolitan visitors who have passed through the islands over the centuries — South Americans, East Indians, Chinese, Europeans and Africans — so there is no single "West Indian" style of cooking. What has evolved, however, is a fascinating hodgepodge of customs and cuisines reflecting their diverse origins.

Blanchard's has been hailed as one of the best restaurants in the Caribbean. Bob and Melinda Blanchard are the creative founders of this tropical dining experience set in Mead's Bay, Anguilla. The cuisine is creative and sophisticated with flavors from the Caribbean, Asia, America and the Mediterranean. Fortunately for us they are sharing their recipes in two recipe books: *Cook What You Love* and *At Blanchard's Table*. These cookbooks are recommended by the staff of Cruising Guide Publications – they are some of our favorites! The following recipes were selected from their books.

MARINATED GINGER SHRIMP WITH LEMON-PARMESAN DIPPING SAUCE

* SERVES 6

FOR THE DIPPING SAUCE
1-1/2 cups Hellmann's mayonnaise
1 tablespoon freshly grated lemon peel
3 tablespoons freshly squeezed lemon juice
1 tablespoon Dijon mustard
1/4 cup freshly grated Parmesan cheese
Salt and freshly ground black pepper

FOR THE SHRIMP
1-1/2 pounds large shrimp
1/4 cup soy sauce
1/2 cup freshly squeezed lemon juice
2 small garlic cloves, minced
1 tablespoon minced peeled fresh ginger
1/4 cup sugar
1/4 cup corn oil

In a medium bowl, mix together the mayonnaise, lemon peel, lemon juice, mustard, and cheese. Add salt and pepper to taste and refrigerate until needed.
Bring a large saucepan of lightly salted water to a boil. Add the unpeeled shrimp, cover, and cook over medium heat until pink and firm, about 2 minutes. Drain well and peel, leaving the tails intact.
In a small bowl, combine the soy sauce, lemon juice, garlic, ginger, sugar, and oil, and whisk until blended. Add the shrimp, toss well, and marinate in the refrigerator for 15 minutes.
Remove the shrimp from the marinade, transfer to a serving bowl, and serve with the dipping sauce.

CHILLED AVOCADO-LIME SOUP WITH SHRIMP AND CHILIES

* SERVES 4

THIS IS A COOL, LIGHT SUMMER SOUP. FOR A RICHER VERSION, SUBSTITUTE HEAVY CREAM FOR SOME OR ALL OF THE MILK. IF YOU'RE NOT A CILANTRO FAN, SNIP SOME FRESH CHIVES OVER EACH BOWL INSTEAD.

10 cooked medium shrimp, chilled, deveined, and sliced horizontally
Salt and freshly ground black pepper
1 tablespoon olive oil
1/3 cup   freshly squeezed lime juice
2 pounds ripe avocados, peeled and chopped
3 cups chicken broth
1 cup milk
1 jalapeño pepper, seeded and minced
Pinch dried red pepper flakes
1-1/2 tablespoons coarsely chopped fresh cilantro, plus more for garnish

In a small bowl, sprinkle the cooked shrimp with salt and pepper, and toss with the oil and 2 tablespoons lime juice. Let stand for 15 minutes.
In the bowl of a food processor, puree the avocados and chicken broth until very smooth. Add the milk and process until blended. Add 3 tablespoons lime juice, the minced jalapeño pepper, and the pepper flakes, pulsing until blended. Add salt, pepper, and more lime juice to taste.
Ladle the soup into bowls, float 5 shrimp halves on the top of each, and garnish with cilantro.

WEST INDIAN GRUB & GROG

MARINATED RED AND YELLOW PEPPERS

* SERVES 6

THESE PEPPERS ARE A STAPLE IN OUR HOUSE. THEY ADD BRILLIANT COLOR AND EARTHY FLAVOR TO ALMOST ANYTHING. SERVE THEM AS AN APPETIZER ALONG WITH MARINATED OLIVES AND A CRUSTY LOAF OF BREAD OR AS A SIDE DISH WITH GRILLED CHICKEN OR FISH. WE KEEP PLENTY ON HAND TO ADD TO SALADS, PASTA, AND SANDWICHES.

3 red bell peppers, cut in half lengthwise and seeded
3 yellow bell peppers, cut in half lengthwise and seeded
3 garlic cloves, minced
2 tablespoons fresh basil, roughly chopped
1 tablespoon fresh rosemary leaves, chopped
3 tablespoons olive oil
1 tablespoon freshly squeezed lemon juice
Salt and freshly ground black pepper

Preheat the broiler or prepare grill. If using a broiler, place the peppers skin side up on oiled sheet pan and cook until the skin is blistered and black. If using a grill, place the peppers skin side down and blacken the skin thoroughly. Transfer the peppers to a large bowl and immediately cover with plastic wrap. Allow the peppers to steam in the bowl until cool enough to handle, 20 to 30 minutes.
Remove the skin from the peppers and arrange them on a serving dish. In a small bowl, combine all the other ingredients and spoon evenly over the peppers. Season with salt and pepper. Cover and refrigerate for at least 1 hour and up to 1 week. Serve at room temperature for the best flavor.

ISLAND RICE WITH CUMIN AND COCONUT

* SERVES 4

TOO OFTEN, RICE IS JUST A BACKDROP FOR SOMETHING ELSE. THIS DELICIOUS VARIATION STANDS ON ITS OWN AND OFFERS GREAT FLAVOR. IF YOU HAVE ANY LEFT OVER, TRY TOSSING IT WITH A LITTLE VINAIGRETTE THE NEXT DAY FOR A SALAD.

1 tablespoon unsalted butter
2 shallots, minced
1 cup long-grain white rice
2 teaspoons ground cumin
1/4 cup shredded, unsweetened coconut
1-3/4 cups chicken broth
1/4 cup raisins
2 tablespoons chopped fresh parsley
Salt and freshly ground black pepper

Melt the butter in a medium saucepan over medium heat, and cook the shallots until soft. Add the rice and cumin, and cook for 2 minutes. Add the coconut, broth, and raisins, and bring to a boil. Cover and cook over low heat until all the liquid is absorbed, 12 to 15 minutes. Fluff with a fork, add the parsley, and taste for salt and pepper. Serve immediately.

REGGAE PORK

NEXT TIME IT'S COLD AND GRAY OUTSIDE AND YOU NEED A SHOT OF SUNSHINE, GIVE THIS A TRY. PUT ON SOME ISLAND MUSIC — BOB MARLEY OR JIMMY BUFFETT WORKS WELL—AND MAKE SOME REGGAE PORK.

Prep time: 36 minutes (including 30 minutes marinating time)
Cooking time: 6 minutes

* SERVES 4

1/4 cup fresh lime juice
1/4 cup plus 2 tablespoons dark rum
¼ cup pineapple juice
1-1/4 pounds pork tenderloin, trimmed of fat and sliced 1/2 inch thick
8 ounces guava jelly
Kosher salt and freshly ground black pepper
Olive oil

In a medium bowl, whisk together the lime juice, 1/4 cup rum, and the pineapple juice. Add the pork and marinate for 30 minutes to 1 hour. While the pork is marinating, warm the guava jelly and remaining 2 tablespoons of rum in a small saucepan. Remove from the heat and set aside.
Remove the pork from the marinade, pat until very dry with paper towels, and sprinkle with salt and pepper. Discard the marinade. In a large sauté pan, warm enough oil to cover the bottom of the pan over medium-high heat. Heat the oil until it is hot but not smoking. Cook the pork, turning only once, for 3 minutes on each side, or until cooked through and lightly browned. Drizzle the pork with the warm guava jelly and rum mixture and serve immediately.

TEQUILA SHRIMP WITH SAFFRON RICE

THIS VARIATION ON A CLASSIC PAELLA IS COLORFUL AND HAS TREMENDOUS DEPTH OF FLAVOR—AND THE PEPPERY SAUSAGE GIVES IT A LITTLE KICK. OUR PREP TIME INCLUDES PREPARING THE SHRIMP BUT IT'S, EVEN EASIER IF YOU BUY SHRIMP THAT'S BEEN PEELED AND DEVEINED.

Prep time: 20 minutes
Cooking time: 40 minutes

* SERVES 6

1/4 cup olive oil
5 medium garlic cloves, thinly sliced
1 large onion, chopped
1 large red bell pepper, chopped
1/2 pound chorizo (Spanish sausage), thinly sliced
3 large ripe tomatoes, chopped
1 (19-ounce) can black beans, drained
1-1/2 cups tequila
1-1/4 cups chicken broth
1-1/2 cups long-grain white rice
1 teaspoon kosher salt
1 large pinch saffron threads
1/4 teaspoon turmeric
1-1/2 pounds large shrimp, peeled and deveined
Preheat the oven to 400°F.
In a large, shallow ovenproof casserole or paella pan, heat the oil over medium heat. Add the garlic, onion, and bell pepper and cook for 4 minutes, stirring occasionally. Add the chorizo and cook for 1 minute. Add the tomatoes and beans and stir well. Increase the heat to high and add the tequi-

la, chicken broth, rice, salt, saffron, and turmeric and stir well again. Cover and bring to a boil. Reduce the heat to medium and simmer for 10 minutes.

Add the shrimp, mix well, and bake uncovered for 15 minutes, or until the shrimp is cooked and the rice has absorbed the liquid.

GRILLED CINNAMON BANANAS

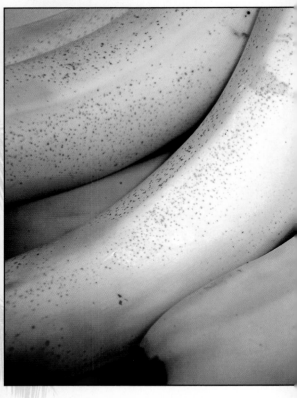

These sweet glazed bananas make a great accompaniment to spicy foods. In the restaurant we serve them every night with our hot Jamaican jerk shrimp, a powerful, spicy dish that has become one of our most popular items. Try to find firm, just ripe bananas. If they're too green, a bitter taste will come through. If they're too soft, they won't hold up on the grill.

Prep time: 5 minutes
Cooking time: 10 minutes
Serves: 8

2 tablespoons unsalted butter
1/4 cup molasses
1 teaspoon Myers dark rum
1 teaspoon ground cinnamon
1 tablespoon honey
4 ripe, firm bananas

Prepare an outdoor grill or heat a grill pan over medium-high heat on the stove.

Place all the ingredients except the bananas in a medium saucepan and cook over a very low heat just until combined. Cut the bananas in half lengthwise, leaving the peels on. Brush the glaze on the cut side of the banana halves and place skin side down on the grill.

Cook until soft, about 8 minutes. Using tongs, carefully turn the bananas over and cook for 1 to 2 minutes on the cut side. Serve immediately, glazed side up.

MANGOES AND CREAM

* SERVES 4

THIS IS ONE OF OUR EASIEST AND MOST POP-
ULAR DESSERTS. PEACHES CAN EASILY BE
SUBSTITUTED FOR THE MANGOES IF YOU PRE-
FER.

3 large ripe mangoes, peeled
1 cup heavy whipping cream
2 to 3 tablespoons granulated sugar
1 teaspoon vanilla extract
light brown sugar, for sprinkling
ground cinnamon, for sprinkling

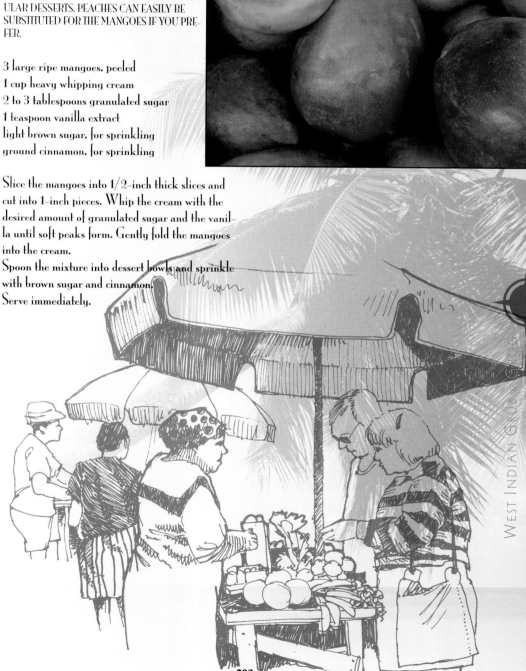

Slice the mangoes into 1/2-inch thick slices and
cut into 1-inch pieces. Whip the cream with the
desired amount of granulated sugar and the vanilla until soft peaks form. Gently fold the mangoes
into the cream.
Spoon the mixture into dessert bowls and sprinkle
with brown sugar and cinnamon.
Serve immediately.

WEST INDIAN GRUB × GLOG

The Origin of Grog

True "grog" had its beginning in the Royal Navy in the 18th century — specifically on August 21, 1740. It is the most traditional of all sea drinks.

Prior to 1740, Pusser's Rum was issued to the men "neat" — that is without water. But Admiral Vernon, the hero of Porto Bello and Commander-in-Chief West Indies was to change all this by the issuance of his infamous Order to Captains No. 349, given on board his flagship HMS Burford on August 21, 1740.

His order refers to the

"...unanimous opinion of both Captains and Surgeons that the pernicious allowance of rum in drams, and often at once, is attended with many fatal effects to their morals as well as their health besides the ill consequences of stupefying their rational qualities.

...You are hereby required and directed...that the respective daily allowance... be every day mixed with the proportion of a quart of water to a half pint of rum, to be mixed in a scuttled butt kept for that purpose, and to be done upon the deck, and in the presence of the Lieutenant of the Watch, who is to take particular care to see that the men are not defrauded in having their full allowance of rum."

The tars had already nicknamed Vernon "Old Grog" from the grosgrain cloak he often wore when on the quarterdeck. The watered rum gave great offense to the men, and soon they began referring to it contemptuously as "grog" from the name they'd already provided Vernon.

Vernon's order provided that every man's half-pint Pusser's Rum allowance be diluted with one quart water. This was later changed to two parts water and one rum. In 1756, the daily ration was increased to one pint per man! Just before the end in 1970, it was reduced to one-eighth pint.

On board another ship of Vernon's squadron, the HMS Berwick, and just after the issuance of Vernon's order, one of the men wrote this poem that became famous throughout England:

"A mighty bowl on deck he drew
    And filled it to the brink.
Such drank the Burford's gallant crew
    And such the Gods shall drink.
The sacred robe which Vernon wore
    Was drenched within the same,
And Hence its virtues guard our shore
    And Grog derives its name."

LIMEY

Tall glass or old-fashioned glass
filled with ice cubes
2 ozs. Pussers Rum
Soda water

Squeeze the juice from one half lime. Add
sugar to taste (optional, but not traditional). Top
off with soda water, stir, and float the expended
lime peel on top.

ROYAL NAVY FOG CUTTER

Ice cubes to fill shaker
2 ozs. Pusser's Rum
1/2 ounce gin
1/4 cup lemon juice
2 tbsps. orange juice
1 tbsp. orgeat syrup
1 tsp. dry sherry
Fruit slices for garnish

THE BIG DIPPER

Ice cubes to fill shaker
1 oz. Pusser's Rum
1 oz. brandy
1 tbsp. lime juice
1/2 tsp. sugar
dash of Cointreau
Club soda

Shake well rum, brandy, lime juice, sugar and
Cointreau. Strain into an old-fashioned glass
with several ice cubes, fill with club soda and stir
slightly. This is a popular drink on Atlantic
crossings just before star time.

EMPIRE TOP

2 parts Pusser's Rum
1 part French Vermouth
1 part Grand Marnier
1 dash Angostura bitters
Crushed ice

Shake all the ingredients well and serve.

DIFFERENT DRUMMER

3 cups orange juice
3/4 cup coffee liqueur
6 orange or lemon slices (garnish)
3/4 cup Jamaican or dark rum
2 dozen ice cubes

Combine ingredients and shake well. Garnish
with orange or lemon slices and serve immediately. Serves 6.

PLANTER'S PUNCH

1 cup cracked ice
3 ozs. Pusser's Rum
1 oz. lime juice
1 oz. sugar syrup
3–5 dashes Angostura bitters
soda water

Shake all ingredients together well and pour
unstrained into tall glass with several ice cubes.
Top off with soda water, stir, garnish with lime
slice and serve with a straw.

THE DEEP SIX

Tall glass filled with crushed ice
2 ozs. Pusser's Rum
1 tbsp. lime juice
1'2 ounce sugar syrup
Champagne

Combine rum, lime juice and sugar, and stir well.
Fill glass with champagne and stir gently.
Garnish with a slice of lime. This is an unusual
drink — smooth, flavorful & powerful.

FORCE 12

Ice cubes to fill shaker
1/4 cup Pusser's Rum
1 oz. vodka
1 tbsp. lime juice
1 tbsp. grenadine
1/4 cup pineapple juice

Shake well and pour into tall glass. Garnish with
fruit slices. This drink is a good test for sea legs.

WEST INDIAN GRUB & GROG

"The Origin of Grog" and the above recipes are provided courtesy of Pussers Ltd., Road Town, Tortola, B.V.I.

Fabulous Island Fruits & Vegetables

A collection of some of the most delicious tropical produce to be found in the Virgin Islands.

Sugar Apple

   A favourite throughout the islands, the sugar apple looks like it wears a coat of armour! Actually when ripe, it breaks open easily and the delicious, custard-like interior can be scooped out by the spoonful or by eating it by the mouthful, taking care to spit out the shiny seeds inside. It is well worth the effort, as the inside is sweet, with a wonderful sort of soft texture.

Guava

This colourful fruit is used for making jams, jellies, and is scrumptious in pies and tarts. The guava is a small, usually round fruit that grows on a tree. The skin is green to yellow-green, and pulp inside is pink or peach to an almost red colour, with lines of seeds. Guava ice cream is a delicacy not to be missed.

Passion Fruit

Despite the connotation of the name, this fruit may be rather baffling to the first time taster. It is actually quite unattractive with a tough, wrinkly, brownish skin and is about the size of a lemon. The interior has a yellow green jellyish pulp with edible brown seeds. When the seeds are removed, the passion fruit essence is used to flavour exotic drinks, ices, tarts and pies, becoming an interesting, perfumey addition to many recipes.

Genip

Looking like a bunch of green grapes, these small, round fruits are a bit more challenging to eat! First the somewhat tough skin encasing the pulp must be pulled off (usually with your teeth). Once the skin is gone, the inside is yours to tug the sweet, sometimes tart pulp from the rather large pit. Although not easy fruits to eat, genips can keep you busy for quite awhile!

Ugli Fruit

Resembling an ugly version of a grapefruit the ugli fruit is light green to a yellowy orange colour, and can be the size of an orange to the size of a large grapefruit. Succulent and dripping with juice it is best eaten the same way as a grapefruit or an orange (the skin is easily peeled). If you have an opportunity to try this wondrous fruit, be sure to enjoy its blessings.

Tamarind

Growing from large, lovely shade trees are the pods of the tamarind tree. Used in many sauces such as Worcestershire, chutney, and piccalilli, tamarind is also used for sweet candies, and jams. One has to develop a taste for this often tart fruit, but, once acquired, it is hard to stop the attachment. To eat you must first crack open the pod, remove the threads and then consume the sticky paste attached to the large seeds.

Papaya

Growing from a tall, slender umbrella-shaped tree, the fabulous "paw-paw" varies from an eggplant shape to an oval or round shape. The colours vary from a green to orange or yellow, but the fruits must be tested by squeezing to ascertain whether it is ripe or not. The texture of the lovely orange, melon like interior of the fruit is almost as heavenly as the taste, especially when sprinkled with a bit of fresh lime. Green papaya still hard to the squeeze, is used as a cooked vegetable in many delectable recipes.

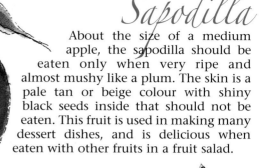

Sapodilla

About the size of a medium apple, the sapodilla should be eaten only when very ripe and almost mushy like a plum. The skin is a pale tan or beige colour with shiny black seeds inside that should not be eaten. This fruit is used in making many dessert dishes, and is delicious when eaten with other fruits in a fruit salad.

Soursop

A very unlikely looking delicacy this fruit is large (often weighing several pounds), with a green, spiny exterior. The shape is like that of a large pine cone irregularly formed. Only very few are eaten fresh, as most are used in flavouring other dishes with it's sweet fragrance, like soursop ice cream, or in tropical fruit drinks with a healthy measure of rum!

Mango

The mango grows from a large, leafy tree that during mango season becomes heavily laden with its scented fruit. Mangos come in many varieties, but are usually best eaten at the beach, where one can jump into the sea to clean off the delicious stickiness. Grafted mangos are less fibrous, and when peeled are a delight. One may see children and adults sucking on mangos to extract the juicy, orange flesh from the fibers and bulky seed in the middle.

Breadfruit

The breadfruit tree is a common sight on many Caribbean islands. Mature fruits have dimpled green skins and grow to 6 inches or larger in clusters on magnificent trees of up to 60 feet in height with huge, long-fingered leaves. Inside, the soft, fleshy fruits are yellowish-brown to white in color and rich in carbohydrates and vitamins A, B and C. Breadfruit can be cooked as a starchy vegetable side dish or in breadfruit breads, puddings and pies. Try it baked with salt, pepper and butter.

Dasheen

This versatile plant grows to a height of four to six feet. The large, handsome, arrow-shaped leaves, sometimes called elephant ears, are similar to spinach. The young, tender leaves are used in callaloo soup, while the tubers, shown here, are generally stubby and similar in size to potatoes. Also called cocoyam, taro, eddo and kalo, the dasheen tubers are usually boiled, roasted or baked and eaten like potatoes.

Christophene

The pear-shaped christophene originated in Mexico where it is known as chayote, and is a member of the gourd family. It can be eaten raw or cooked and is crisp, juicy and nutty flavored, with a taste like fresh, young squash. Large christophenes may be stuffed with a mixture of bread crumbs, meat, cheese, onions, herbs and seasonings and broiled or baked.

Aubergine

This egg-shaped member of the potato family is a common plant throughout the Caribbean, as it relies on the warm climate and plentiful rain supply to support its growth. The large, glossy fruits are known by various other names, including Chinese eggplant, Jew's apple, egg fruit, melongene, garden egg and mad apple. The skin colors range from dark purple to mottled purple-and-white. Served as a vegetable, the ripe aubergines may be cubed and boiled or cut into strips or slices, battered and fried. Comprised of over 90 percent water, aubergines are low in both calories and nutritional value.

MEDICAL INFORMATION

Emergency Numbers
British Virgin Islands
911, 999, VISAR 767 (SOS)
Peebles Hospital
284-494-3497
US Virgin Islands 911
Roy Lester Schneider Hospital
340-776-8311

The sailing area comprising the Virgin Islands stretches from St. Thomas in the U.S. Virgin Islands to Anegada in the British Virgin Islands. Therefore, it is reassuring to know that good medical help is never far away. Both St. Thomas and Tortola have well-equipped hospitals should a serious injury occur, but the majority of minor boating mishaps require only the attention of a physician; hospitalization is seldom required. Accidents do happen, however, and when they do, it is good to know what facilities are available and where they are located.

When you are cruising or vacationing in the Virgin Islands, the last thing which you anticipate is sickness or injury. These notes are based on years of experience in practice in these Islands treating the visitor who unexpectedly becomes sick. They are not intended to replace any good first aid book issued by the Red Cross or St. John's Ambulance Brigade.

If you have a medical condition that requires ongoing medication, check with your physician before leaving home to ensure that you have enough medication to last during your holiday. Please carry the medication with you in your carry-on luggage, as checked baggage can go astray (check airline requirements first). Most commonly used medications are available at the local pharmacies or at the local hospitals, however, you will have to see a local doctor to obtain a prescription.

Peebles Hospital in Road Town, Tortola is a small modern hospital with an operating room, x-ray department, pharmacy and laboratory and can handle most routine emergencies. The hospital is fully staffed with very competent physicians. There are other clinics in the islands listed in the directory. In the event of a more serious illness or accident the St. Thomas hospital is only 15 minutes by air and 35 minutes by air from Puerto Rico; air evacuation can be arranged if necessary. There is also a resident physician in Virgin Gorda.

In St. Thomas, the Roy Lester Schneider Hospital is located close to Charlotte Amalie and is also a modern, fully staffed hospital that, besides offering the normal facilities as does Peebles Hospital, they also have a recompression chamber for diving accidents.

The waters around the islands give you some of the best sailing, snorkeling, and scuba diving in the world. Enjoy it, but cultivate a deep respect for it.

Sunburn

Probably the commonest ailment. This area is classified as subtropical, and the sun can be very harmful if taken in large doses at the beginning of vacation. On a boat there is a lot of reflected sunlight from the surface of the water.

Wear a long-sleeved shirt and light, long pants part of the day for the first few days. Socks will protect the tops of your feet and wearing a T-shirt while swimming will protect your back. Use plenty of sunscreen lotion — the higher the SPF factor, the better the protection.

If, in spite of these precautions, you suffer a severe burn, cover up and use an anti-allergic cream such as Benadryl or Phenergan. Solarcaine or other burn lotion, liberally applied, and a couple of aspirin or acetaminophen every four hours or so will diminish the pain.

If the burn develops blisters, leave them intact as long as possible to protect the sensitive tissues beneath. Once the blisters have burst, apply an antibiotic ointment to prevent infection.

Eye Conjunctivitis

Wind, dust, overchlorinated water in pools, aerosol sprays, etc., can cause mild to moderate discomfort. Symptoms include constant watering of the eye(s) with redness due to vascular congestion. Wash the eyes with clear water and use decongestant eye drops every four hours. Wear sunglasses as a preventative measure.

Foreign Body In The Eye

When examining the eye for a foreign body, a good source of light is necessary.

Lay the patient on his back and have an assistant hold a flashlight from the side of the eye. Check the lower lid first by pulling the lid down with the thumb. The upper eyelid can be examined by having the patient look down towards his feet. Hold the upper eyelashes with the thumb and forefinger and roll the lid back over the shaft of a Q-tip. Gently remove the foreign body with a moist Q-tip and instill eye drops afterwards. Do not use a dry Q-tip as it can damage the surface of the eye.

Bowel Upset Constipation

Constipation is rarely a problem in the tropics but may be worrisome during the first few days while acclimatizing to a new diet and the crowded quarters on a boat. Eat plenty of fruit and drink fruit juices, prune juice, and plenty of other fluids. If these remedies are unsuccessful, try some Milk of Magnesia or a mild laxative of your choice. If the condition persists, call a physician.

Diarrhea

Diarrhea is a common ailment on a tropical vacation, probably due to a change in diet and the availability of many exotic fruits. If you suspect the drinking water, boil it before drinking. If the diarrhea lasts more than a day, rehydrate using a glucose/salt solution like Gatorade or a solution of 1 pint water with 1/4 teaspoon salt and 1 tablespoon sugar, and stick to clear liquids only for 24-36 hours. If the diarrhea is accompanied by fever, contact a physician, who will probably prescribe an intestinal antibiotic.

Burns

Minor burns can be treated with a simple antibiotic ointment and covered with vaseline gauze and then gauze dressings held in place by a bandage. If blisters appear, leave them intact as long as possible; puncturing them may lead to infection. If the burn appears to have penetrated through the skin layer, consult a physician.

Fish Hooks

The best way to remove a fish hook is to cut the shaft of the hook with wire cutters and pull the hook, point first, through the skin with a pair of pliers. Treat afterwards as a puncture wound with antibiotic ointment and gauze dressing.

Fractures

The immediate first aid treatment is to immobilize the limb and use an analgesic or painkiller to relieve pain. Splints can be improvised from everyday items such as pillows, magazines, broom handles, or paddles, padded and tied firmly around the limb. In suspected fractures of the neck or back, lay the patient flat and prevent any movement, rolling or otherwise, by the use of pillows or other supports. Seek medical attention as soon as possible.

Headaches

May be due to too much to drink the night before, eyestrain (wear sunglasses), sinusitis from swimming and diving (take aspirin, acetaminophen or sinus tablets every four hours), or from too much direct sun (wear a hat). Bed rest and icepacks will relieve the ache. If the symptoms do not resolve in 24 hours, seek the advice of a physician.

Sprains

The early application of icepacks to the affected area during the first 8 hours will greatly reduce the amount of swelling. Elevate the limb on a pil-low and apply an ace bandage from the affected area to above it. Stings from Sea Urchins, Jellyfish or other.

Aquatic Creatures

First and foremost, watch where you are going. A weedy or stony approach to a beach means you may find sea urchins — don't step on them.

If you do get stung, do not attempt to dig the stinger out, as this can cause a secondary infection. Dab tincture of iodine on the stingers, and take antihistamines to reduce the reaction. One easy method we have heard of to reduce the sting of jelly fish, is to use meat tenderizer (take some with you in your first aid kit or in the galley) as a poultice.

There are no lethal creatures in these waters, but there are a few with self- protection devices that can give you a nasty painful sting.

Cystitis & Urinary Tract Infections

Urinary infections are most frequently caused by sitting around in wet bathing suits. Drink plenty of fluids — cranberry juice is a favorite home remedy. A doctor will likely prescribe a urinary tract antibiotic.

Insect Bites

For bites of mosquitoes, sandflies, no-see-ums or blister bugs, apply an anti-allergic cream, such as Phenergan or Benadryl, to the area.

For prevention, there are a wide variety of insect repellent sprays, lotions and creams which are very effective when applied to exposed skin, especially in the late afternoons or early evenings, when the cooler temperatures lure these insects from their hiding places.

Suggestions for a Marine Medical Kit

If you will be cruising out of sight of land for any length of time, a first aid kit is essential. The following items will meet most of your medical requirements:

- Ace bandages
- Antacid tablets
- Antibiotics (ampicillin, erythromycin, tetracycline, etc.)
- Antibiotic ear drops
- Antibiotic eye drops & ointment
- Antihistamines (Benadryl 25 mg., Phenergan 25 mg., etc.)
- Anti-seasickness medication (Dramamine, patches, etc.)
- Antiseptic powder or cream
- Aspirin, acetaminophen (Tylenol, etc.), ibuprofen (Nuprin, Advil, etc.)
- Assorted dressings: Rolled gauze, gauze squares, bandage strips, roll bandages, cotton, adhesive tape, triangular bandage, butterfly strips, safety pins, etc.

- Azo gantrisin or Septrin
- Insect repellant sprays
- Laxatives (Milk of Magnesia, etc.)
- Lomotil tablets 2.5 mg.
- Oil of cloves
- Paregoric
- Rubbing alcohol
- Solarcaine
- Sunburn relief cream
- Sunscreen lotions
- Thermometer

Allergic Dermatitis

The leaves of several tropical plants such as manchioneel or oleander, especially after rain, can produce a severe skin reaction. Apply antihistamine cream and take Phenergan or Benadryl 25 mg., 4 times a day.

The manchioneel tree produces a fruit resembling a small green apple, which is highly poisonous. Do not eat it.

Earache

Ear discomfort is frequently due to wax buildup after swimming, snorkeling and diving. The mixture of salt water and wax can create swelling which may cause temporary deafness.

If you are subject to wax formation in the ear canal, visit your physician and have him or her syringe your ears before vacation. Frequently a few drops of warm olive oil in the ear will soften the wax and alleviate the symptoms.

Earache associated with a runny discharge may denote an infection in the canal and will usually respond to antibiotic ear drops with hydrocortisone used 4 times a day. There are numerous preparations on the market containing isopropyl alcohol and boric acid crystals, which are helpful for drying the ear canals after swimming.

Fishing in the Virgin Waters

The vast numbers of sailors who cruise the Virgin Islands waters each year attest to the fact that there is a seldom quelled sense of adventure lurking in all of us; but few who come to these islands in search of excitement ever really delve below the sparkling surface of the turquoise and indigo waters to meet the equally cosmopolitan inhabitants below.

The colorful underwater residents come in every size, shape and character from mean-toothed barracuda to genially smiling grouper, and the annual pelagic visitors are just as varied; sleek, powerful marlin, graceful sailfish and vivid, rainbow-hued dolphin.

The range of gamefishing is therefore broad enough to please every type of angler, whether their inclination is towards a peaceful, reflective stroll along a quiet beach to cast for bonefish or the lusty adventure, so glamorized by Hemingway, tossing about on the high seas to battle with solitary billfish or giant tuna.

Fishing can be a very enjoyable supplement to a sailing vacation and one of the beauties of the sport is that a lucky novice has as much chance as an expert of landing a good sized fish. As the saying goes, "gamefishing is the only sport in which a complete novice has a realistic chance at a world record."

The modes of fishing in the Virgin Islands can vary from jetty fishing (guaranteed to keep the kids occupied for hours) to the dedicated pursuit of the Atlantic blue marlin, requiring boat, tackle and a skilled crew. Generally, however, the fishing available can be categorized into three main areas: shoreline angling, inshore fishing and blue water trolling.

Shore Fishing

Shore fishing and the variety of sport this provides is probably the least documented and the least utilized of all the types of fishing in the Virgin Islands, and yet for zealots of this king of sport, the area really has it all. The quarry includes bonefish, tarpon and permit, fish that in other parts of the world have as many ardent followers as the blue marlin, yet the potential in these waters is largely untapped and relies mainly on the reports of a few who, without the availability of a guide, still manage to locate enough of these wary demons of the shallows to return year after year.

Dougal Thornton

Fresh water casting gear, fly rod or spinning tackle can be put to good use along the shoreline. In the lagoons and shallow banks a variety of smaller fish can be found, and the meandering channels that wind sluggishly through walls of mangroves are a haven for jacks, parrot fish, schools of snappers, lady fish and the occasional barracuda or grouper.

Live shrimp are excellent bait for fishing off these banks, but good results can also be obtained with strips of fish, flies, small spoons, feathers or spinners.

Off rocky ledges snapper can be enticed with feath-ers or bucktailed jigs, and with spinning tackle and light test line the battle must be won quickly before the fish dives for cover to cut the line on a sharp-edged cranny.

Off the beach, the shallows are sometimes frequented by jacks, mackerel and runners for which ordinary fresh water casting tackle with surface lures and six to eight pound test line is ideal.

The same type of tackle can be used to hunt bonefish, permit and tarpon in the surf or on banks and flats where the angler can wade out into the warm shallows to peer eagerly into the weed for the flash of silver.

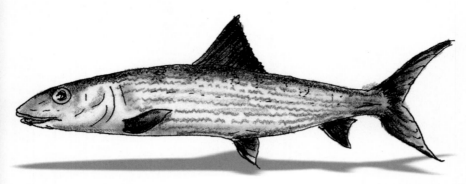

Bonefish

The bonefish can be found in shallow flats or off quiet beaches, feeding like a grey ghost along the bottom. A narrow, streamlined fish with a pointed snout, it ranges from 3-16 pounds, with an average size of about 5 pounds. It is a fussy eater with a highly suspicious nature, fickle and difficult to persuade; however, it can be tempted with conch, crab or shrimp and artificial lures such as streamer flies. Small feathers or bucktails can be successfully used with spinning tackle, but accurate casting and skillful working of the lure helps considerably. Because of its nervous disposition better results can be achieved by stealthy wading rather than poling out into the shallows in a dinghy.

The scientific name for bonefish, Abula vulpa means white fox, an accurate name for this wily, fast-moving fish which, when hooked, produces an astonishing turn of speed, zig-zagging with sizzling fury in one of the most exciting battles to be found in angling.

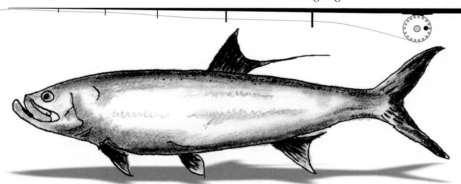

Tarpon

These bulky, energetic fish, the largest member of the herring family, can be found in a variety of feeding grounds including harbours, reefs, shallow flats and creeks. They are a good-sized fish ranging from 20 to 280 pounds, but are more commonly found at less than 80 pounds. They tend to snooze through the day in holes and deep creeks and feed at night, when they can be heard splashing and leaping in pursuit of their prey — small fish, crabs and grass shrimps. Fly rod plugs and spinning gear are sure to produce some good sport with these hefty adversaries who are very willing to plunge after a variety of baits, tackle and fishing modes. The larger specimens require a considerably weightier test line, yet still give excellent sport. Local fishermen should be consulted for advice on the best areas and tackle for tarpon.

Permit

Largest of the pompanos, the permit ranges in size between 5 and 50 pounds, though is more common between 12 and 25 pounds. It is a flat-sided fish with an angry frown which warns that, for its size, it possesses surprising strength. It can be found bottom feeding, looking for crabs, sea urchins, clams, starfish and shrimp in the surf, the creek estuaries or on the reefs. Permit are fast feeders, flitting from one spot to another with flashing birdlike movements, always alert and on the go.

Permit can be taken on artificial lures, live bait or, if conditions are right, a skillfully used fly. Besides frequenting the shallows they like to feed in waves crashing over a reef or in curling breakers on sandy beaches.

Inshore Fishing

Inshore fishing covers a multitude of species and equally diverse methods of capture. By far the most popular method is trolling around shallow reefs and headlands with the principal quarry being the kingfish or mackerel. At a slower speed, trolling with a 59-pound test line and strip bait, whole baits or spoons, large grouper of up to 75 pounds or snapper between 10 and 20 pounds can be caught.

Most practical for the yachtsman is bottom or still fishing which can be done more easily from a sailboat. This can produce fine catches of snapper and grouper, hogfish, grunts, hinds and many other bottom dwellers. For the still fishing enthusiast one just needs to anchor over any of the deeper reef areas — say 16 to 20 fathoms — and drop over a handline or two, or maybe a leadhead jig and the fish will do the rest. In calm weather drifting rather than anchoring will always produce better results. Strips of cut fish are commonly used as bait, but small live bait is by far the best and easily obtained by swiping the results of the kids' jetty fishing.

Chumming conch or tiny bits of any fish will often get the action going as the smaller fish will start to feed, stimulating the larger ones into striking at the bait.

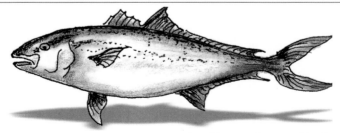

Amberjack

The amberjack is a long fish with heavy shoulders and tapered body. Like the bonefish it has crushers instead of teeth. When hungry or excited it displays feeding stripes — a black band across each side of the head. They range in size from 20 to 150 pounds, more usually between 30 and 40.

Known for its dogged stubbornness and line-cutting tactics, amberjack provides first class sport on any tackle. Live bait is best, although the amberjack can readily be persuaded to gulp a properly worked bucktail or feather jig, and can also be tempted towards the surface with popping plugs or spinning lures. These fearless fish are often found around wrecks, travelling in small groups or schools at a fair depth. When hooked they rush for the bottom, but if one can be brought up, often the rest of the school will follow, allowing other anglers an excellent chance for a good battle.

Barracuda

This sleek, wolfish, sharp-toothed fish is one of the most easily captured in the area. Found everywhere from deep ocean to shallow flats, the barracuda is a voracious and impulsive feeder, happy to pounce on practically any bait offered. The usual specimen is about 12 pounds, but often goes over 50 and occasionally up to 80 pounds.

Barracuda are most often caught when anglers troll the reefs and "drop offs" for other gamefish. Despite the ease with which it can be caught, "cuda" is not a popular prey in the Virgin Islands, where it not only is considered inedible but also has a stench which can make the entire boat smell like a garbage tip. Nevertheless, if an angler is prepared to throw it back promptly, barracuda gives some good sport on light tackle.

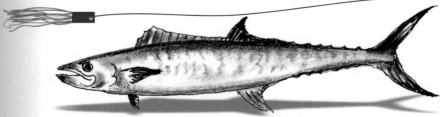

Kingfish

The kingfish is actually a member of the mackerel family and a fine food fish, sought by commercial fishermen as well as sportsmen. Ranging from 4 to 80 pounds it is more often found between 7 and 20. Like the amberjack, the kingfish prefers the depths but will race upward in pursuit of a trolled lure often clearing the surface of the water in its enthusiasm. When drifting or still fishing, plug casting gear or spinning tackle can tempt the kingfish, as can a carefully worked feather or bucktail jig. Having a similar shape to the speedy wahoo, kingfish can be tremendous sport on light tackle.

Blue Water Trolling

Made famous the world over by the likes of Hemingway and Zane Grey, and more recently in the Virgin Islands by a string of world records, blue water trolling is by far the most popular method of angling in the area and also the most advanced as far as providing services for the would-be angler. The technique is to trail behind the boat a variety of baits and artificial lures at speeds usually ranging from four to eight knots and occasionally faster, working a pattern back and forth across the edge of the continental shelf.

This edge, or "drop-off" as it is usually known, plunges from an average depth of 25 fathoms to in excess of 300 fathoms, and in places is within two miles of the Virgin Islands group. Ocean currents striking this formidable cliff create a huge upswelling of microscopic food from the depths and, in turn, a food chain of small fish and larger predators. It is for the sepredators that the offshore angler is looking and the results of his search depend on such things as weather, moon and tide and of course, most importantly, the skill of the captain and crew. To go after the bigger pelagic (ocean roaming) species it is necessary to use a fishing boat, equipment and skilled crew. These can be chartered with ease throughout the Virgin Islands.

The various types of pelagic fish one normally encounters here include blue marlin, white marlin, sailfish, dolphin fish or dorado, wahoo, tuna and bonito.

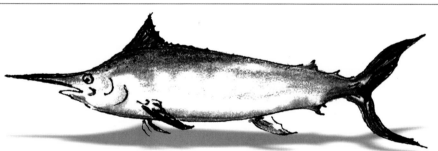

FISHING

Blue Marlin

Found in the Virgin Islands from July to September, the Atlantic blue marlin, grandaddy of the fleet, probably the most difficult of the pelagic fish to locate, to tempt into striking, to hook successfully and then to land. A marlin can get really mad at a bait, so mad that it keeps coming back over and over again to "kill" it or swallow it, smashing at it with its powerful bill. Anyone observing this fury will surely be hooked themselves. The challenge of this extraordinary fish matches its size which ranges from 90 to over 1,000 pounds. Up to

500 pounds is most common.

To tempt these solitary billfish that roam where there is plenty of space in the deep, a whole 2-5 pound mackerel, bonefish or mullet is used as bait. These, or large artificial lures, are trolled from outriggers to skip enticingly across the surface of the waves. Often a "teaser" is dragged behind the boat to create additional commotion.

Some anglers use light tackle — 30 to 50-lb. test line — or a medium 80-lb., but the majority prefer a heavier 130-lb. line. A hooked marlin is perhaps the most exciting fish in the world, leaping out of the water in enormous bounds, "tail-walking" on the surface, shimmering with rushes of bright colour in its fury. A "green" fish (one brought in so quickly that it isn't even tired) has been known to wreck a boat without much difficulty and the fight can be long and arduous, sometimes lasting for several exhausting hours that require grim determination and constancy from the angler.

However, the satisfaction of catching and tagging one of these monsters is well worth all the tossing around on high swells, the empty hours of no fish and the hard physical work involved.

Sailfish

Easily recognized and distinguished from other billfish by the enormous dorsal fin, the sailfish ranges from 20-140 pounds in size. It first arrives in the Virgin Islands in December, peaks in January and early February and generally leaves by March.

Its habits are somewhat different from the other pelagic fish in that it prefers to feed in shallow waters of 20 fathoms or so. Small ballyhoo or strips of fish trolled at 5-7 knots are a very effective enticement and, for the expert, a live bait worked in the right manner can produce good results.

With an average weight in these waters of 30-40 pounds, sailfish are not normally eaten and are usually released.

Like the blue marlin, when the sailfish becomes excited, as when going for the trolled bait, it frequently "lights up," as waves and waves of iridescent blue ripple up and down its body. When hooked, the sailfish puts on a magnificent acrobatic display, its slender body leaping out of the water with extraordinary grace and beauty.

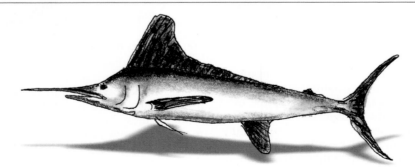

White Marlin

The smaller cousin of the big blue, the white marlin ranges between 40 and 60 pounds. The methods of capture are the same as for the bigger marlin, although, of course, the tackle is lighter (20-50 pound test), and the bait smaller.

Like sailfish, white marlin readily strike a variety of artificial lures or even a simple yellow-feathered lure trolled in the wake.

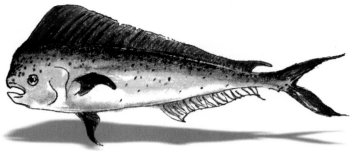

Dolphin

Although also named dolphin, this fish bears no resemblance to the porpoise. The dolphin start to arrive in numbers in late March, and depart in late May, though they are caught occasionally year-round. For the light tackle enthusiast few fish can give such a good account of themselves leaping and somersaulting repeatedly into the air, their brilliant blue and golden bodies flashing in the sunlight. They also jump in long leaps to catch their prey which, due to their sharp eyes, they can spot from quite a distance.

Dolphin are always greedily on the move and will savage almost any offering trolled at a good clip. They range in size from 5-85 pounds, most commonly from 10-20. On 8 or 12-lb. test line and spinning tackle the dolphin can give a spectacular battle, the aerial display being followed by a dogged broadside fight. It is quite common to have every rod on the boat bending when these fish are around, for they like to school, particularly around floating flotsam or driftwood. Dolphin also provide some of the best table fare in the islands.

Tuna

There are several types of tuna around the Virgin Islands, the black fin being the most common. Usually weighing from 5-15 pounds, they tend to school in large numbers. Their compact bodies are powerful and speedy, always providing some hard action, with the angler only too aware that, if it is not boated quickly, the tuna will fall prey to a marauding shark; and sharks just love tuna!

Growing considerably larger than the blackfin tuna, the Allison or yellowfin tuna reaches weights in excess of 300 pounds, and, pound for pound, can match any other fish in the sea for brute strength and pigheadedness. Around the Virgin Islands the Allison is seldom found over 100 pounds and more usually around 40 pounds. They can be caught all year round, although the larger specimens seem to show up around June. The Allison will feed on almost any trolled offering, from the favourite ballyhoo through a whole range of strip baits and artificial plastics and feathers.

Tuna are steady, stubborn opponents which, once hooked, will usually sound several hundred feet and there engage the angler in a tiring and dogged fight. On the right test, the tuna will provide some of the best sport in gamefishing.

FISHING

Bonito

The usual size of the oceanic bonito is between 10 and 20 pounds, though they range between 3 and 40 pounds. The smaller fish are popular as live bait for marlin, but the bonito can be a worthwhile catch in itself, the large schools often providing plenty of action for a boatful of fishermen.

Like the blackfin tuna, the bonito feeds on bait fish, which can be found in clusters of thousands. The feeding frenzy leaves scraps floating in the churning water which are promptly dived on by quarreling seabirds. It is these birds, hovering over the feeding schools, which will give away the presence of tuna or bonito. If the boat can get there before the birds finish feeding, feathers, or lures trolled rapidly around the roiling mass will almost certainly be snatched.

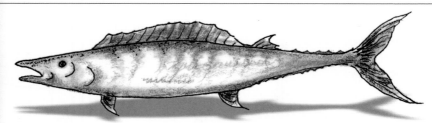

Wahoo

One of the most elegant fish to be found in the islands, the wahoo is sleek and torpedo-shaped, its upper body tiger-striped in shades of blue, its pointed mouth lined with razor-sharp teeth. This long, lean body slashing through the water has the appearance of a marine projectile. It ranges in size between 10 and 150 pounds, but is more often found between 30 and 50.

The wahoo is world famous for its immensely powerful strike and fantastic speed. Light tackle, 12 to 30 pound test, will guarantee the best sport, but 50 to 80 pound test is often used as 60 or 80-pound wahoo are not unusual.

They can usually be found singly or in small groups, prowling along the edge of a drop off, and will readily attack any trolled offering be it real or artificial. Wahoo have also been known to go after the teaser itself. Although present all year round they do predominate from late October through December.

For the competitive angler, the various gamefishing clubs of the Virgin Islands and Puerto Rico offer numerous tournaments throughout the year. The majority of these are run during July, August and September, when the blue marlin season is at its peak.

B.V.I.:
BVI Yacht and Anglers Club
284-494-3286

U.S.V.I.:
Virgin Islands Game Fishing Club
St. Thomas, USVI 00801
340-775-9144

Courtesy of HIHO

REAL ESTATE IN THE VIRGIN ISLANDS

British Virgin Islands

For many a property investor in the B.V.I. the love affair begins on the first day of the first charter when, upon clearing the harbor, the decision to go to port is as difficult as the decision to go to starboard, because in every direction there is a new anchorage to be explored.

For some, a whirlwind romance ensues, with the decision to purchase property transpiring within a week or two; for others it is a long and pleasurable engagement, the visitor returning year after year, each time promising himself that next year he will purchase property.

Why this enduring love affair with the B.V.I. for so many people?

Certainly there are a number of obvious reasons, such as a perfect climate, miles and miles of pristine sailing waters and an underwater habitat to rival that of almost any resort area. Add to these an extremely stable and self-determining government, numerous tax advantages and proximity to both the U.S.V.I. and Puerto Rico. The U.S. dollar economy is one of the biggest selling point in the British Virgin Islands.

The reasons go beyond the obvious, however — they also include a proud and friendly people and an environment that, as one of nature's finest achievements, is protected against outside intrusion or influence unless these are for the common good of the people of the B.V.I.

Around us is the land and the sea, and the use or abuse to which we subject these elements has a far-reaching and permanent effect on the environment. It doesn't take long for the potential investor, looking for his home in the sun, to realize that it is the local government's program of directed and controlled development that has maintained the relaxing and unhurried atmosphere that prevails in the B.V.I.

Having made the decision to buy, the question of just where to purchase property is relatively simple, as properties are available the whole length and breadth of the B.V.I. on over a dozen different islands. Making contact with a local real estate agent at this point will considerably cut the search time needed and will also provide the investor with up-to-date information on the laws and government requirements pertaining to property purchase. Though many of the local agents market the same properties, by "shopping around" you may find a property that no one else has.

In short, the purchase of property in the B.V.I. revolves around a Non-Belonger Land Holding License which is issued by the government after consideration of certain factors, including how much property is involved. The purchaser, if a non-belonger (not a citizen of the B.V.I.), is required to develop the property in less than three years, and may also have a financial commitment to invest in the development or improvement of the property.

Apart from a careful scrutiny of potential buyers, the government's main concern is the sale of previously undeveloped land; its chief concerns are how many acres are involved, what the intended development consists of, and how much money will be spent in the Territory on the project.

The licensing procedure is relatively straightforward with a developed property such as an existing residence. Non-belongers owning homes that they may want to rent when they are off the island must apply for a business license first. With larger projects that will bring money into the territory, the government is amenable to expedient approval.

Throughout the B.V.I. there is a wide range of existing houses and condominiums for sale. For those intent on building, there is a limitless variety of sites to choose from, either on the waterfront or on one of the many hillsides that make up the islands. Most investors opt for the hillsides, to take advantage of the spectacular views and also benefit from year-round trade winds — a definite advantage in the summer.

Building a house in the B.V.I. is not the trial it used to be. With regular shipping from both England and the U.S. mainland, the variety of building materials, fixtures and fittings now available has eased the burden on local architects and contractors, who can now purchase building materials locally that are required for the average residence. Building is still expensive, however, with concrete blocks being the only material locally produced.

Although far less demanding than Stateside or British authorities, the local Building Department and Planning Authority do have guidelines and regulations, which must be followed. It is recommended that a local architect be consulted during the planning stages, preferably before the land is purchased. Generally, the guidelines control building setbacks, sewage disposal, cistern requirements and hurricane proof construction, together with special applications such as for jetties and land reclamation.

Most of the banks in the B.V.I. are active in the home mortgage market, although their individual policies do vary from time to time, often in relation to the prime lending rate. Represented in the B.V.I. are FirstCaribbean International, Chase Manhattan Bank, ScotiaBank, Banco Popular of the B.V.I. and several more (please see a complete listing in the directory). Since the investor's main concern is normally capital appreciation the B.V.I. has always been and should continue to be a good investment.

The British Virgin Islands may not be for everyone and the area is certainly an expensive place to live; but the people of the B.V.I. do live well and enjoy not only the magnificent environment but also many other advantages.

The B.V.I. is a close-knit, friendly society, and there is no lack of facilities. Considering the combined activities of the Sports Club with its squash and tennis division, the Yacht Club with its sailing, angling and rugby division, both Lions and Rotary clubs, soccer, baseball, golf and cricket clubs, a women's club, botanic society and drama group, the only problem can be having enough time left to relax and take a vacation!

There's always something happening in the B.V.I., but it's also a perfect place to relax and do absolutely nothing — so if the pressures of the big smoke have been getting you down, the B.V.I. just may be for you.

United States Virgin Islands

When the United States bought St. Thomas, St. Croix and St. John from

Denmark in 1917, it cost them less than $300 an acre. Inflation has taken its toll since then, and today the average price for a home in the Virgin Islands is over $500,000. By modern real estate standards, however, buying property here is

still an excellent investment.

With some of the finest weather and scenery to be found under the protection of the U.S. flag, the U.S.V.I. has a great deal to offer the prospective buyer. Stunning views are complemented by beautiful beaches, fascinating historical buildings, good restaurants and a leisurely approach to life.

Because the tourist industry is so vital to the island economy, there are plenty of facilities for sports, entertainment and the arts. Both St. Thomas and St. Croix have top quality golf courses, and sailing is, of course, an integral part of the lifestyle throughout the Virgins.

The U.S. Virgin Islands differ enormously in their character. St. Thomas is the busiest of the three; it contains the headquarters of most of the major businesses in the U.S.V.I., most of the government agencies and most of the people.

Charlotte Amalie is the commercial heart of the U.S. Virgins; the town bustles with tourists and traffic, and the harbor teems with yachts, cruise ships and visiting naval vessels. As a consequence, St. Thomas offers the broadest range of facilities and events and a choice of shops, restaurants, hotels and a variety of entertainment.

St. Croix is somewhat quieter. Set apart from the rest of the Virgin Islands it is, in fact, the largest of the group and was once the main agricultural producer. The miles of gently rolling hills are dotted with ancient sugar mills and gracious colonial homesteads like Whim Great House and Sprat Hall.

The historic buildings of Christiansted and Frederiksted still look out over a slower pace of life, and the attractions of this island have persuaded many talented artists and musicians to make it their home.

St. John, the quietest of them all, once belonged to Laurence Rockefeller, who donated it to the United States under the proviso that most of it be designated as a National Park. Consequently the island is very unspoiled and, with its uncluttered beaches and untouched hills, it truly lives up to its name as a Virgin Island. In terms of property investment, this pristine quality means that the available real estate is often the most expensive, the most highly restricted and the most exclusive in the U.S. Virgins — and often the most spectacular, too.

Visitors considering the purchase of property in the U.S.V.I. must first choose which island most suits their taste, and then examine the alternative types of property. Whether to buy land and build, whether to renovate an old building or invest in a new, whether a self-contained residence or a condominium is best, are some initial questions. The choices are considerable and an experienced realtor can give valuable advice at this stage.

In some ways an undeveloped home site may be the easiest way to start. There is no time limit for how long land can be held before development must begin, and so the new owner can take his time in deciding on the kind of home he wants and financing.

Buying a finished home, of course, saves time. Condominiums are a popular choice; they can generate a healthy income if rented as vacation units and usually have excellent amenities, such as swimming pools, beaches, tennis courts,

ownership. There is always adequate security, and all the details of rental and maintenance are taken care of by the management.

An alternative to purchasing a condominium outright is time-sharing, which provides a refinement of the traditional condominium ownership. Instead of holding the unit year-round, the buyer can own it for as little as two months per year.

Perhaps better suited to those who want to spend a greater proportion of their time in the islands, an individual residence offers more privacy and space. Most sites are at least half an acre and keen gardeners can take advantage of the profusion of fast-growing tropical

golf courses, restaurants, etc.

Most condominiums offer an on-site management team whose function is to advertise the apartments as resort hotel rooms, book reservations on a rotating or pool basis, provide maid service, do the accounting and disburse income to the owners. Management fees vary from 35% to 60% of the gross income, however, and there is generally a monthly maintenance charge, depending on the size of the unit. Typically this covers upkeep of the exterior of the building and the grounds, pool service, cleaning, gardening and insurance.

The major advantage of having a condominium is the relatively worry-free plants to create colorful and imaginative surroundings.

Single-family homes are as varied in type as they are in price., which ranges from about $350,000 to $1.5 million and above. Maintenance on a home is generally less expensive than on a condominium and mortgage interest, maintenance and property taxes are all tax-deductible items. The government maintains an efficient system of surveys and titles, and title insurance can also be arranged though local attorneys.

Anyone can buy real estate in the U.S.V.I. There are no restrictions on nationality or on speculation purely for investment purposes. Land can be held for

any length of time and no development plan is required by the government.

Land use, however, is another matter. It is dictated by zoning laws, deed restrictions and building permit requirements, including approval by the Coastal Zone Management Committee. The ease with which this approval is obtained is largely dependent on the location of the property and the type of development proposed.

The Coastal Zone Management is the organization responsible for keeping the U.S.V.I. looking good enough to be described as the "American paradise." They have a scale of restrictions designed to preserve the beauty of the island by limiting such things as density, height of building, type of construction and so on. The severity of the limits varies according to the area.

For example, the majority of St. John's land belongs to the National Park Service. The remaining land available for development is R1 density, which means no more than two dwelling units per quarter acre. These are mostly concentrated around Cruz Bay and Coral Bay areas.

Other restrictions may include details like clothesline placement and other visual features. Fortunately, St. John has excellent architects and builders, making building a home remarkably hassle-free.

St. Thomas and St. Croix have more medium and high density residences available, as well as extensive business and commercial areas. The choices for potential real estate buyers are wide. Many

begin by trying out something from the range of rental and leasing arrangements which, allows the participants to try the lifestyle before making a heavier commitment.

The advantages of V.I. living are less tangible—the islands are obviously sunny, pretty and cosmopolitan, but for many people the fascination runs deeper. They find themselves returning again and again, spending longer periods of time and scraping their savings together to buy a foothold. Down here, the islanders call it "getting sand in your shoes," and a sailing vacation is often just the beginning.

People go on to buy real-estate in the Virgin Islands because they want to make an investment and because they like the lifestyle and the environment. From an investment point of view, the chances for worthwhile return are good.

So if you get home and unpack to find half the beach in your docksiders, it could be that your next visit to the Virgin Islands will include "just checking it out" at the nearest real estate office.People go on to buy real estate in the Virgin Islands because they want to make an investment and because they like the lifestyle and the environment. From an investment point of view, the chances for worthwhile return are good.

So if you get home and unpack to find half the beach in your docksiders, it could be that your next visit to the Virgin Islands will include "just checking it out" at the nearest real estate office.

RESTAURANTS & BARS

Arriving at a restaurant by dinghy is a unique and special experience for most. This is one area where it is not at all unusual to see people arriving for dinner with wet bottoms from the dinghy ride in to shore! The Virgin Islands offer many restaurants and bars that cater to sailors. The food ranges from casual, served on the beach, to sophisticated and elegant, but almost all have unforgettable views of these exquisite islands. Credit cards are taken in most establishments, but some of the more casual restaurants do not have credit card capabilities. Reservations are also important at many restaurants, again wise to check first. Many restaurants have shorter hours or close completely during the slow season, so please check before you make plans. We have tried to include year-round hours for your convenience, but it is always better to double check.

We have included most of the restaurants that are accessible by dinghy and a few others that you wouldn't want to miss. For a more complete listing pick up some of the free tourist literature available in the airports, marinas and hotels.

*Asterisk denotes restaurants accessible by dinghy, or within easy walking distance of a dinghy dock. The others may require the services of a taxi or rental car.

BRITISH VIRGIN ISLANDS

Jost Van Dyke

*Abe's, Little Harbour, VHF 16, 495-9329 or 9529 On the eastern end of the bay, Abe's serves West Indian fare for lunch and dinner, also open for breakfast daily. Check or their pig roasts. Reservations for dinner requested.

*Ali Baba's, Great Harbour, 495-9280, VHF 16, Baba serves breakfast, lunch and dinner West Indian style. Reservations for dinner requested by 6pm.

*Corsairs, Great Harbour, 495-9294, Laid back atmosphere with rustic fare, open daily from 7am until...(See our ad on page 100)

*Foxy's Beach Bar, Great Harbour, 495-9258, The famous Foxy's on the beach at the eastern end serves lunch, and dinner with reservations by 5pm. Catch Foxy himself entertaining with his Calypso ballads. Foxy's has its own dinghy dock. (See our ad on page 97)

*Foxy's Taboo, Diamond Cay, 495-9258, VHF 16, Beautiful view, serving Mediterranean fare specializing in fresh seafood. Open breakfast, lunch and dinner. Reservations requested. (See our ad on page 102)

*Harris' Place, Little Harbour, 495-9302, Serves breakfast, lunch and dinner. Good place for lobster and fish.

*One Love Beach Bar, White Bay, 495-9829, Located on the beach this is a great place for a cold drink! Open daily

*Rudy's Rendezvous, Great Harbour, 495-9282, VHF 16. Open daily for breakfast, lunch and dinner. Dinner is from 6-9pm, specializing in seafood. Reservations are required. Located on the very western end of the beach.

*Sandcastle, White Bay, 495-9888, VHF 16. Serves breakfast, lunch and a four course dinner by candle light. Reservations for dinner requested by 4pm. Visit the Soggy Dollar Bar famous for the delicious Painkiller.

*Sidney's Peace and Love, Little Harbour, 495-9271, West Indian dishes and seafood served. Open for breakfast, lunch and dinner from 9am.

*Wendell's World, Great Harbour, 495-9969
Casual fare on the beach including burger, wings and sandwiches – open all day.

Tortola, Cane Garden Bay

*Big Banana Paradise Club, 495-4606,
Open daily from 7am until 11pm, on the beach, with a breezy atmosphere, they serve breakfast, lunch and dinner.

*Elm Beach Bar, 494-2888,
Open daily on the beach for lunch from 11am and dinner from 6-9pm.

*Myett's Garden & Grill, 495-9649,
Amongst the almond trees on the beach the grill offers fish, lobster, steak, chicken and vegetarian meals. Breakfast, lunch and dinner are available daily. Entertainment often. (See our ad on page 105)

*Quito's Gazebo 495-4837,
On the   beach next to the dinghy dock, Tuesday through Sunday, lunch starting at 11am and dinner starting at 6pm. Reservations are recommended, but walk-ins are welcome too. Quito entertains several nights in the week, often with his band.

*Rhymer's 495-4639, VHF 16,
the pink building on the beach serving breakfast, lunch and dinner.

*Stanley's Welcome Bar 495-9424,
On the beach by the tire swing, Stanley's is open for happy hour (3-7pm), lunch and dinner. Open starting at 10:00am until..... Casual and relaxed atmosphere.

Tortola, West End

*Blue Parrot Café, 495-4811,
Located in a courtyard at Soper's Hole Marina, they serve, gourmet breakfasts, coffees, cakes and afternoon tea.

Frenchman's Cay Hotel, 495-4844,
On Sir Francis Drake channel serving breakfast, lunch and dinner. A short walk from Soper's Hole. Pool and tennis privileges for diners. Reservations requested for dinner.

*Jolly Roger, 495-4559,
Next to the West End ferry dock; Jolly Roger serves breakfast, lunch and dinner from 7:30am until late. The setting is casual and a good place for pizza and burgers. During season, there is live music on the weekends.

*Pisces Restaurant & Bar, 495-3154,
Open 8am-10pm daily, serving West Indian cuisine. It is just across the street from Soper's Hole Wharf & Marina.

*Pusser's Landing West End, 495-4554,
Great food on the water at Soper's Hole, Pussers serves lunch from 11am until 3pm and snacks all day. Happy hour begins at 5pm. For dinner they offer, lobster, steak and seafood, serving from 6pm to 10pm. Reservations requested. (see our ad on the inside covers)

Other restaurants near West End

Bomba's Shack, Capoons Bay, 495-4148,
Famous for his full moon and 1st of the month parties on the beach, the bar is comprised of flotsam and jetsam accumulated over the years. Very casual atmosphere and they often have beach BBQ's on Wednesdays and Sundays. Please call to find out if they are serving food. Open from 10am until....

BVI Steak, Chop and Pasta House, 494-5433,
This restaurant, at Heritage Villas, is perched high with dynamic views of Carrot Bay, Apple Bay and Long Bay. They serve lunch and dinner.

Coco Plums, Apple Bay, 495-4672,
Coco Plums serves international meals with a West Indian flare. They are open for breakfast, lunch and dinner on some nights only.

Long Bay Hotel & Resort, Long Bay, 495-4252,
The '1748' restaurant serves breakfast, lunch and dinner from 7:30am until 9:30pm. The more elegant Palm Terrace serves dinner from 6:30 to 9:30pm with reservations, and the bar stays open until 11pm. There is also the upstairs Pasta House open for dinner from 6:30-9:30 on Tuesdays and Thursdays with reservations.

Mauricio Handler

Mrs. Scatliffe's, Carrot Bay, 495-4556,
Mrs. Scatliffe specializes in West Indian style food and Caribbean seafood "cooked in her own style". Reservations are required by 5pm of the evening you would like to dine, as her menu changes daily.

Sebastian's On the Beach, Little Apple Bay, 495-4212, Beachside dining on the north shore. Serves breakfast, lunch, happy hour and dinner. Open from 7am until 10pm. Reservations requested.

Sugar Mill Hotel, Apple Bay, 495-4355,
Gourmet meals are served in an old sugar mill with a romantic atmosphere. They offer breakfast (8-10am), lunch (12-2pm), and dinner (6-8:30). Reservations required.

Nanny Cay

*Genaker Café, Nanny Cay, 494-2512 ext.2339,
In the marina plaza, this casual restaurant serves breakfast from 7-11am, and lunch from 11:30am to 5pm. They also have happy hour every day from 4pm to 7pm.

*Peg Leg Landing, Nanny Cay, 494-0028,
Overlooks Sir Francis Drake Channel, this whimsical restaurant serves lunch, happy hour and dinner. Lunch starts at 10:30am, the bar opens at 4:30 and dinner service begins at 7:00. Happy hour is between 5 and 7pm daily. Reservations recommended.

Struggling Man's Place 494-4163,
A local restaurant on Sea Cow's Bay a short walk from the marina serves West Indian fare for lunch and dinner.

Road Town

*Callaloo, Prospect Reef, 494-3311,
 Upstairs overlooking the harbor, serves breakfast, lunch and gourmet dinner with reservations.

*Capriccio di Mare, 494-5369,
Across from the ferry dock on the waterfront, serves breakfast, lunch and dinner Italian style. Good cappuccino and pastries for breakfast and pasta and salads. From 8am to 9pm Monday through Saturday.

*Captain's Table, 494-3885,
At Inner Harbour Marina serves lunch and dinner daily, as well as happy hour. Open from 10am-10pm. Reservations recommended. Fresh live lobster is available to choose from the lobster pool.

*The Dove, 494-0313
The Dove serves gourmet meals from their quaint West Indian building on Main Street. They are open Tuesday through Saturday for dinner from 6pm.

Happy hour starts at 5pm. Reservations are recommended.

*Fort Burt, 494-2587,
Spectacular views of Road Harbour, the New England Culinary students serve delicious and elegant meals. The offer breadfast, lunch and dinner with reservations.

*Le Cabanon, 494-8660,
Covered patio dining in a French bistro serving French cuisine. Open for lunch and dinner. Casual dining. Please reserve for dinner.

*Lime 'n Mango, 494-2501,
Across the street from the Footloose Dock, in the Treasure Isle Hotel. Serves breakfast, lunch, and dinner with Caribbean and Mexican fare. Cool and breezy location.

*Maria's By the Sea, 494-2595,
On the harbor serving breakfast, lunch and dinner from 7am until... Dinner reservations requested. West Indian cuisine specializing in conch, lobster, steak and liver. Air-conditioned or terrace dining.

*Mariner Inn 494-2333,
At the Moorings Marina this recently renovated airy restaurant serves breakfast, lunch and candlelit dinners daily overlooking the marina. Reservations suggested for dinner.

*The Pub, 494-2608,
At Fort Burt Marina with dinghy dock, serves burgers and sandwiches for lunch and steak, fish etc. for dinner. Open Monday through Saturday from 7am until 10pm and on Sunday from 5pm.

*Pusser's Pub, 494-3897,
On the waterfront, the Pusser's Pub serves traditional English pub food, pizza and deli sandwiches. Air-conditioned. Open from 11am to 10pm daily. (see our ads on the inside covers)

Maya Cove

*Calamaya, 495-2126,
Features Mediterranean and Caribbean menu on the dock at Hodges Creek Marina. Serves breakfast, lunch, happy hour with tapas, and dinner.

*Fat Hog Bob's, 495-1010,
A Caribbean barbecue, Fat Hog Bob's serves steak, ribs and fish. Casual atmosphere on the water with a great view.

*Pelican's Café, 495-1515,
Overlooking Maya Cove serves breakfast, lunch and dinner Monday through Saturday from 7:30am to 10:30pm. International menu.

East End

Bing's Drop Inn Bar, 495-2627,
Has a late night bar menu and is also a good dance spot.

*Eclipse, 495-1646,
Fresh seafood specialties, as well as steak and pasta. Open for dinner daily from 5pm to 10pm.

*Harbour View Restaurant, 495-2797,
Fine dining for lunch and dinner above the Harbour View Marina with a view and a breeze. Reservations requested for dinner.

Secret Garden, 495-1834,
Open for lunch and dinner in the gardens of an old plantation great house. Open daily except on Tuesday from 12pm to 9pm.

Tamarind Club, 495-2477,
Serves international and West Indian food in an open air setting, close to Josiah's Bay. Open for breakfast, lunch and dinner.

Beef Island

*D' Best Cup,
a 5-minute walk from the airport on Trellis Bay, serves espresso drinks, ice cream, smoothies, pastries, beer, wine, sandwiches and snacks. They also have a gift shop.

*De Loose Mongoose, 495-2303, VHF 16,
On the beach at Trellis Bay at the Beef Island Guest House. Serving breakfast, lunch and dinner. Hearty food, casual surroundings. Moorings available.

*The Last Resort, 495-2520, VHF 16,
Bellamy Cay, lunch and happy hour served on the patio. Dinner is fusion style cuisine with live musical entertainment nightly. Fun gift shop open during lunch and dinner. Reservations requested.

*Royal BVI Yacht Club, 494-8140,
At Road Reef Marina is open to the public for dining. Lunch is served from 12 to 3:00 and dinner is from 6pm.

*Scuttlebutt Bar & Grill, Prospect Reef, 494-3311,
Downstairs, serves casual food for breakfast, lunch and dinner.

*Spaghetti Junction, 494-4880,
Overlooking the water from their new location at Baugher's Bay they serve fine Italian cuisine Monday through Saturday from 5pm to 10pm. Reservations suggested. Don't miss the Bat Cave bar – a happening place with entertainment often.

*Village Cay Dockside, 494-2771,
Overlooking the docks and harbor, casual fare for breakfast, lunch & dinner. Open from 7:30am. Good frozen drinks at the lively bar. (See our ad on page 130)

*Virgin Queen, 494-2310,
Not far from Village Cay serving West Indian, pizza, and European fare. Open from 11am to midnight, and from 6pm until late on Saturday night.

Brandywine Bay

*Brandywine Bay Restaurant, 495-2301, VHF 16,
Elegant dining with a Florentine flair on the terrace overlooking the Sir Francis Drake Channel. Moorings are available for dinner guests. Reservations requested.

Moorings available. Call from the hotline next to the dock for water taxi service. (See our ad on page 156)

Marina Cay

*Donovan's Reef, 495-1175,
Scrub Island, serves international and Caribbean cuisine. Open 2:30-10pm. Reservations requested. Ferry service is available for parties of over six people.

*Pusser's Marina Cay, 494-2174, VHF 16,
Pusser's offers free ferry service to this tiny island. Or if arriving by boat, moorings are available. A great island setting, with a delicious array of choices. Lunch and dinner daily. Also check out the Company Store. (see our ad on page 161)

*Trellis Bay Cybercafé, 495-2447,
Serves fresh juices, smoothies, sandwiches on home-cooked bread, and pizza. Open daily from 7am-11pm.

Norman Island

*Pirates Bight, 496-7827,
Bar and grill on the beach serving Caribbean and continental cuisine daily and home-made desserts. Open from 11am.

*The William Thornton, 494-0183, VHF 16,
Floating bar/restaurant anchored in the Bight. Serves lunch and dinner daily from 11am until... Casual food, fun location. Reservations requested.

Courtesy of HIHO

Peter Island

*Lazy Iguana Beach Club, 494-2872, VHF 16
Located in Buttonwood Bay, Great Harbour, they have an assorted menu for lunch and dinners by request. Open from 10am.

*Peter Island Yacht Club, 495-2000,
Elegant dining in the Tradewinds Restaurant. Check on the dress code. They serve lunch and dinner with reservations. Lunch and dinner are also served on the beach at Deadman's Bay Bar & Grill (casual). Moorings and dockage available – check first for mooring fees.

Cooper Island

*Cooper Island Beach Club, VHF 16, 495-9084
Lunch and dinner are served in Manchioneel Bay, next to the beach, daily with a fantastic sunset view. Moorings are available. (See our ad on page 182)

Virgin Gorda
The Valley (Spanish Town)

*Bath & Turtle, 495-5239,
Located at the Virgin Gorda Yacht Harbour,
casual surroundings serving lunch and dinner. A fun and convenient location. Free lending library and liquor store on the premises. (See our ad on page 193)

*Chez Bamboo, 495-5752,
Refined dining Creole style. Next to the Yacht Harbour. Serving dinner with reservations. Open from 3-10pm. Great spot for sunsets. (See our ad on page 193)

*Fischer's Cove 495-5252,
On the beach in the Valley offering West Indian cuisine. They serve breakfast, lunch and dinner. This is a good spot for sunsets.

*Giorgio's Table, 495-5684,
Great location in beautiful Savannah Bay. Italian and Mediterranean cuisine served daily. Open from 12pm for lunch and dinner from 6:30. Reservations requested for dinner.

*Leverick Bay Restaurant, 495-7154,
Lunch is served downstairs at the beach bar, and dinner is served upstairs. Open from 11am-9pm daily. Happy Hour is from 5pm – 7pm. (See our ad on page 199)

Little Dix Bay Hotel, 495-5555,
Refined dining at this world renowned resort. Lunch and dinner with reservations. Casually elegant dress requested.

Mad Dog, 495-5830,
Near the Baths this airy bar is a great place for drinks and sandwiches. Open from 10am to 7pm.

Mine Shaft Café, 495-5260,
Located on Coppermine Road, serves casual fare for lunch and dinner. Open daily at 10am.

Rock Café, 495-5482, VHF 16,
Nestled in amongst the famous boulders of the Baths you can eat outside or inside the air conditioned dining room. Their specialties are Italian and Caribbean food and they are open from 4pm to midnight daily. (See our ad on page 196)

*Top of the Baths, 495-5497, VHF 16,
At the top of the famous Baths with a spectacular view to the west of Drake Channel. Serving breakfast, lunch and dinner.

Wheelhouse, 495-5230,
Serves breakfast, lunch and dinner. West Indian food with a casual atmosphere located at Ocean View Hotel.

North Sound

*Bitter End, 494-2745, VHF 16,
Welcomes yachtsmen, serves breakfast, lunch and dinner in The Clubhouse, snacks in the Emporium. Frequent entertainment. Moorings available. (see our ad on the inside back cover)

*Fat Virgins Café, 495-7052,
Located on the service dock on the west side of Biras Creek. Open for breakfast, lunch & dinner with a wide array of offerings.

*Saba Rock Resort, 495-7711, VHF 16
Two bars, a restaurant, long dinghy dock, and moorings available. Serving lunch from 12 and dinner from 6pm, including an all-you-can-eat buffet in the evening. Live music often. Reservations requested. (See our ad on page 202)

*Sand Box Beach Bar & Restaurant, 495-9122/9123, VHF 16,
Prickley Pear, open for lunch and dinner. Free boat pick up from Gun Creek or Leverick Bay by request, moorings available. Beach bar and grill, casual atmosphere.

Anegada

*Anegada Grill House, 495-8002,
VHF 16, At the Anegada Reef Hotel specializing in grilled lobster and fish, serving breakfast, lunch and dinner. Dinner reservations required. (see our ad on page 209)

Big Bamboo, 495-2019,

On the shore at Loblolly Bay serving lunch, dinner upon request. Monitors VHF 16

Cow Wreck Beach Bar, 495-9461, VHF 16,
Serves lunch and dinner at Lower Cow Wreck Beach, seafood plus burgers and ribs.

Dotsy's Bakery & Sandwich Shop, 495-9667,
Serve breakfast, lunch and dinner from 9am to 7pm. Located in the settlement.

Flash of Beauty, 495-8014, beautiful view on the beach of Loblolly Bay. Serves sandwiches and fresh seafood from 10am.

*Lobster Trap, 495-9466, VHF 16,
On the beach at Setting Point, featuring grilled seafood serving lunch and dinner. Reservations by 4pm please.

*Neptune's Treasure, 495-9439, VHF 16,
At Setting Point, serves breakfast, lunch and dinner, including fresh fish and lobster. (see our ad on page 213)

Pomato Point, 495-9466, VHF 16,
Serves seafood including barbecued lobster. Overlooking the beach, serves lunch and dinner. Call for reservations.

Potters by the Sea, Setting Point, 495-9182,
Serves fish, lobster, chicken and ribs for lunch and dinner. Reservations requested by 4pm.

U.S. VIRGIN ISLANDS
Cruz Bay
Asolare, 779-4747,
Serves Asian, French cuisine. Open daily from 5:30pm-8:45pm. Reservations recommended.

Banana Deck, 693-5055,
Overlooking Cruz Bay, American/Caribbean fare, open for lunch and dinner, reservations.

Chloe & Bernard's, 714-6075,
Upscale open-air dining at Gallow's Point, serving European cuisine, weekly entertainment. Reservations recommended.

Duffy's Love Shack, 776-6065,
American food, casual island atmosphere, handcrafted tropical drinks, open daily, food served 12pm-10pm, Mon.-Sat., opens 3pm on Sundays. One block from ferry dock.

*Fish Trap Restaurant, 693-9994,
A short walk from the ferry dock in a tropical setting in the Raintree Court. Inspired cuisine. Serving dinner

Mauricio Handler

*Stone Terrace, 693-9370,
Elegantly inspired international cuisine served from 6-10pm Tuesday through Sunday. Bar opens at 5pm. Reservations suggested. Waterfront dining.

*Sun Dog Café, in Mongoose Junction, 693-8340,
Serving lunch in the courtyard, menu includes homemade soups, salads and over-stuffed sandwiches.

Tage, 715-4270,
Two blocks from the ferry dock, across from field. Serves gourmet cuisine.

Coral Bay

*Shipwreck Landing Restaurant, 693-5640,
Open for lunch and dinner daily on the bay in a breezy locale.

*Skinny Legs, 779-4982,
In Coral Bay, serves sandwiches, burgers, and seafood.

*Voyages, 774-1566,
French Cuisine open for dinner.

St. Thomas, Red Hook

Agave Terrace Restaurant & Bar, 775-4142,
At Point Pleasant Resort, serves dinner from 6-10pm daily, local lobster, fish, steaks and pasta. Entertainment Tuesday and Thursday. Reservations.

*Café Wahoo, 775-6350,
On the water at the Picola Marina next to the ferry dock. Open for dinner, Euro-Carib cuisine. Open daily from 6pm-10pm.

*Caribbean Saloon, 775-7060,
Overlooking the marina serving lunch and dinner and late, late menu. Mainly steak, pasta and seafood.

Duffy's Love Shack, 779-2080,
Open 11:30 am-2 am daily, food served continuously. Opposite the St. John Ferry, American food, casual island atmosphere, hand-crafted tropical drinks.

East End Café, 715-1442,
Serves Italian cuisine. Open every day for lunch and dinner from 11am-10pm. Located at the far end of American Yacht Harbor, a 2-minute walk from the ferry dock.

Tuesday through Sunday from 4:30 through 9:30pm. www.mongoosejunctionstjohn.com

*Gecko Gazebo, in Mongoose Junction, 693-8340 www.mongoosejunctionstjohn.com Courtyard across from Gazebo building, sit, relax and enjoy a cool tropical drink at the open-air bar overlooking beautiful Mongoose Junction.

*The Lime Inn, 776-6425,
In the Lemontree Mall for lunch and dinner in an airy spot in the middle of the Bay.
www.mongoosejunctionstjohn.com

*Mongoose Restaurant & Bar/ Northshore Deli, 693-8677, Serves breakfast, lunch, dinner & Sunday brunch sandwiches, homemade salads, and baked goodies. www.mongooserestaurant.com

*Morgan's Mango, 693-8141,
Across from the Nat'l Park Dock. Dinner served from 5:30pm. Caribbean cuisine, reservations recommended.

*Panini Beach Trattoria, 693-9119,
On the beach in Cruz Bay near Wharfside Village, this Italian restaurant is casual and open-air with some great Italian food. It is a good place to watch the boats and ferries in Cruz Bay.

*Paradiso Restaurant, in Mongoose Junction, 693-8899, Open daily for dinner from 5:30 - 9:30. Casually elegant dining. Contemporary American cuisine. Reservations recommended.

Rhumb Lines, 776-0303,
Pacific Rim and tropical cuisine, Meada's Plaza, open Wednesday-Monday, lunch and dinner. Live entertainment on Saturday.

*The Frigate, 775-6124,
Across from American Yacht Harbor serving steak and seafood for dinner nightly.

*Latitute 18°, 779-2495,
At the Fanfare dock across from the ferry dock. Casual ambiance, check for entertainment.

*Mackenzie's Restaurant & Tap Room, 779-2261,
Upstairs in the American Yacht Harbour building. Serves lunch and dinner daily.

Off the Hook, 775-6350,
Caribbean cuisine, and seafood caught daily by local fisherman. Open daily for dinner, 6pm-10pm. Casual atmosphere, reservations recommended.

*Sopchoppy's Pub, 774-2929,
Open daily from 4pm to 10pm for casual fare—pizzas, calzones, wraps and salads.

*Whale of a Tale, 775-1270,
On the top floor of American Yacht Harbor with an extensive seafood and pasta menu.

XO Bistro, 779-2069,
Serves fine wines and light fare, intimate bistro-style atmosphere. Open nightly from 6pm-midnight.

The Lagoon

*Dottie's Front Porch,
Informal outdoor patio serving from 6:30pm-10pm. Home cooked meals, great desserts. Please no credit cards.

*Windjammer, 775-6194,
In the Compass Point Marina, German-American fare open for dinner Monday through Saturday from 6pm.

*Bottoms Up, 775-4817,
Light fare and drinks at Independent Boatyard and Marina for breakfast, lunch, dinner and drinks.

Pirates Cove, 714-2135,
Open-air setting, casual dining, great food for breakfast, lunch and dinner daily. Located at Pirates Cove Marina.

Secret Harbor

*Blue Moon Café, 779-2262,
On the water at Secret Harbor, dinghy over for good wine and a great dinner. Reservations requested.

Frenchtown

Noche, 774-3800,
New Southwest cuisine, patio bar or air-conditioned dining. Open nightly.

Oceana Restaurant & Wine Bar, 774-4262,
Waterside at Villa Olga. Offers fresh seafood from around the world, also serves steaks.

Epernay Wine Bar & Bistro, 774-5348,
Menu includes sushi, pasta, appetizers, and desserts. Open Monday – Wednesday, 5pm-1am, Thursday – Friday until 2am. Saturday 6pm-2am.

Tuscan Grill, 776-4211,
Italian cuisine in a stylish atmosphere. Serves pastas, seafood and steak. Open Monday through Saturday, 11:30am-11:30pm.

Alexander's, 774-4349,
Serves Austrian, International, Euro-Caribbean cuisine. Serves lunch and dinner Monday through Saturday. Closed on Sundays.

Craig & Sally's, 777-9949,
Italian and eclectic cuisine with an International flair. Intimate atmosphere, large wine selection. Open for lunch Wednesday-Friday, for dinner Wednesday-Sunday.

Hook, Line & Sinker, 776-9708,
Casual and friendly waterfront dining serving lunch and dinner Monday through Saturday, and Sunday brunch 10am-2:30pm. Specializes in seafood, also serves burgers, pastas, and steak.

Charlotte Amalie

There are so many restaurants in Charlotte Amalie to discover, and many more restaurants than we could possibly list. We suggest you start with the many free tourist publications that list the dining establishments and details. Bon Appétit!

Crown Bay

*Tickles Dockside Pub, 776-1595,
Located in the Crown Bay Marina, serves breakfast, lunch and dinner. Extensive menu, live entertainment. Christiansted

Christiansted

*Baggy's Marina Bar, 713-9636, At St. Croix Marina in Gallows Bay, a casual, breezy spot serving breakfast, lunch and dinner from Monday through Saturday and Sunday for brunch.

*Commanche, 773-2665, On Strand Street, a Christiansted favorite for thirty years. Harbor view, second floor, serving lunch and dinner Monday through Saturday.

Dougal Thornton

*Kendricks, 733-9199, Located in a historic West Indian cottage serving an inspired array of dinner selections and wine. Open for dinner Monday through Saturday. Reservations requested.

*Stixx on the Waterfront, 773-5157, Downtown Christiansted with a fabulous harbor view from the deck. Serving breakfast, lunch and dinner daily. Moderately priced, good selection.

Salt River

*Columbus Cove, 778-5771, In the Salt River National Park overlooking the Salt River Marina. Open for breakfast, lunch, happy hour and dinner. Saturday and Sunday try their brunch.

*Green Cay, 773-9949, Overlooking the Green Cay Marina, serving drinks at the piano bar and dinner with a good selection of wine. Reservations requested.

St. Croix
Christiansted

*Bacchus, 692-9922, a gourmet restaurant in Christiansted town with a prize-winning wine list. Dinner except Sunday and Monday. Reservations suggested.

Breezes, 773-7077, At Club St. Croix west of Christiansted. An airy, colorful and casual restaurant open for lunch and dinner daily. Reasonable prices.

*Giovanni's Piacere, 692-5360. Choose indoor or outdoor Italian dining in the heart of Christiansted. Open for lunch and dinner. Reservations suggested.

*The Golden Rail, 719-1989, At St. Croix Marine in Gallows Bay, a casual, breezy spot serving breakfast, lunch and dinner from Monday through Saturday and Sunday for brunch. Blues band jams

Sunday afternoons.

*Kendricks, 733-9199, Located in a historic West Indian cottage/courtyard serving an inspired array of dinner selections and wine. Open for dinner Monday through Saturday. Reservations requested.

*Luncheria, 773-4247, In historic Apothecary Courtyard in Christiansted. Moderately priced Mexican food in a casual outdoor setting. Open 11am-9pm daily except Sunday.

*Rumrunners, 773-6585. Right on the waterfront in Christiansted Harbor, this reasonably priced restaurant serves good food three meals a day, seven days a week.

*Savant, 713-8666. Dine in or out every evening but Sunday on a fusion of Thai, Mexican and Caribbean cuisines. Reservations suggested.

*Stixx, On the Waterfront, 773-5157, Downtown Christiansted with a fabulous harbor view from the deck. Serving breakfast, lunch and dinner daily. Moderately priced, good selection.

*Tivoli Gardens, 773-6782, On Strand St., Christiansted. Upstairs in a breezy garden setting. Lunch Monday-Friday and dinner every night from 6 to 9:30. The owner plays guitar and sings songs of the 60s every night.

*Tutto Bene, 773-5229, Just east of Christiansted and south of Gallows Bay. Good Italian food in a spacious upstairs setting. Open for dinner every night from 6-10. Reservations suggested.

Frederiksted

Beachside Café, 772-1266, At Sand Castle on the Beach Hotel south of Frederiksted, a great place to watch the sunset. An open air bistro serving lunch/brunch and dinner. Live jazz Saturday nights. Reservations recommended.

*Blue Moon 772-2222. Right across from the waterfront park in Frederiksted town, this restaurant is in a restored Victorian house and is famous for its jazz on Friday nights and during Sunday brunch. Reservations suggested.

*Le St. Tropez 772-3000 is St. Croix's only French restaurant. Located in a charming courtyard on King Street, it is open for lunch during the week and for dinner every night but Sunday. Reservations suggested.

*Motown 772-9882 serves local West Indian food, specializing in seafood. It is on the waterfront Stand Street.

Sunset Grill:772-5855. On the beach north of town, open for lunch and dinner daily, closed Mondays in the off-season. You're welcome to use hammocks, beach chairs, showers and changing rooms and can choose to have dinner right on the sand. There's a beach party every full moon. Reservations suggested.

*Turtles Deli 772-3676 is a unique deli and coffee shop, with gourmet sandwiches served on home-made bread in a setting right on the beach. (There is another Turtles Deli in a Company Street courtyard in Christiansted.)

Green Cay

Cheeseburger in Paradise, 773-1119, Near Green Cay Marina. A popular, friendly spot open from 11am to 10pm daily. Casual food and daily specials in addition to great burgers. Moderate prices. Live music Thursday through Sunday starting at 7pm.

*Deep End Bar, 773-4455 is part of the Green Cay Marina/Tamarind Reef Hotel complex. A casual open-air restaurant, it is open every day for breakfast, lunch and dinner.

*Galleon, 773-9949, Overlooking the Green Cay Marina, an air-conditioned setting for lunch and dinner daily. Soft dinner music at the piano bar most evenings. Reservations suggested.

Salt River

*Columbus Cove, 778-5771,
In the Salt River National Park overlooking the Salt River Marina. Open for breakfast, lunch, happy hour and dinner. Saturday and Sunday try their brunch.

CRUISING GUIDE PUBLICATIONS' VIRGIN ISLANDS DIRECTORY

This directory is arranged in two sections: BVI and USVI. The two largest British Virgin Islands are listed first, followed by the other, smaller islands, in alphabetical order, followed by the U.S. Virgin Islands in alphabetical order.

British Virgin Islands General Information

To call from outside the BVI, dial 1-284 plus 7 digits.

Airlines

Air Sunshine	495-8900
American Eagle	495-2559
Cape Air	495-2100
Caribbean Star	494-2347
Caribbean Sun Airlines	495-2347
Caribbean Wings	495-6000
Fly BVI	495-1747
Island Birds	495-2002
Island Helicopters	499-2663
LIAT	495-1187
Tortola Travel Services	494-2215

Ferries

Inter-Island Boat Services	495-4166
Marina Cay	494-2174
Native Son	495-4617
New Horizon Ferry Service	495-9278
North Sound Express	495-2138
Nubian Princess	495-4999
Peter Island Ferry	495-2000
Road Town Fast Ferry	494-2323
Saba Rock Ferry	495-7711
Smith's Ferry Service	495-4495
Speedy's	495-5240

Miscellaneous

Ambulance/Fire/Police	999/911
VISAR	767 (SOS)

BVI Customs	494-3475
BVI Immigration	494-3471
BVI Chamber of Commerce & Hotel Association	494-3514
BVI Dept. Conservation & Fisheries	494-5681
BVI Ports Authority	494-3435
BVI Post Office	494-3701x4996
BVI Tourist Board	494-3134
Cable & Wireless	494-4444
CCT Boatphone	444-4444
BVI Registrar	494-3492
Virgin Islands Search & Rescue (VISAR)	494-4357 (494-HELP)
VHF 16, or dial .767 (SOS), 999 or 911	

Tortola

Auto/Bicycle/Moped Rentals

Alphonso Car Rental	494-8746
Avis Rent-A-Car	494-3322
Budget Rent-A-Car	494-8902
Coconut Car Rental	495-4939
Courtesy Car Rental	494-6443
D & D Car Rental	495-4765
Del's Jeep & Car Rental	495-9356
Denzil Clyne Jeep & Car Rentals	495-4900
Dollar	494-6093
Hertz Rent-A-Car	495-4405
Honey Bee Auto Rental	494-3666
Hopkins Equip. & Rentals	494-3925
International Car Rentals	494-2516
ITGO Car Rental	494-5150
JRB Auto Rentals	494-8654

Jerry's Car Rental 495-4111
National Car Rentals 494-3197
Palestina Car Rental 494-0976
Tola Rentals 494-8652
Virgin Island Motors 494-4085
West End Car Rental 494-1483

Banks
Banco Popular 494-2117
Development Bank of the VI . 494-3737
First Bank Virgin Islands 494-2662
FirstCaribbean Int'l Bank . . . 494-2171
ScotiaBank 494-2526
The Chase Manhattan Bank . 495-6267
VP Bank Limited 494-1100

Charters
Barefoot Yacht
Charters 784-456-9526
BVI Yacht Charters 494-4289
The Catamaran Company . . . 494-6661
Conch Charters 494-4868
Horizon Yacht Charters 494-8787
King Charters 494-5820
The Moorings 494-2331
North South
Yacht Vacations 494-0096
Pro Valor Charters . . . 1-866 PROVALOR
Sunsail 495-4740
Tortola Marine
Management 494-2751
VIP Power &
Sail Yacht Charters 776-1510
Virgin Traders 495-2526
Voyage Charters 494-0740

Courier Services
Cape Air 495-2100
Caribbean Star Airlines 494-4964
DHL Worldwide Express 494-4659
FedEx 494-2297

Diving, Snorkeling
Aqua Venture Scuba
Services 494-4320
Blue Water Divers 494-2847
Caribbean Images
Snorkelling Tours 494-1147
Caribbean Undersea
Adventures 443-7336
Dive BVI 495-9363
Dive Tortola 494-9200
Sail Caribbean Divers 495-1675
UBS Dive Center 494-0024
Underwater Safaris 494-3235

Electronics
Caribbean Technology 494-3150
Cay Electronics 494-2400
CCT Wireless 444-4444
Radio Doctor Services 494-3219
Sea Recovery Caribbean 494-3150
Varieties & Electronics 494-3798

Emergency/Medical
Ambulance/Fire/Police 999, 911
VISAR (Virgin Islands Search &
Rescue) . . . . 767 (SOS)
. . . . (494-4357)
Dr. Adamson, Oral Surgeon . 494-3274
B&F Medical Complex 494-2196
Bougainvillea Clinic 494-2181
BVI Red Cross 494-6349
Eureka Medical Clinic 494-2346
Medicure Health Centre 494-6189
Smile Crafters 494-2196

Fishing Charters
Caribbean Fly-Fishing 494-4797

Haul-out
Frenchman's Cay Shipyard . . 495-4353
Tortola Yacht Services 494-2124

Jewelers

Caribbean Jewellers	495-4137
Colombian Emeralds Int.	494-7477
Samarkand Jewellers	494-6415
The Jewelry Box	494-7278
Torneau Watch Shop	494-7477

Laundry

Brackwell's Laundromat	495-2369
Speed Clean Coin Laundry	494-9428
Sylvia's Dry Cleaners	494-2230
West End Laundromat	495-4463

Lodging

Beef Island Guest House	495-2303
Fort Recovery Estate Villas	495-4467
Frenchman's Cay Hotel	495-4844
Hodge's Creek Marina Hotel	494-5000
Icis Villas	494-6979
The Lighthouse Villas	494-5482
Mainsail Resort, Marina & Spa (Open 2007)	813-254-3110
Maria's By The Sea	494-2595
The Moorings Mariner Inn Marina Hotel	494-2331
Myett's Restaurant Gift Shop & Inn	495-9649
Nanny Cay Resort & Marina	494-2512
Ole Works Inn	495-4837
Rhymer's Cane Garden Beach Hotel & Restaurant	495-4639
Soper's Hole Marina & Inn	494-0740
Treasure Isle Hotel	494-2501
Village Cay Marina/ Hotel & Restaurant	494-2771

Machine Shops

Nautool Machine Ltd	494-3187
T&W Machine Shop	494-3342
Triton Marine Services	494-4252

Marinas

Fort Burt Marina	494-4200
Frenchman's Cay Marina	495-4050
Inner Harbour Marina	494-4289
Mainsail Resort, Marina & Spa (Open 2007)	813-254-3110
Manuel Reef Marina	495-2066
MegaServices Marina	
The Moorings	494-2331
Nanny Cay Resort & Marina	494-2512
Penn's Landing Marina	495-1134
Soper's Hole Wharf & Marina	495-4589
Village Cay Marina	494-2771
Wheatley's Harbour View Marine Center	495-1775

Marine Chandleries

Al's Marine	494-4529
Budget Marine	www.budgetmarine.com
Cay Electronics	494-2400
Clarence Thomas Ltd	494-2359
Golden Hind at Tortola Yacht Services	494-2756
Island Marine Outfitters	494-2251
Island Water World	www.islandwaterworld.com
Marine Consultants & Surveyors BVI	494-0600
Marine Power Service Ltd	494-2738
Napa Auto Parts	494-2193
Parts & Power	494-2830
Paint Factory	494-1800
Richardson's Rigging	494-2739
Virgin Island Marine Refinishing	494-0361
Wickham's Cay Rigging	494-3979

Marine Contractors & Brokers

Moor Seacure	494-4488

Marine Repair Services

Bristol Boatworks 494-1806
Island Marine Outfitters 494-7169
Johnny's Maritime
Services 494-3661
Marine Consultants
& Surveyors BVI 494-0600
Parts & Power 494-2830
Penn's Landing Marina 495-1134
Tortola Yacht Services 494-2124
Tradewind Yachting
Services 494-3154
Woods Marine Services 495-2066
Wycliffe & Sons 494-2738

Marine Surveyors

Caribbean Marine
Surveyors 494-2091
John M Cope Marine
Surveys 494-3373
Robert W. Hirst & Co 494-2399

Miscellaneous

AB Inflatables 494-3154

Outboard Motors

Tradewind Yachting
Services 494-3154
Trellis Bay Cybercafé 495-2447
Wycliffe & Sons 494-2738

Pharmacies

B&F Medical Complex 494-2196
Medicure Ltd 494-6189
O'Neal J R Ltd 494-2292
Vanterpool Enterprises 494-2702

Power Rentals & Sales

Cane Garden Bay
Pleasure Boat 495-9660
Island Time 495-9993
M&M Powerboats 495-9993

Propane

Popeye 494-3989
O'Neal Gases Ltd 494-2825
Shell Baugher's Bay Depot . . 494-2258
Shell Fish Bay 494-1182

Provisioning

Bobby's Supermarket 495-2140
Caribbean Cellars 494-4649
Dock Side Food Market 494-1096
The Gourmet Chandler 494-2894
Gourmet Galley 494-6999
Harbour Market 495-4541
K-Mark's Foods 494-1824
One Mart Foods 494-4649x249
Port Purcell Market 494-2724
Rite Way Food Markets 494-2263
Sailor's Ketch 495-1100
TICO 494-2211
Trellis Bay Market 495-1421

Radio Stations

ZBVI 780AM 494-2250
ZROD 103.7FM 494-5832

Real Estate

BVI Development Consult. . . 494-2000
Caribbean Realty 494-3999
Gordon & Associates 494-3072
Icis Real Estate 495-9003
Island Real Estate 494-3186
Premier Caribbean Properties
. . . . 800-260-3554
Romney & Associates 494-3352
Smiths Gore Overseas 494-2446
Trude Real Estate 494-2500

Sail Makers

Doyle Sailmakers 494-2569
North Sails 494-9420
Quantum Sails 494-1124

Shopping

Aragorn's Studio	495-1849
Bolo's Dept. Store	494-2867
Cantik	494-7927
Cockle Shop	494-2555
Coconut Sun & Arawak	494-5240
"D" Best Cup	449-2194
Focus Targeted Marketing	495-9135
Latitude 18	494-7807
Myett's Restaurant, Gift Shop & Inn	495-9649
Sea Urchin	494-4108
Sunny Caribbee Spice Co.	494-2178
Yacht Shots	494-0175

Sports

HIHO Watersports	494-7694
Last Stop Sports Center	494-0564
Tortola Sports Club	494-3457

Taxis

BVI Taxi Stand	494-6456
Beef Island Taxi	494-1694
McLean's Tours (Island's Friendliest Driver)	494-5397
Cell: 496-6535, mcleantours@yahoo.com	
Nanny Cay Taxi Stand Association	494-0539
Quality Taxi Association	494-8397
Road Town Taxi Stand	494-8294
Wheatley's Transport	494-5669

Travel Agencies

Tortola Travel Services	494-2777
Travel Plan/ Caribbean Sun Airlines	495-2209
Travel Plan Ltd	494-2347

Woodworking

BVI Marine Services	494-2393
The Carpenter's Shop	495-4353
E&S Yacht Maintenance	495-7500
Frenchman's Cay Shipyard	495-4587
Omega Caribbean	494-2943
The Woodshop	494-2393

Yacht Brokers & Dealers

BVI Yacht Sales	494-3260
Caribbean Connections	494-3623
Caribbean Yacht Management	494-7055
Catamaran Charters	494-6661
Ed Hamilton & Co	800-621-7855
Horizon Yacht Charters	494-8787
LateSail Limited	www.latesail.com
Southern Trades	494-8003
Swift Yacht Charters	508-647-1554
Tortola Marine Mgmt	494-2751
Tortola Yacht Sales	494-2124

Yacht Refinishers

BVI Painters	494-4365
Caribbean Refinishing Co	494-3353
Frenchman's Cay Shipyard	495-4353
Sea Hawk Paints	727-523-8053
Tony's Marine Refinishing Services	494-0140
Virgin Island Marine Refinishing	494-0361
Yacht Restoration Co	494-0803

Virgin Gorda

Auto/Bicycle/Moped Rentals

Flying Iguana	495-5277
Island Style Jeep & Car Rental	495-6300
L & S Jeep Rental	495-5297
Mahogany Car Rental	495-5469
Penn's Car Rental	495-5803
Potter Gafford Taxi	495-5960
Speedy's Car Rental	495-5240

Chandleries
Chandlery at Virgin Gorda
Yacht Services 495-5628
Clarence Thomas Ltd. 495-5091
Virgin Gorda Yacht Harbour
Ship's Store 495-5513

Diving, Snorkeling
Dive BVI Ltd. 495-5513
Kilbride's Sunchaser Scuba. . 495-9638
Mahogany Watersports 495-5469

Laundry/Dry Cleaners
Stevens Laundry &
Dry Cleaners 495-5525

Lodging
Bayview Vacation
Apartments 495-5329
Biras Creek Resort 494-3555
Bitter End Yacht
Club Hotel. 494-2746
Fischer's Cove Beach Hotel. . 495-5252
Leverick Bay Resort 495-7421
Little Dix Bay Hotel 495-5555
Mango Bay Resort 495-5672
Necker Island 494-2757
Olde Yard Village 495-5544
Paradise Beach Resort 495-5871
Saba Rock Resort 495-9966
Virgin Gorda Villa Rentals . . . 495-7421

Marinas
Biras Creek Estate 494-3555
Bitter End Yacht Club 494-2746
Leverick Bay Resort
& Marina 495-7421
Virgin Gorda
Yacht Harbour 495-5500

Miscellaneous
American Express 494-2872

BVI Tourist Board 495-5181
Public Library 495-5518

Pharmacies
Medicure Ltd. 495-5479

Provisions
Bitter End 494-2746
Buck's Food Market
Yacht Harbour 495-5423
Chef's Pantry. 495-7154
North Sound Superette 495-7424
Roadtown Wholesale
of Virgin Gorda 495-5028
Rosy's Supermarket 495-6765

Real Estate
Trude Real Estate 495-5648

Sailing, Water Sports
Bitter End Yacht Club 494-2746
Leverick Bay Watersports . . . 495-7421
Power Boat Rentals 495-5542
Speedy's Fantasy. 495-5235

Sailmakers
Next Wave Sail & Canvas. . . 495-5623
Airforce Sails,
Sailnet, Inc . . . . www.sailnet.com

Shopping, Gifts
Thee Artistic Gallery 495-5104
Fat Virgin's Café & Gift Shop . 495-5923
Flamboyance
Perfume Shoppe 495-5946
Nauti Virgin Beachtique 495-5428
Paradise Gifts & Herbs 494-5454
Reeftique, Bitter End
Yacht Club 494-2746
Saba Rock Gift Shop 495-7711
Virgin Gorda Craft Shop 495-5137

Anegada

Lodging
Anegada Reef Hotel 495-8002
Bonefish Villa & Tours 495-8045
Neptune's Treasure
Hotel & Restaurant 495-9439

Diving
Dive BVI 495-5513

Shopping
Anegada Reef
Hotel Gift Shop 495-8002
Sue's Boutique 495-8062

Cooper Island

Lodging
Cooper Island Beach Club . . 495-9084

Provisions
Deliverance 494-0765

Shopping
Seagrape Boutique 495-3634

Diving
Sail Caribbean Divers 495-1675

Jost Van Dyke

Provisions
Harris' Place 495-9295
Nature's Basket (no phone)
Rudy's Rendezvous 495-9282

Shopping
Foxy's Foxhole 495-9275

Peter Island

Diving
Dive BVI Ltd 495-5513

Provisions
Deliverance 494-0765

Lodging
Peter Island Resort
& Yacht Harbour 494-2591

Marinas
Peter Island Resort
& Yacht Harbour 494-2591

Shopping
Peter Island Resort 494-2591

Marina Cay

Diving
Dive BVI 495-9363

Lodging
Marina Cay Hotel 495-9363
Pusser's 494-2174

Shopping
Marina Cay Boutique 495-9791
Pusser's Company Store 494-2467

U.S. Virgin Islands
General Information

To call from outside the VI, dial
1-340 plus 7 digits.

Airlines
Air Center Helicopters (charter)
. . . . 340-775-7335
Air Sunshine 340-776-7900

American Airlines 800-474-4884
American Eagle 800-474-4884
Bohlke International Airways
(charter) 340-778-9177
Cape Air 800-352-0714
Caribbean Sun 800-744-7827
Continental 800-231-0856
Delta Airlines 800-221-1212
LIAT 340-774-2313
Seaborne Aviation Inc. . 340-773-6442
Spirit Airlines 800-772-7117
Sun Country 800-359-6786
US Airways 800-428-4322
United 800-864-8331

Miscellaneous
Smith's Ferry 775-7292
Transportation Services
of St. John 776-6282
USVI Coast Guard 776-3497
. . . . 774-1911
USVI Customs 774-6755
. . . . 774-1719
USVI National Parks Service
Visitor Information Center . . . 776-6201

St. John

Auto/Bicycle/Moped Rentals
Cool Breeze Jeep 776-6588
Delbert Hill Jeep Rental Taxi
and Tow Service Inc. 776-6637
Hertz 693-7580
O'Connor Car Rental 776-6343
Penn's Jeep Rental 776-6530
Spencer's Jeep Rentals 693-8784
St. John Car Rental 776-6103
Varlack Car Rental 776-6412

Banks
Banco Popular 693-2777
First Bank 775-7777
Scotia Bank 776-6552

Charters
Proper Yachts 776-6256
Royal Overseas
Yachting Co., Ltd 877-693-9292

Diving, Snorkeling
Cinnamon Bay
Watersports Center 776-6330
Cruz Bay Watersports 776-6234
Low Key Watersports 693-8999
Paradise Watersports 779-4999

Emergency/Medical 911

Lodging
Caneel Bay 715-6600
Cruz Inn 693-8688
Gallows Point Suite Resort . . 776-6434
Westin Resort 693-8000

Marine Repair & Supplies
Budget Marine 774-2667
Coral Bay Marine Service . . . 776-6859
Island Marine Outfitters 776-0753
Island Water World . . . .
www.islandwaterworld.com

Provisions
Marina Market 779-4401
Starfish Market 779-4949

Real Estate
American Paradise
Real Estate 693-8352
Cruz Bay Realty 693-8808
Holiday Homes of
St. John Inc. 776-6776
Islandia Real Estate 776-6666
Town & Country
Real Estate 693-7325

Sailing, Water Sports

Big Planet Adventure
Outfitters 776-6638
Cinnamon Bay
Watersports Center. 776-6330
Coral Bay Water Sports 776-6859
Cruz Bay Water Sports 776-6234
Hurricane Alley 776-6256
Low Key Watersports 693-8999
Proper Yachts 776-6256
St. John Windsurfing 776-6052
Windseekers Parasailing . . . 776-7048

Sailmakers

Canvas Factory & Lee Sails . 776-6196
Coral Bay Sails,
Marine Services 776-6665

Shopping, Gifts

Bajo El Sol Gallery
& Studio 693-7070
Batik Caribe 776-6465
Batik Kitab 776-7828
Bamboula Collections 693-8699
The Best of Both Worlds 693-7005
Big Planet Adventure
Outfitters 776-6638
Bodywear Fashion Jewelry . . 776-8363
Bougainvillea 693-7190
Canvas Factory 776-6196
Caravan Gallery. 779-4566
Caribbean Casting Co.,
Jewelers 693-8520
The Clothing Studio 776-6585
Columbian Emeralds
International 776-6007
Cruz Bay Clothing Co. 693-8686
Cruz Bay Photo Center 779-4313
Donald Schnell Studio 776-6420
Dreams & Dragonflies 779-4212
Fabric Mill. 776-6194
Freebird Creations 693-8625
Galeria Del Mar 693-9399

I Catchers Sportswear 776-7749
Island Fancy 776-6940
Kariba Fine Jewelry 693-9380
Lee Sails. 776-6196
Little Planet Kids' Stuff 776-7828
Mongoose Junction 776-6267
Mongoose Trading Co. 776-6993
Nell 693-8444
Pink Papaya 693-8535
R&I Patton Goldsmithing . . . 776-6548
Shae Designs 776-0669
St. John Glassworks 693-9544
St. John Spice 693-7046
Verace 693-7599
Wicker, Wood & Shells. 776-6909

St. Thomas

Attractions
Coral World 775-1555

Auto/Bicycle/Moped Rentals
American Yacht Harbor. 775-6454
Avis 774-1468
Budget Rent-A-Car 776-5774
Dependable Car Rental. 774-2253
Discount Car Rental. 776-4858
Discount Scooter Rental 776-4858
E-Z Car Rental. 775-6255
First Rent-A-Car 776-3730

Banks
Banco Popular 693-2777
ScotiaBank 774-0037
First Bank 775-7777

Charters
CYOA 777-9690
Fanfare Yacht Charters 715-1324
Island Yachts 775-6666
Regency Yacht Vacations . . . 776-5950
VIP Power &
Sail Yacht Charters. 776-1510

Diving, Snorkeling

Admiralty Dive Center.	777-9802
Aqua Action	775-6285
Blue Island Divers	774-2001
Caribbean Divers.	775-6384
Chris Sawyer Diving Center	777-7804
Coki Beach Dive Club	775-4220
Dive In.	775-6100
St. Thomas Diving Club	776-2381
Underwater Safaris.	774-1350
Water World Outfitters	774-2992

Electronics

Boolchand's Electronics	776-0302
Cellular One	777-7777
Electronics Unlimited	714-4798
Vitel Cellular	779-9999
Vitelcom	776-9900

Emergency/Medical

Ambulance/Fire/Police.	911
Decompression Chamber. . .	776-2686
Dr. Boaz.	774-8998
Doctors-On-Duty	776-7966
Richard A. Lloyd, dentist. . . .	774-8155
Pearle Vision Express.	774-2020
Red Hook Family Practice. . .	775-2303
St. Thomas Hospital	776-8311
Stuart M. Wechter, dentist. . .	774-1420
Walk In Medical	775-4266

Haul-out

Haulover Marine	776-2078
Independent Boat Yard	776-0466

Laundry/Dry Cleaning

Island Laundry & Dry Cleaning	774-4567
One-Hour Martinizing.	774-5452
Rodgers Laundromat	776-9697
Washboard Laundry	774-8276

Liquors

Al Cohen's Discount Liquors	774-3690
A.H. Riise Gifts & Liquors . . .	776-7954
Universal Liquor & Gifts	776-3287

Lodging

Blackbeard's Castle	776-1234
Bluebeard's Castle Hotel. . . .	774-1600
Island Beachcomber Hotel . .	774-5250
Island View Guest House . . .	774-4270
Mafolie Hotel.	774-2790
Sapphire Beach Resort.	775-6100
Secret Harbor Beach Resort.	775-6550

Mail Drop

Fed Ex	774-3393
Nisky Mail Boxes.	774-7055
Red Hook Mail Services	779-1890
St. Thomas Communications	776-4324

Marinas

American Yacht Harbor.	775-6454
Compass Point Marina.	775-6144
Crown Bay Marina.	774-2255
Fish Hawk Marina	775-9058
Frenchtown Marina, CYOA . .	777-9690
Haulover Marine Yachting Center	776-2078
Independent Boatyard	776-0466
Pirates Cove Marina.	774-4655
Red Hook Marina	775-6454
Saga Haven Marina.	775-0520
Sapphire Beach Marina	775-6100
Vessup Point Marina	779-2495
Yacht Haven Marina (Opens fall of 2006)	774-6050

Marine Repair & Supplies

Budget Marine.	779-2219
Caribbean Battery	776-3780

Caribbean Inflatable
Service 775-6159
Crown Bay Maritime
Center 774-2255
Island Marine Outfitters 714-7860
Island Water World
. . . . www.islandwaterworld.com
Island Rigging
& Hydraulics 774-6833
La Vida Marine 776-0466
Lighthouse Marine 774-4379
Offshore Marine 776-5432
Reefco Marine
Refrigeration 776-0038
Ruan's Marine Service 775-6346
Tropical Marine 775-6595
Virgin Islands Canvas 774-3229
VI Tecno Services 776-3080
Yanmar Diesels
Island Yachts 775-6666

Miscellaneous
Animal Hospital
St. Thomas 775-3240
Atlantis Submarines 776-5650
Emy Thomas Books 778-1952
Frank's Lock & Key
Service 774-1094
Lock-It Please, locksmiths . . 775-9790
Moore Veterinary Clinic 775-6623
Nisky Business Center 774-7055
Rush-It, Inc. Courier 776-9414
Saunders Veterinary Clinic . . 777-7788
Vitel Cellular 776-8599

Pharmacies
Doctor's Choice Pharmacy . . 777-1400
Family Heath Center 776-3805
Frenchman's Reef Drug
Store 776-8681
Frenchtown Drug Center 774-1466
Havensight Pharmacy 776-1235
Nisky Pharmacy 776-4759

St. Thomas Apothecary 774-5432
Sunrise Pharmacy 775-6600

Provisions
A&F Bakery 776-5145
Bachman's Bakery 774-4143
Daylight Bakery 776-1414
E&M Grocery 774-6836
Marina Market 779-2411
Natural Food Grocery
& Deli 774-2800
Pueblo International 776-4415
Shop Rite Grocery 774-2645
Solberg Supermart 774-7606

Real Estate
Calypso Realty 774-1620
Century 21 777-5700
Stout Realty 776-7653

Sailing, Water Sports
Atlantis Submarines 776-5650
Nauti Nymph Power Boats . . 775-5066
West Indies Windsurfing . . . 775-6530

Sailmakers
Manfred Dittrich
Canvas Works 774-4335
Quantum Sails 777-5638
The Sail Loft (Doyle) 775-1712

Shopping
Amsterdam Sauer Jewelry . . 774-2222
Bambini Fine Art Gallery . . . 775-4766
Blue Diamond 776-4340
Bobby's Jewelers 776-1748
Boolchands 776-0794
Caribbean Sportswear 774-1607
Cardow Jewelers 776-1140
Cartier, Les Must, Jewelers . . 774-1590
Coin D'Oro Jewelers 774-2275
Colombian Emeralds 777-5400
Cosmopolitan, Apparel 776-2040

Cruzan Rum 775-1275
Crystal Shoppe 777-9835
Dockside Bookshop 774-4937
Dolphin Dreams 775-0549
The English Shop 776-3776
Jonna White Art Gallery 774-1201
Last Mango in Paradise 998-2639
Little Switzerland 776-2010
Mango Tango
Art Gallery 777-3060
Ninfa's Gift Shop 774-0460
Nita's Jewelry & Gift
Shop 776-3042
Phil's Paradise 774-5549
Poor Richard's
Tropical Boutique 776-1344
A.H. Riise 776-7954
Scandinavian Center 776-5030
S.O.S. Antiques 774-2074
Soft Touch Boutique 776-1760
H. Stern Jewelers 776-1223
Tillett Gardens Art
& Craft Gallery 775-1929
Trident Jewelers 776-7152
Tropicana Perfume
Shoppe 774-0010

Taxis / Transportation
Carey Limousine 775-9035
Dohm's Water Taxi 775-6501
East End Taxi 775-6974
Independent Taxi 774-0394
St. Thomas Taxi Assoc. 776-3577
Wheatley Taxi 775-1959

St. Croix

Auto
Avis Rent-A-Car 713-1347
Budget Rent-A-Car 778-9636
Centerline Car Rental 778-0450
Hertz Rent-A-Car 778-1402
Olympic Rent-A-Car 773-8000
Thrifty Car Rental 773-7200

Banks
Banco Popular 693-2777
Bank of St. Croix 773-8500
First Bank 775-7777
ScotiaBank 773-1013
V.I. Community Bank 773-0440

Diving, Snorkeling
Anchor Dive Center 778-1522
Cane Bay Dive Shop 773-9913
Dive Experience 773-3307
Dive St. Croix 773-3434
N2 the Blue 713-1475
SCUBA 773-5994
Scuba Shack 772-3483
Scubawest 772-3701

Electronics
Glentronics 778-6505
Mike's Electronics 778-6655
Radio Shack 778-5667

Emergency / Medical
Ambulance/Fire/Police 911
St. Croix Hospital 778-6311
St. Croix Hospital Decompression
Chamber . . . . 778-6311 ext. 2664
Frank T. Bishop, M.D. 778-0069
Charles A. Braslow, M.D. . . . 719-4455
Rodney A. Fabio, Jr.,
Dentist 778-6900
Daniel T. Kenses, Dentist . . . 692-9770
Arakere Prasad, M.D. 778-7788

Laundry / Dry Cleaning
C&J Laundromat 773-2036
Johannes Laundry 778-7602
Neighborhood Laundry 778-6138
Sunny Isle Laundromat 778-6606
Tony's Laundromat 772-4580
WFB Laundromat 773-9788

Liquor, Beer, Wine
BACI Duty Free 773-5040
S&B Liquor 772-3934
Village Liquors 773-8157
*Also available in supermarkets
and grocery stores.
Kmart. 692-5848/719-9190

Lodging
Best Western Holger
Danske. 773-3600
Breakfast Club. 773-7383
Buccaneer Hotel 773-2100
Cane Bay Reef Club. 778-2966
Carambola Beach Resort . . . 778-3800
Caravelle Hotel 773-0687
Carrington's Inn. 713-0508
Chenay Bay Beach Resort . . 773-2918
Cottages by the Sea. 772-0495
Divi Carina Bay Resort
& Casino 773-9700
Frederiksted Hotel 772-0500
Hibiscus Beach Hotel. 773-4042
Hotel on the Cay 773-2035
King Christian Hotel. 773-6330
The Palms 778-8920
Pink Fancy Hotel 773-8460
Tamarind Reef Hotel. 773-4455
Waves at Cane Bay 778-1805

Marinas
Green Cay Marina 773-1453
Salt River Marina. 778-9650
St. Croix Marine. 773-0289

Marine Repair & Supplies
The New Paint Locker 773-0105
St. Croix Marine. 773-0289

Miscellaneous
Blue Mountain
Purified Water 778-6177

Mobile Locksmith 778-1099
Security Lock & Safe,
locksmiths 773-5000

Provisions
Cost U Less 692-2220
Cruzan Rum. . . . . . . www.cruzanrum.com
Foodtown 692-9990
Plaza Extra 778-6240
Pueblo Supermarket. 773-0118
Schooner Bay Market Place . 773-3232

Real Estate
Coldwell Banker 778-7000
Farchette & Hanley 773-4665
Landmark Realty 773-6688
R&R Realty 773-7740
ReMax 773-1048

Sailmakers
Airforce Sails. . . . . www.sailnet.com
Calypsew Canvas 719-2398
Wesco Awning
& Marine Canvas. 778-9446

Shopping, Clothing
Coconut Vine. 773-1991
Foot Locker. 778-3585
Kmart. 692-5848/719-9190
Purple Papaya 713-9553
Quiet Storm. 773-7703
Urban Threadz. 773-2883

Shopping, Gifts
Folk Art Traders 773-1900
Gone Tropical 773-4696
Many Hands. 773-1990
Royal Poinciana 773-9892
Tesoro 773-1212
Violette's Boutique
(cosmetics, perfumes) 773-2148
Whim Museum Shops. . . . .
713-8102/772-5668

Taxis

Antilles Taxi Service. . . . 773-5020
Caribbean Taxi Service. . 773-9799
Cruzan Taxi 773-6388
St. Croix Taxi 778-1088

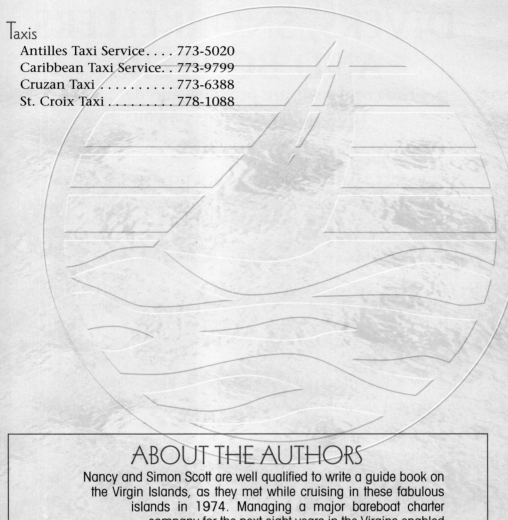

ABOUT THE AUTHORS

Nancy and Simon Scott are well qualified to write a guide book on the Virgin Islands, as they met while cruising in these fabulous islands in 1974. Managing a major bareboat charter company for the next eight years in the Virgins enabled them to see things through the eyes of both the cruising yachtsman and the charterer.

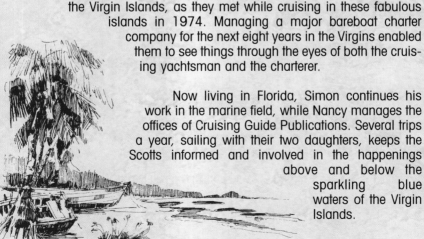

Now living in Florida, Simon continues his work in the marine field, while Nancy manages the offices of Cruising Guide Publications. Several trips a year, sailing with their two daughters, keeps the Scotts informed and involved in the happenings above and below the sparkling blue waters of the Virgin Islands.

DIVERS, SNORKELLERS AND BOATERS

The coral reefs are precious and delicate. Their future depends on you.

Worldwide coral reefs are suffering degradation from various factors — pollution, over fishing, excess nutrients...tourist activity.

PLEASE TAKE CARE NOT TO INFLICT FURTHER DAMAGE

TOUCH NOTHING — The slightest touch with hands, fins or equipment can irreparably damage coral polyps, the tiny animals that build the coral reefs. Remember most corals only grow a half inch per year.

REMAIN HORIZONTAL in the water and snorkel in water over your depth. Snorkeling on shallow reefs can easily inflict damage to the coral and cause personal injury. In a vertical position, your flapping fins are killers! They break coral and stir up sediment that can smother the coral polyps. For equipment adjustment, swim out and away from the coral into deep water.

UNSURE, UNEASY — Wear a float vest, and practice your skills off a sandy beach.

LOOK, ENJOY AND LEAVE — Take nothing dead or alive from the reef.

DO NOT ANCHOR ON CORAL — Use mooring buoys where available, or anchor on a sandy bottom. Anchors, chain and line should not touch coral (dinghy anchors included). If there is no sandy bottom don't anchor, but leave an attendant in the dinghy while the rest of the party snorkel or dives.

FEEDING THE FISH — Caution, you may be injured! Feeding can make fish aggressive and dangerous. It also upsets species distribution and may introduce disease.

PHOTOGRAPHERS — Avoid cumbersome rigs. Don't brace yourself on the coral to take a photo. Damaging the reef even inadvertently for the sake of a photo is not worth it.

DIVERS — Adjust buoyancy. Secure all dangling gauges, consoles, and octopus regulators. Know where your fins are. Air bubbles trapped in caves will destroy marine growth. Bubbles rising on a vertical rock can scour, don't get

THINK, CARE AND ENJOY. HELP THE
REEF GIVE CONTINUING ENJOYMENT

A Message From ARK (Association of Reef Keepers)

CRUISING GUIDE PUBLICATIONS

Safely guiding yachtsmen through the Caribbean for over twenty years.

Order Form On Back

VIRGIN ANCHORAGES
color aerial photos and color graphics $29.95

LEEWARD ANCHORAGES
aerial photos of anchorages from Anguilla thru Dominica
$29.95

CRUISING GUIDE TO THE LEEWARD ISLANDS with GPS Coordinates (9th Edition) by Chris Doyle $29.95

CRUISING GUIDE TO THE WINDWARD ISLANDS with GPS Coordinates (12th Edition) by Chris Doyle $29.95

CRUISING GUIDE TO THE VIRGIN ISLANDS (12th Edition) by Simon and Nancy Scott $31.95

CRUISING GUIDE TO TRINIDAD AND TOBAGO PLUS BARBADOS (3rd Edition) by Chris Doyle $25.95

GENTLEMAN'S GUIDE TO PASSAGES SOUTH 8th Edition with GPS coordinates - The "Thornless Path to Windward." by Bruce Van Sant $29.95

CRUISING GUIDE TO CARIBBEAN MARINAS AND SERVICES
This essential reference guide includes details and contact information for marinas and marine repair facilities from the Bahamas through the Caribbean. Don't leave port without it! $19.95 or $10.00 with the purchase of any other book.

CRUISING GUIDE TO VENEZUELA & BONAIRE (2nd Edition) by Chris Doyle. Provides anchorage information, GPS and full color charts. $27.95

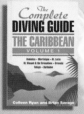

he Windward Islands $29.95   Puerto Rico & The Virgin Islands $29.95

COMPLETE DIVING GUIDE TO THE CARIBBEAN
by Brian Savage and Colleen Ryan. These definitive guides clearly describe dive sites with detailed dive plans aided by spectacular color photos.

CARIBBEAN YACHTING CHARTS
Recently surveyed with the yachtsman in mind.
Includes GPS coordinates.
CYC #1 Virgin Islands - St. Thomas to Sombrero $79.95
CYC #2 Northern Leeward Islands - Anguilla to Antigua $79.95
CYC #3 Southern Leeward Islands - Guadeloupe to Martinique $79.95
CYC #4 Windward Islands - St. Lucia to Grenada $79.95

1-800-330-9542 • www.cruisingguides.com • Email: info@cruisingguides.com

ORDER FORM - CRUISING GUIDE PUBLICATIONS

☐	$31.95	CRUISING GUIDE TO THE VIRGIN ISLANDS
☐	$29.95	VIRGIN ANCHORAGES - available early 2009
☐	$29.95	LEEWARD ANCHORAGES - available early 2009
☐	$29.95	WINDWARD ANCHORAGES - available early 2009
☐	$29.95	CRUISING GUIDE TO THE LEEWARD ISLANDS
☐	$29.95	SAILOR'S GUIDE TO THE WINDWARD ISLANDS
☐	$25.95	CRUISING GUIDE TO TRINIDAD AND TOBAGO PLUS BARBADOS
☐	$27.95	CRUISING GUIDE TO VENEZUELA & BONAIRE
☐	$29.95	GENTLEMAN'S GUIDE TO PASSAGES SOUTH

COMPLETE DIVING GUIDE TO THE CARIBBEAN

☐	$29.95	The Windward Islands
☐	$29.95	Puerto Rico & The Virgin Islands

☐	$9.95	Laminated Virgin Island Planning Chart

CARIBBEAN YACHTING CHARTS

☐	$79.95	CYC #1 Virgin Islands - St.Thomas to Sombrero
☐	$79.95	CYC #2 Northern Leeward Islands - Anguilla to Antigua
☐	$79.95	CYC #3 Southern Leeward Islands - Guadeloupe to Martinique
☐	$79.95	CYC #4 Windward Islands - St. Lucia to Grenada

For More Visit Our Website at
cruisingguides.com

ORDER FORM

To order, check the appropriate boxes - fill out coupon and send check or money order to: Cruising Guide Publications, P.O. Box 1017, Dunedin, FL 34697-1017. Florida residents add 7% sales tax. See schedule for shipping charges. All books are shipped within 10 days of receipt of order. Orders only 800-330-9542.

SHIPPING & HANDLING:

For U.S. Orders Totaling	ADD	Larger orders will be charged according to weight and shipped via United Parcel Service.
Under $15.00	$ 4.50	
$15 - 29.99	6.00	
$30 - 44.99	7.00	
$45 - 60.00	9.00	

International Shipping via Airmail or United Parcel Service. Foreign duties, insurance and taxes are the customer's responsibility.

$ _____ Total Merchandise

$ _____ Sales Tax 7%
Florida Residents Only

$ _____ Shipping & Handling

$ _____ Total Enclosed

Name _____

Address _____

City_____ State _____ Zip_____

Daytime telephone (   ) _____

Email _____

Prices subject to change w/o notice

Advertisers Directory

The PUSSER'S Landing, Soper's Hole, West End, Tortola

FUN!

at the PUSSER'S LANDING®

**Across from the Customs Dock, West End, Tortola
Dockage, Fuel, Water, Ice & Moorings available.
The best place to clear in and out of the BVI.**

✓Dine on the deck, or just enjoy the day's sunset with a Pusser's Painkiller in a take-home mug.

✓Or enjoy more elegant dining upstairs at our Crow's Nest Restaurant with some of Tortola's best food, at fair prices!

The Pusser's Painkiller Mug

✓Shop at our BIG Pusser's Co. store with its full line of Tropical & Nautical clothing, and unique gifts & accessories for men and women. And many other fine shops.

✓A full marina next door: fuel, ice, water, slips & moorings

and Dance & Dine to Live Music on Fri, Sat, & Sun Nites!

PUSSER'S LANDING, Channel 16 or 495-4554
No better food, drink and fun on Tortola!